Tourism Destination Management
Principles and Practices

ABHINAV KAMAL RAINA
JINLIN ZHAO
DEEPIKA GUPTA

KANISHKA PUBLISHERS, DISTRIBUTORS
NEW DELHI-110 002

KANISHKA PUBLISHERS, DISTRIBUTORS
4697/5-21 A, Ansari Road, Daryaganj
New Delhi-110 002
Phones : 2327 0497, 2328 8285
Fax : 011-2328 8285
E-mail: kanishka_publishing@yahoo.co.in

Tourism Destination Management:
Principle and Practices

First Published 2010

ISBN 978-81-8457-218-6

PRINTED IN INDIA

Published by Madan Sachdeva for Kanishka Publishers, Distributors, 4697/5-21A, Ansari Road, Daryaganj, New Delhi-110 002, Typeset by Sunshine Graphics, Delhi, and Printed at Rajdhani Printers, Delhi.

Preface

Travel and Tourism industry refers to all businesses that cater to the needs of the travelling public. The overall hospitality industry thus, primarily refers to organizations that provide loading or accommodation and food services for people when they are away from homes. Many businesses in this sector are engaged with Destination activities and offer various products and services that can be shared by the travelling and non-travelling publics. Lodging properties all over the world offer space for food services, meetings and entertainment and are utilized by non-travellers. Another set of hospitality operations such as private clubs, casinos, cruise ship, vending and theme parks provide hospitality options for many travellers and non-travellers.

Over the years travel patterns are evolving. Travellers could generally be divided in types as travellers for business and those travellers for pleasure. However there is often a blurring of this distinction. In the early times people used to travel on short business trips and relatively longer family vacations.

Today, increasingly business travellers take family members to conference and conventions. The length of pleasure trips has decreased. The change in travel patterns have not lessened the need for the products and services provided by organizations in the hospitality industry and businesses. Hotels and restaurants must still meet the needs of both those who travel and those summers have become more sophisticated and as competitive hospitality organizations increasingly find more creative ways to serve their guests. Meeting management is also an integral part of the hospitality industry because meetings represent a very big business. There are various businesses or trade establishments that provide education lobbying group purchase and other services for other members who share common professional hobby or other interests. Many associations in the west have regional and national meetings and even conventions or trade shows.

Also in the present competitive set up many resorts offer all the amenities of a full service hotel or additional attractions to make them a primarily destination for travellers for example resorts may feature golf, spas, skiing, horseback riding, tennis, and ocean front or other attractions sufficient to entertain guest for several days or even for longer periods. Even time share properties also called interval ownership properties allow persons to purchase partial year ownership of the lodging property. But this practice is generally seen in the western part of the globe. Another set of accommodations for visitors to parks and other nature conservations that are more formal.

Apart from these set of faculties a tourist destination is expected to provide easy and safe mode of journey, comfortable and affordable living accommodation, good quality food and service recreation, rest, and health care at reasonable prices. There can be no growth in the long-term basis in this industry if modern directions which cater the needs of modern tourists are not met.

The present study is based on study conducted by the author Dr. A.K. Raina on the *Destination Competitiveness at Florida International University School of Hospitality Management* in 2005 and the Ph.D. doctorial work of Deepika Gupta under my supervision. The present book presents a comprehensive view and analytical understanding to form a strategy for tourism promotion on sustainable terms.

AUTHORS

Contents

1

Introduction to Travel and Tourism

All beings, whether human or animal, want a change either for a longer period or for a shorter period of time. It is natural on all human beings to move from one place to another for a purpose being social, natural, political, cultural or religious and so on.[1] Travel is an ancient phenomenon. From the very earliest times, travel has fascinated human beings all over the world. Man has been travelling from the very earliest times. Most of the travel in the beginning of the human race was a simpler affair. Travel in the distant past was not a thing of pleasure, as it is the case now. The traveller of the past was a businessman, a pilgrim, a scholar in search of ancient texts and even a curious person looking forward to new and exciting experiences.[2] The early history of tourism is the story of growth and the mobility of man.[3] In the pre-historic era and later, man looked for things as he travelled for food, shelter even for the curiosity sake. From the very beginning, the main reasons for travel have been to extend one's knowledge and to understand about different peoples, places and countries, to study their culture, customs, life-style and heritage. Drama, poetry, art, architecture, culture, Olympic Games all promoted tourism in its own way during beginning of the 12th century. With the advent of science and technology[4] and growth in the transportation and communication, tourism became the fashion of the neo-rich class in the coming years. It has now grown from the pursuits of a privileged few to a mass movement of people.

During the 18th and 19th century in India pilgrim travel assumed a great unusual significance. Religious motivators dominated the travel. Thus, religion played a crucial role in tourism in earlier times and even in present times. Today, because of the availability of fast and inexpensive travel facilities, travel has become more accessible even for the common masses.[5] Travel is thus an activity of movement of people that deserves approbation of all persons. It can further be called as activity of movement of visitors and travellers. It is also considered as a temporary movement of people to destination outside of the place where they normally live and work. Further tourism can also be called as not only the activities to a human being but it is also a process of involving people. Thus, tourism is a constructed break from normal life. It may be identified with the recreation of life and also be as a modern ritual in which people "get away from", particularly from the usual work (which include the home as well as the work place). Tourism activity can be viewed in three phases: *(a) the beginning* (when the tourist separates/moves out of his home), *(b) the middle* (the period of his movement when he comes across new places for experiencing change) and *(c) the end* (the process of his returning to home after the end of the tour).[6] Tourism activity passes through stages of *preparation, liminality* and *reincorporation*. It gives to its tourists a new state of psychological satisfaction just as religious ceremonial does.

The phenomenon of Indian travel are seen in the Indian methodological descriptions of stories examples being, the exile of Rama, Sita and Lakshman, the punishment of the Pandvas, the adventures of Krishna, even Sudama going to his court in search of help. We have Gods and Goddess, minor deities or their attendants roaming at across the heavens and descending to the earth to rescue their worshippers and so on. Also travel account of some illustrious historical figures whose accounts of life are well documented like those of Gautam Buddha, Mahavir, Chandra Gupta Maurya, Ashoka or his son or daughter further adds the presence of early travellers in India. There are also quite a few ancient tales depicting sea trips by the traders and others.[7] Trade and commerce remained a strong force for many travellers to undertake long journeys to one place to another. This was followed by an urge to search new lands and to seek new learning in ancient and distant lands. There are many references of great researchers who spent many formidable years of their lives in search of knowledge[8] namely Vasco-de-Gama, Columbus, Alexander the Great and Marco Polo. Other examples of early travellers being Young Macro Pole left Venice in year 1271 with his father and uncle. The first medieval traveller to reach the orient was perhaps Benjamin of Tendela, a Jewish Scholar. Another famous traveller who recorded interesting accounts of his travel experience was the Batutah, who wrote detailed diary of his travel experiences. He was born in Tangier in 1304 A.D. In 1325 A.D. he left his home and passing through various countries in Africa and West Asia, crossed the Sindhu in 1333 A.D. Mention may also be made of the famous Portuguese chronicle the commentaries of the Great Alfonso D' Albuquerque. Later on in the sixteenth and seventeenth centuries many more European monks, travellers and adventures visited India and many other places in search of knowledge and spirituality.[9]

An Ancient Phenomenon of Travel

The growth of the tourism can be viewed under different periods.

Transition Period

During this period more people started moving from rural to urban areas which brought more leisure and recreational facilities. People became richer and had more disposable income which encouraged and developed tourism. Transportation and communication systems improved with revolutionary developments in technology. More travel agents and tour operators came up. In India after independence destinations were reachable to tourists and railway network connected the whole country reachable to tourist. Today, India is considered as 'Travel for change destination."[10]

Pre-industrial Travel System Era

This was the period before wide scale industrialisation in the world. It was also the time before the development of railway within the two continents. During this era there were no regular scheduled transportation services and there was little travel and tourism. Travellers made their own arrangements with many suppliers. Travel was arduous and often dangerous. It was the era of the stagecoach and the wayside inn, only a small proportion of the population had the money or the reason to travel.

Nature Railway System Era

This era was one in which the railways began to expand scope of their operations into running hotels and providing other travel-related services. The railway began to market their services more aggressively. Travel agencies and tour operating companies were formed. Thomas Cook was one of the innovators in this field during this era, beginning his company's activities in the 1940s in the U.K. More people were travelling in this era than in the one before.

Express Travel System Era

During this era express services became increasingly available, meaning that the trains or other forms of transportation did not stop at every station or terminal but only at the major ones. This enhanced the speed of travel and encouraged more travel and tourism than before.

Modern Tourism Travel System Era

The modern tourism travel system era spanned the period of 1945 to 1987. It is still prevalent today, but some fundamental changes have taken place since the energy crises years began in 1973 and 1974. Car ownership continued to grow at a rapid rate, mainly at the expense of long distance rail travel. Mass air travel was another Post-World War II phenomenon and the introduction of wide-bodied jets in 1970 further increased air travel and tourism. The "mass tourism" philosophy and marketing approaches were certainly prevalent during the 1950s and 1960s. The period of 1945 to 1965 is generally considered to be the baby-boom era, when a large segment of today's population was born and these people passed through their childhood.

Post-Mobility Adjustment Era

Van Duren's post-mobility adjustment era was initiated in 1973-74 as a result of the OPEC – generated oil embargo and the increasing fuel prices that ensued. This author's point was that the events of the energy crisis fundamentally modified travel patterns in North America and elsewhere. Transportation and travel have then evolved over the years in six or perhaps seven distinct eras. The first six years were marked by continuing growth in travel both for business and pleasure/personal reasons and by constant advances in transportation and communications technology. In the modern era, although technological advances are still with us the growth curves of travel and tourism have experienced some reverses or at least shown some moderation in the rates of growth.

Religion as a Motivator

The differentiation between tourist and pilgrim has prompted E. Cohen (1979) to draft distinguish between modern pilgrim and pleasure seeker's. The former seek values in their journey's either as (1) *Existential pilgrim,* who leave modern life to become absorbed in a new spiritual setting; as (2) *Experimental pilgrims,* who quest for an alternative lifestyle especially through engaging in its authenticity; or as (3) *Experiential pilgrims,* who look for meaning in the life of other through an enjoyment of its authenticity.[11] Travel for religious purposes granted a significant importance during the middle period. The practice of travelling for religious purposes became a well established custom in many parts of the world. By the end of the medieval period more and more pilgrims were travelling to the main shrines in Europe and the rest of the world. The spread of Hinduism, Christianity and Islam subsequently led to various pilgrims making their journey to the holy places. Religion was a great unifying force between the nations and thus pilgrimage strengthened the religious bonds. It provided the impetus for a stay at home. Agrarian society broke out its geographical boundaries and prompted people to visit places associated with religion.[12]

In the Christian world, for instance, a visit to Jerusalem on the Vatican is considered to be very prosperous. In the Arab-Muslim world, the pilgrimage to Mecca or some other religious centres is considered to be a great act of faith. In India there are many pilgrimage centres and religious places of all the major religions of the world where every year a large number of pilgrims from all over the world come. As per the recent studies it has been noted that about 7 per cent of tourists in India visited purpose being pilgrimage.[12] In India, pilgrim travel has assumed the great importance. Emperor Ashoka had special memorials set up at each spot and also rest houses where travellers even today can pause and refresh themselves.[14]

In India religious tourism is a large business–with more than twenty five lakh temples spread across the country. Religious matters most in India, and so does religious tourism. Around eight to ten crore domestic tourists visit religious places every year, generating more than Rs. 15000-20000 crores annually from religious and pilgrimage tourism. In India tourism permits an assimilation as perpetuation, distinctive language, literature, music, art, architecture, philosophy and understanding cultures. Religion thus plays and continues to play a crucial part in travel development.[15]

The Origin and Concept of the Annual Holidays

The concept of annual holiday was another important landmark which encouraged many visitors to undertake travel in large numbers during the eighteenth and nineteenth century. In Europe the eighteenth and nineteenth century became the great age of travel takeoff. The annual holiday was the fore-runner to the paid holidays, which later was responsible for the development of tourism.[16] The term holiday derives of course from holy days, days associated with religious observances, though now it is generally used in a secular sense meaning a respite from the routine of work and a day life and a time of leisure, amusement and recreation. Features of ancient Rome public holidays were among the most enjoyable events. The most enjoyable public holiday was the 'Saturnalia' the feast of Saturn celebrated in December, when all classes indulged in feasting and frolic. Also in Europe certain days commemorating religious festivals and saint's days became holy days on which there was cessation from the work.[17] In the year 1952 in England an Act was passed during the regime of Edward the VI for the keeping of holidays and fasting days." Subsequently, public and semi-official offices in England frequently closed on certain saint's days. There were, however, no general public holidays until the time of the Industrial Revolution.[18]

The industrial revolution brought the drastic change in social and economic set up of large population.[19] Today 'travel bug' in the modern parlance had its seeds in the ancient past. Although the purpose and motives for travels in the subsequent periods underwent a great change but the urge to travel has always been there. The growth and development of travel has been closely linked with the growth and development of society as a whole. The travellers of the ancient past were in fact the explorers in search of knowledge of different places of people, their cultures and their traditions along with traders. In fact these very developments paved the way for growth of travel in the subsequent time.[20] It has been customary to believe that in late medieval and early modern period the population was largely immobile. Development in the transportation and communication in the past fifty years or so has, however, tended people to be more mobile and more travel prone. Nevertheless, it is probably still true to say that the majority of people still lives within the fairly narrow horizons and only a small population, however, did move about." Modern tourist loves travel for searching new recreations. Changes in the mental attitude, a new outlook towards pleasure and enjoyment and the secularization of social life and the creation of new centres of accommodation and entertainment[21] are essential for the further growth of modern tourism.

Growth, Meaning and Nature of Tourism

Tourism is the vital breath in the human activity while making a prolonged journey from one place to another. It is a human desire to make a round of the places of interest like religious, spiritual, natural, beautiful places, monuments, ancient cities, historical sites, pilgrimage centres and other places that raises curiosity. The charm of inquisitiveness is found in the sphere of tourism. A tourist is anxious to exert himself to study and survey, to investigate and learn, to find and observe the natural phenomenon and human skill around the Globe. Therefore, tourism is a triadic composition of social, cultural and natural phenomenon which has emerged as one of the world's largest industry. It is of course the fastest growing industry where human spirit is deeply involved to know more and more about the mysteries of nature in wanting.

The origin of the word 'Tourist' can be traced from the Latin word 'Tornus' meaning a tool for describing a cycle. This word dates back to the year 1292 A.D. which speaks of the fascination of man and his urge to discover the unknown, to explore new and strange places and to seek the change of environment and a strong will to undergo new experiences. The 17th century concept of the term 'Tourism' was concerned about travelling from one place to another, which would involve a journey touching the principal parts of the country or a region. These principal parts could be places connected with socio-religious life for the sake of curiosity to see the new places.[22] Before going into the detail of subject matter it will be more feasible to define a tourist by I.U.O.T.O. as "A tourist is a person travelling for a period of 24 hours or more in a country other than that in which he usually resides."

1. *According to Lickorish*—"All persons staying for more than 12 months and less than 24 hours should be excluded from the category of tourist."[23]

2. *According to League of Nations*—"The term tourist shall in principle be interpreted to mean any person travelling for a period of 24 hours or more in country other than that in which he usually resides."[24]
3. *I.U.O.T.O. now W.T.O.*—"Tourist that is temporary visitor staying at least 24 hours in the country visited and the purpose of whose journey can be classified under the following headings:

   (*a*) Leisure: recreation, holidays, health, study, religion and sport.
   (*b*) Business, family mission and meetings.
   (*c*) Excursions."[25]

4. *The United Nations Convention Concerning Customs Facilities for Touring*—"Any person without distinction as to race, sex, language or religion who entered the territory of a contacting state other than that in which that person normally resides and remains there for not less than 6 months in the course of 12 months period for legitimate non-immigrant purpose such as touring, recreation, sports, health, family reasons, study religious pilgrimages or business."[26]
5. *According to Tourist Statistics, Government of India, Department of Tourism, New Delhi*—"A visitor is defined as a person who travels to a country other than that in which he had his usual residence but outside his/her usual environments for a period not exceeding 12 months and whose main purpose of visit is other than that exercise of an activity remunerated from within the country visited. This definition is subdivided into:

   (*a*) *Same day visitor:* Visitors who do not spend the night in a collective or private accommodation in the country visited.
   (*b*) *Tourists:* Visitors who stay at least one night in a collective or private accommodation in the country visited."[27]

The origin of the word 'Tourist' dates back to 1292 A.D. It has come from the word 'tour' a number of experts have defined the term:

1. Tourist is voluntary/temporary traveller, travelling in the

expectations of pleasure from the novelty and change experienced on a relatively and non-recurrent round-trip.[28]

2. 19th Century Dictionary defines tourist as a person who travels for pleasure of travelling out of curiosity and because he has nothing better to do.[29]
3. Dictionnaire Universal says tourist a person who makes a journey for the sake of curiosity for the fun of travelling or just to tell others that he has travelled.[30]
4. The League Committee finds tourist any person visiting a country other than in which he usually resides for a period of less than 24 hours.[31]

Tourist and not to be Tourist

Tourists are

- Persons travelling for pleasure, domestic reasons, health, convention.
- Persons travelling for business purpose.
- Persons arriving in the course of a sea cruise even when they stay less than 24 hours.

Not to be Tourist

- Persons arriving with or without a work to take up an occupation or engage in any business activity in the country.
- Persons coming to establish a residence in the country.
- Students in boarding.
- Persons domiciled in one country and working in adjoining country.
- Persons passing though a country without stopping even if the journey takes more than 24 hours.

Definitions of Tourism

1. *According to W.T.O.* – "Tourism comprises the activities of persons travelling to and staying in places outside their usual environment for not more than one consecutive year for leisure, business and other purposes."[32] W.T.O. report distinguishes the following type of tourism:

   (i) *Domestic Tourism*: Involving 'residents' (visiting) of a country visiting their own country.

(ii) *Inbound Tourism*: Involving 'non-residents' visiting a country other than their own.
(iii) *Outbound Tourism*: Involving 'residents' of a country visiting other countries.

These three basic forms of tourism can in turn be combined to derive the following categories of tourism:

(a) *Internal Tourism*: Which comprises domestic tourism and outbound tourism.
(b) *National Tourism*: Which comprises domestic tourism and outbound tourism.
(c) *International Tourism*: Which comprises inbound and outbound tourism.[33]

2. *According to Krapf and Hunziker*—"Tourism is the sum of phenomena and relationship arising from the travel and stay of non-residents, in so far as they do not lead to permanent residence and are not connected with earning activity."[34]
3. *According to Bukarat and Medlik*—"Tourism denotes the temporary and short movement of people to destinations outside the places where they normally live and work and their activities at those destinations."[35]
4. *Another board definition formulated by IASET and the Tourism Society of Cardiff in 1981*—"Tourism may be defined in term of particular activities selected by choice and undertaken outside the home environment. Tourism may be or may not be involved overnight stay away from home."[36]
5. *According to Dr. Zivadin Jouice*—"It is a social movement with a view to rest, diversion and satisfaction of cultural needs."[37]
6. *According to L.J. Lickorish*—"Tourism embraces all movements of people outside their community for all purposes except migration or regular daily work. The most frequent reason for this movement is for holidays but it will also include, for example, attendance at conferences and movement on sporadic or infrequent business purpose."[38]
7. *According to McIntosh and Goldner*—"Tourism is the sum of the phenomenon and relationship arising from the interactions of tourists, business, host governments and host communities in the process of attracting and hosting their tourists and other visitors."[39]

8. *According to Hermarn V. Schullard*—"The sum of total operators, mainly of an economic nature, which directly relates to the entry, stay and movement of foreigners inside and outside a certain country, city or region."[40]
9. *According to Tourism Society in Britain*—"Tourism is the temporary short-term movement of people to destinations outside the places where they normally live and work and their activities during the stay at these destinations; it includes movement for all purpose as well as day visitors or excursions."[41]
10. *According to Foster and Douglas*—"Tourism is an activity involving in a complex mixture of material and psychological elements. The material ones are accommodation, transportation, the attractions and entertainment available. The psychological factors include a wide spectrum of attitudes and expectations."[42]

Figure No. 1.1: Classification of Travellers

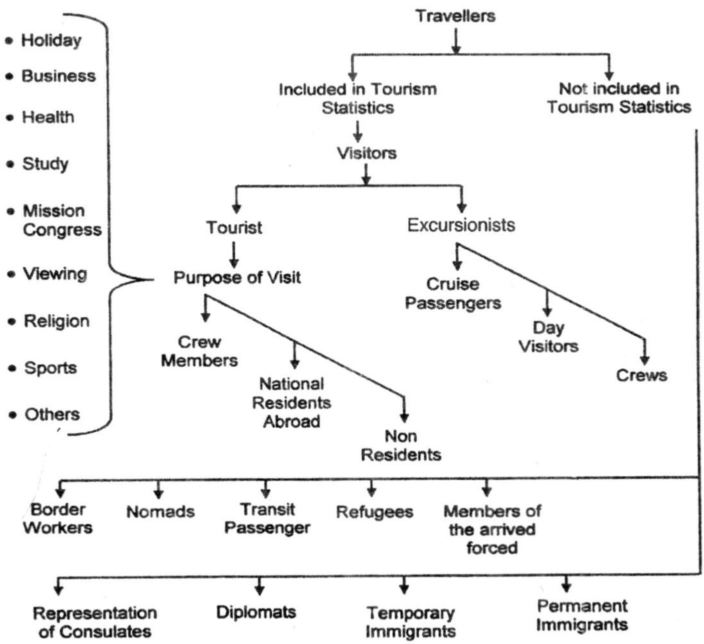

Source: W.T.O. Madrid—1981.

Nature of Tourism

Tourism research has indicated the change in the nature of tourism over the years. In the first place, the whole concept of pleasure travel has changed quite strongly during the past four decades. Foreign travel in the past was for the wealthier, leisured and well-educated members of society who enjoyed travel for its own and for self-recognition. The present day traveller has a different kind of background and his ideas about 'travel' are altogether different. Today's traveller comes from a wider socio-economic background and his tastes and desires are much more varied; his leisure time is much more restricted and accordingly, he wishes to pack into it as much as possible. Secondly, there has been what is aptly termed the "democratization" of leisure pursuits, winter sports for example, were not so very long ago and activity almost exclusively confined to the weather members of the population.[43] The commercialization of many hobbies or leisure time activities has made these available to the common people. Large numbers of people are now moving abroad to participate in thrilling and extraneous activities of mountaineering, water-skiing, underwater swimming, pony-trekking etc.[44] Growth of 'social tourism' has also changed the nature of tourism over the years. This kind of tourism is responsible for the opening up and development of new areas "organized for very large groups of visitors, specially-designed for low-price accommodation, entertainment and other services, 'social tourism' is able to bring movements in the large numbers of tourists all over the globe."[45]

The Basic Components of Tourism

Tourism does not exist in isolation. It has reliable basic components without which it cannot operate. In order to understand tourism, it is necessary to know the various components which together make tourism.[46] These components can be divided into four parts: (See Figure 1.2)

Attraction and amenities are also the very basic of tourism. Attraction and amenities help to tourists to be motivated for going out to special places of interest. But of course the needs and tastes of tourist vary widely: the attraction of one place to some people may be unattained to others.[47] Peters has drawn up an inventory of the various attractions which are of significance in tourism.

Figure No. 1.2: Basic Components of Tourism

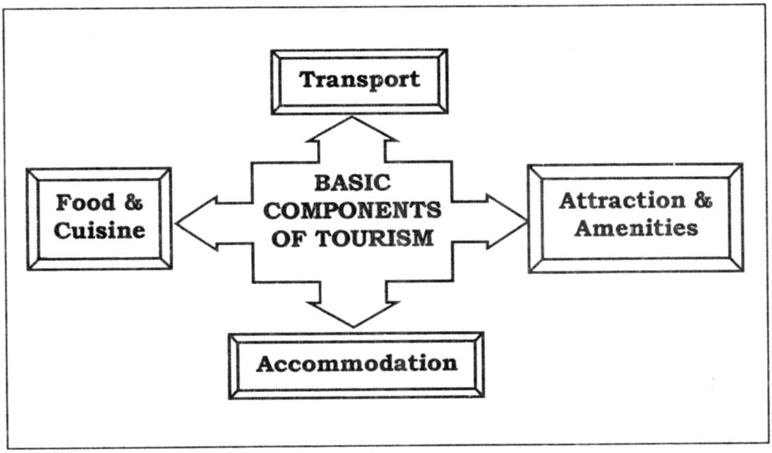

Peter's Inventory of Tourist Attractions

1. Culture	Sites and areas of archaeological interest: historical building and monuments, place of historical importance, museums, modern culture; political and educational institutions; and religious institutions.
2. Traditions	National festivals, arts and handicrafts, music, folklore, native life and customs.
3. Scenic	National parks, wildlife flora and fauna, beach resorts, mountain resorts.
4. Entertainment	Participation in and viewing of sports amusement and recreation parks, zoos and aquariums, cinemas and theatres, nightlife, cuisine.
5. Other Attractions	Climate, health resorts, unique attractions not available elsewhere.

Source: M. Peters, International Tourism, Hutchinson, 1969, p. 148.

H. Robinson in his book *"A Geography of Tourism"* holds that the attractions of tourism are to a large measure geographical in their character.

Geographical Components of Tourism

1. Accessibility and location	
2. Space	*(a)* Land forms e.g. mountains, canyons, cord reefs, cliffs etc. *(b)* Water e.g. rivers, lakes, dams, waterfalls, geysers, glaciers, sea etc. *(c)* Vegetation e.g. forests, grassland, pastures, lees, moors, deserts etc.
3. Scenery	
4. Climate	Sunshine, clouds, temperature conditions, rain and snow
5. Wildlife	*(a)* Animal life e.g. birds game reservoirs, zoos *(b)* Hunting and fishing
6. Settlement Features	*(a)* Tourist cities, villages *(b)* Historical remains and monuments *(c)* Archaeological remains
7. Culture	Ways of life, traditions, folklore arts and crafts

Source: Geography of Tourism, H. Robinson, 1979, p. 42.

Above mentioned components of tourism as described by H. Robinson plays the very important role which geography plays in the tourism activity. In tourism studies, much attention is usually directed to the economic aspects of the industry. But the recognition to the role of geography in the tourism development must not be ignored.[48]

Elements of Tourism

Apart from above mentioned tourism component, the following elements of tourism are essential in the development of tourism.

1. *Fine Weather*

For holidaying fine weather is an important component since it plays an important role in making a vacation a pleasant experience. More of tourists from countries with extremes of weather visit sea beaches in search of good weather and sunshine. Development of spas and resorts along the seacoasts in many countries were a result of visitor urge to enjoy good weather and sunshine.[49] In Europe countries such as Spain, Italy and Greece and states such as California and Florida in the United States which are able to guarantee fine weather in summer and in fact capitalizing on this have become important areas of tourism.[50] Sea beaches of India, Sri Lanka, Thailand, Australia are yet more examples of what good weather can do. All these areas in fact, capitalizing on good weather have become important tourist sports. There are other places inviting winter climate, winter warmth and sunshine and are thus also important centres of tourist attractions, and have become the important winter holiday resorts with variety of winter sports facilities.[51] In countries with tropical climates many upland cool areas have been developed as 'hill station resorts'. A fine example of this could be a beautiful hill station of Gulmarg, Kashmir in India. Climate, thus, adds significance to tourism.[52]

Figure No. 1.3: Elements of Tourism

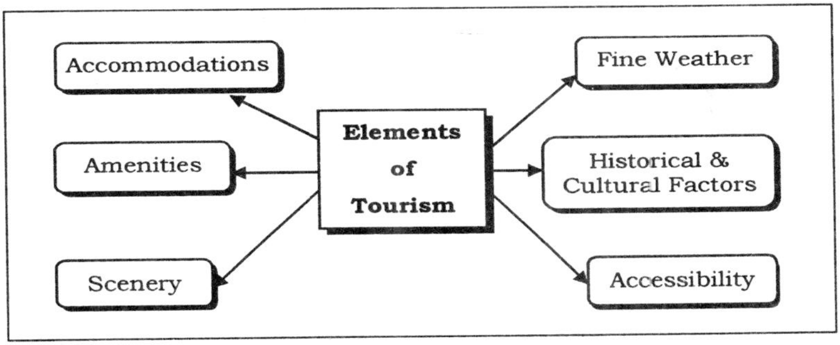

2. *Scenery*

Scenic attractions are considered the second most important element of tourism. Scenery and landscape consisting of mountains, lakes, waterfalls, glaciers, forests, deserts etc. are strong forces attracting visitor to visit there. Breath taking mountain scenery and the coast scenery exert an attraction for both the domestic and international tourists.[53] The wonderful and excellent mountain ranges provide an atmosphere of peace and calm. Visitor visiting the northern slopes of the Alps in Switzerland and Austria and Southern slopes in Italy and also Himalaya Mountain slopes in India and Nepal remain charmed by their magnificence. Natural wonders as the Grand Canyon in the United States, the Geysers of Iceland, the glaciers of Alps, the forests of Africa, the mighty rivers, the lakes and the deserts are a source of great interest to many tourists and have become the basis of an expanding tourist industry.

3. *Historical and Cultural Factors*

Historical and cultural factors largely add to the tourists' interests. A fairly large number of tourists of such a place like the birth place of William Shakespeare in England on the city of the Agra in India because of the world wonder Taj Mahal or Pisa in Italy because of its famous learning tower.[54] Most of tourists visit India because of its long historical and cultural heritage. Any foreign visitor visits England or London not because it is the largest city in the country and the capital, but because of its historical association and traditions and its many cultural attractions. In the similar way the visitor in France includes Paris in his travelling as he does Rome and Moscow in a visit to Italy and the Soviet Union respectively. Mostly countries are using the legacy of their historical past as their major tourist attraction.[55]

4. *Amenities*

Amenities can be grouped either *(i)* natural e.g. beaches, sea bathing, possibilities of fishing, opportunities for climbing, viewing etc. and *(ii)* man-made e.g. entertainment of every kind and facilities which cater for the special needs of the visiting tourist.[56] Very nice sandy beaches, sheltered in sunshine having palm and coconut trees growing there and offering good bathing conditions form very homely and sympathetic atmosphere for tourism motivation. Other natural amenities as sheltered water for the purpose of sailing or rowing and good opportunities for fishing and shooting are also equally important for tourist motivation.[57]

5. *Accessibility*

Accessibility means comfortable easy and fast approach to a tourist destination. Tourist attractions of whatever type would be of no importance in case their locations are not easily accessible as means of transport. The tourist destinations which are located nearer to the tourist generating marketing and can be easily reached by air, receive the maximum number of tourists. Distance factor also plays an important role in tourists' choice of a destination. The distances that are longer and lead to distant areas cost more in the way of expenses on travel as compared to short distances and nearby areas. Therefore efforts must be to make tourist destinations easily accessible that too in shorter distances by the introduction of mega highways. Easy accessibility will remain always the important factor for the growth and development of the tourist movement.

6. *Accommodation*

The demand for accommodation away from one's home is met by a variety of facilities. The term 'accommodation' is loosely used to cover food and lodging. The types of accommodation have to sustain considerably in the usę of boarding houses and small private hotels. The large hotels are managing more or less to keep their share of holiday trade especially in big city and popular tourist areas. Elsewhere particularly in the more traditional holiday resorts and in some seaside resorts in Europe, these are having a lean time. In recent years some changes have been reflected in the type of accommodation and there has been a growing demand for more informal types of accommodation.[58] New types of accommodation particularly holiday villages, apartment houses, camping and caravan sites and tourist villages etc. have become very popular in recent years.

Growth and Development of Modern Tourism

Instruments of Tourism Growth

The following are the major instruments of modern tourism growth:

- *Sociological Improvements* manifest through the greater desire and increased opportunities for education, improved health conditions and entertainment, recreation, cultural leisure.
- *Economic Improvement* brings about improvements in standard of living with more discretionary funds. Increase in personal consumption and consumer spending and a desire for new resorts, new attractions and new facilities.
- *Technological Development* in transport, communications, accommodation and other sectors accelerate the fascination for tourist.
- *Political Stability* brings national and international peace, accelerate travel and tourism world travel is a fundamental expression of international cooperation and is a powerful force for trade for cultural and political enrichment. Tourism is a peace-elastic phenomenon for all the nations.[59]

Figure No. 1.4: Instruments of Tourism Growth

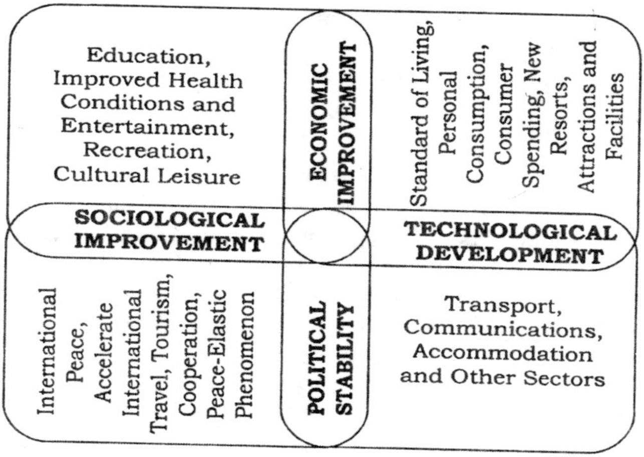

Factors Influencing the Growth of Tourism

Socio and economic factors like income, age, education and cost are thus crucial in the evolution of tourist demand. The most comprehensive list of factors influencing the growth of tourism, however comes from *Loui's Erdi (1970)* of the Swiss Federal University. The list includes:

Figure No. 1.5: Model of Tourism Growth Factors

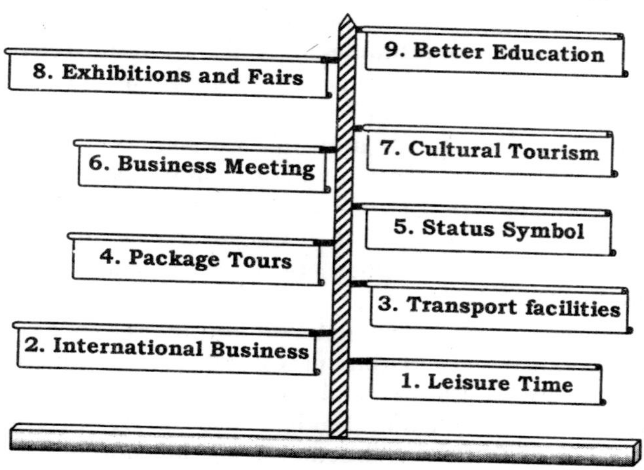

1. Greater affluence and more leisure time.
2. Better and cheap transport facilities.
3. Growth in international business.
4. Package tours.
5. Travel has become a status symbol.
6. Conferences and business meeting.
7. Concept of cultural tourism.
8. World exhibitions and trade fairs.
9. Better education.

From the above list of factors influencing the growth of tourism we can identify the basic motivations for modern day tourism as well.[60]

Tourism: As an Industry

Tourism drives its meaning from Hebrew word 'torah', which means to search to learn. Inquisitiveness is an inherent trait of human personality. To know alien cultural, natural surroundings and to explore new horizon has been constant endeavour of human beings. This process has resulted into the development of tourism in human history. Trade and exploratory tourism has opened the gate of cultural transmission and accelerated the process of economic interaction and development. Thomas Cook laid the foundation of modern tourism in 19th century. Today it has developed as an industry.

Tourism is a basic and most desirable human activity deserving the praise encouragement of all people and all governments. In early years of this century tourism was not looked as industry but as a collection of businesses and to provide essential services to the travellers. Today tourism is a multi-facet activity. It embraces all those industries which have been called upon at various stages of the process of supply of goods and services. In fact, tourism industry is regarded as fragmented industry. The agencies, organisations and businesses which are included in the tourist industry are as under:

(a) *Direct providers of services* examples being airlines, hotel, ground transportation, travel agents, restaurants and retail shops.
(b) *The second category* is the support services to direct suppliers

e.g. specialised services as tour operators, laundry services, service contractors, travel research organisation, hotel management, firms etc.

(c) *The third category* consists of developmental organisation that includes planners, government organisation, financial institutions, vocational training institutes etc. They do not cater to day to day needs of travelling but their plans and activities help in promoting tourism related activities.[61]

Today, 'tourism' has become organized and more competitive industry. Tourism today enjoys the protection of various respective governments and the support and promotional efforts of the official and the private sectors. Tourism is a very important means of earning foreign currency. Foreign exchange receipts from international tourists are major earner of foreign currency and exceed the receipt from any other single industry. Tourism has given rise to a full range of economic activities and services on the domestic front. Entertainment, arts and crafts manufacture and sale of gifts and souvenirs, trinkets and their eating places, bars and restaurants and not the least sightseeing and excursion trips are all important aspects of modern tourism. All these are in the services sectors of the economy generally except for manufacture of products for sale or exchange. Tourism generates and provides full-time or part-time employment to a large number of persons, infrastructural improvements and it may help regional development. That is why most of the states in India have declared tourism and hotels as an industry.[62]

At the global level, the potential of tourism has been recognised in 1967. U.N. General Assembly dedicated the year 1967, the 'International Tourist Year'. The assembly advocated that tourism deserves incentive of all people and government. Tourism is generally described as 'smokeless' and 'employment generating industry'.[63] In the new millennium tourism has been progressing as the largest industry of the coming years. The growth of international tourism was slow in the first half of the 20th century, but quite rapid and phenomenal since the 1980s. Contribution of domestic tourism is assumed to be 9 times greater than international tourism. By 2020 the volume of international tourists will be 1.6 billion, which will generate 2000 billion dollars. Tourism has not only economic significance, but has greater socio-cultural and political impacts as well.[64]

Figure No. 1.8: A Model of the Tourist Industry

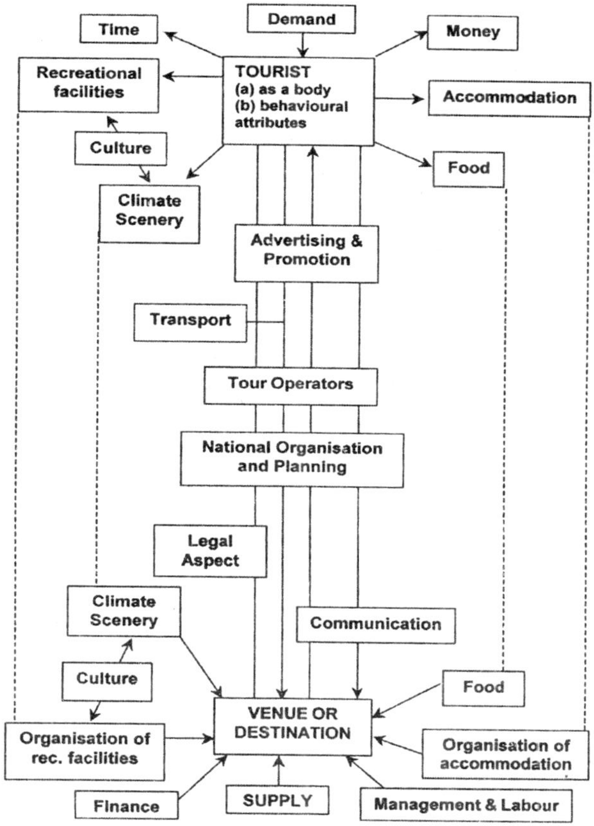

Source: "A Geography of Tourism", H. Robinson 1979, p. xxx.

Tourism Industry in India

India's large geographical diversity, bright culture and heritage, colourful fair and festivals, snow capped mountains, a large coastline, and monumental attractions that make this country a tourist paradise. But the rate of development of tourism in the country has been quite dismal. Tourism economy in India accounts for 9.1 per cent of the GDP support, 10 per cent of the total employment in the country and generates 15 per cent of the total exports from the country. Tourism industry is the third largest net foreign exchange earner after gem, jewellery and readymade garments. Tourism has emerged as an instrument for employment generation, poverty alleviation and sustainable human resource development. The significant feature of this industry is that it employs a large number of men and women educated, uneducated, skilled or unskilled generate employment opportunity particularly in remote and backward areas, and it contributes to national integration. The employment multiplier figure in the tourism sector is 2.36, i.e. a direct employment of one person in tourism creates jobs for 2.36 persons in other sector of the economy. Presently Indian share in the world tourism has been 0.78 per cent only. However, in the new millennium, tourism has entered into the priority zone of government policy and planning. To provide new dimension the Government of India must accord the status of "Export house" to this industry.[65]

The components of tourism industry are varied ranging from small-scale business operating at local levels to multinationals. These different components are closely linked to each other. This linkage is there in spite of the competitions within one set of components. Modern tourism is a result of intermixing and combined efforts of various components.

There is a clear-cut picture of mass character of tourism in a modern world and the travels undertaken are at least part with reference to undertaking exploration, discovery, pilgrimage or migration. Tourism is a mass movement of people from the home location to some other temporary location for a few days to few weeks. Modern tourism can be analysed into eight main categories:

1. For relaxation and refreshment of body and mind, which is becoming ever, more necessary in modern life style because of speed, stress and strain.
2. For health purpose: to secure fresh air and sunshine.
3. For active participation in a wide variety of sporting activities such as walking, mountaineering, skiing, sailing, fishing, shooting, trekking etc.
4. For sheer pleasure, fun and excitement, the individual's need for pure pleasure is very strong indeed; and 'travel' and 'holiday' make a simple way of satisfying this demand.
5. For interest in foreign parts, especially in places having important historical or cultural associations or places holding special festivals in art, drama, music etc.

Figure No. 1.9: Components of Tourism Industry

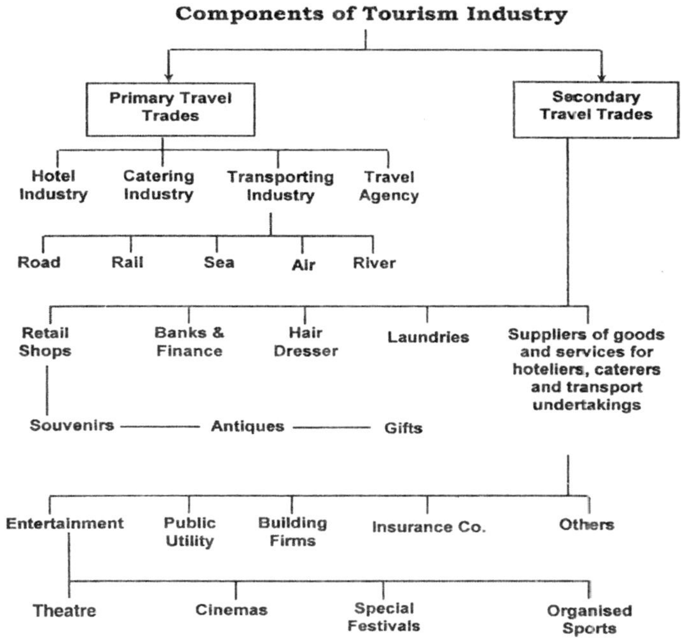

6. For interpersonal reasons: to visit one's relatives, to meet new people and seek new friendships or even to escape for a while for one's usual associations.
7. For spiritual purposes as, for example, going on pilgrimages to scared religious sites or holy places.
8. For professional or business reasons: e.g. attending conventions related to the professions, industry or commerce or to some organisation to which the individual belongs.[66]

REFERENCES

1. Sharma, K.C.—"Tourism Policy Planning, Strategy", Pointer Publishers, Jaipur, 1996, p. 1.
2. Bhatia, A.K.—"Tourism Development: Principles and Practices", Sterling Publishers Pvt. Ltd., New Delhi, 1982, p. 1.
3. Anand, M.M.—"Tourism and Hotel Industry in India: A study of Management", Prentice Hall of India Pvt. Ltd., New Delhi, 1976, p. 2.
4. Batra, G.S. and Dangwal, R.C.—"Tourism Promotion and Development: New Advances", Deep and Deep Pub. Pvt. Ltd., New Delhi, 2001, p. 11.

5. Raina, A.K. and Agarwal, S.K. – "The Essence of Tourism Development: Dynamics Philosophy and Strategies", Sarup & Sons, New Delhi, 2004, p. 14.
6. Raina, A.K. & Jain, Neelu – "Dynamics of Tourism: Concepts, Philosophy and Strategies", Kanishka Publishers, Distributors, New Delhi, 2004, p. 7.
7. Bhatia, A.K. – "Tourism Development: Principles and Practices", Sterling Publishers Pvt. Ltd., New Delhi, 1982, p. 2.
8. Hicks, M.K. and *et. al.*, – "Tourism", Heinemann, London, 1968, p. 30.
9. Bhatia, A.K. – "Tourism Development: Principles and Practices", Sterling Publishers Pvt. Ltd., New Delhi, 1982, p. 3.
10. Bhatnagar, S. – "Front Office Management", Frank Bros. & Co. (Publishers), New Delhi, 2002, p. 10.
11. Malhotra, R.K. – "Nature and Tourism", Cyber Tech Pub., New Delhi, 2006, p. 28.
12. Bhatia, A.K. – "Tourism Development: Principles and Practices", Sterling Publishers Pvt. Ltd., New Delhi, 1982, p. 5.
13. Sharma, J.K. – "Tourism Planning and Development: A New Perspective", Kanishka Pub. Distributors, New Delhi, 2000, p. 44.
14. Singh, Ratan Deep – "Dynamics of Modern Tourism", Kanishka Pub., New Delhi, 1998, p. 44.
15. Times of India, New Delhi, Friday, May 26, 2006, p. 11.
16. Bhatia, A.K. – "Tourism Development: Principles and Practices", Sterling Publishers Pvt. Ltd., New Delhi, 1982, p. 7.
17. Robinson, H. – "A Geography of Tourism", McDonnell and Evans, London, 1976, pp. 4-5.
18. Singh, Ratan Deep – "Dynamics of Modern Tourism", Kanishka Pub., New Delhi, 1998, p. 50.
19. Robinson, H. – "A Geography of Tourism", McDonnell and Evans, London, 1976, p. 5.
20. Bhatia, A.K. – "International Tourism: Fundamental and Practices", Sterling Pub. Pvt. Ltd., New Delhi, 1991, p. 9.
21. Pimlote, Jar – "The English Man's Holiday's", Faber & Faber, 1947, pp. 22-23.
22. Raina, A.K. & Jain, Neelu – "Dynamics of Tourism", Kanishka Publishers, New Delhi, 2004, p. 11.
23. Licorish L.J. and Kershaw A.G. – "Travel Trade: Practice", Press London, 1958, p. 15.
24. Bhatia, A.K. – "International Tourism", Sterling Publishers Pvt. Ltd., New Delhi, 1991, p. 60.
25. International Union of Official Travel Organisation: Conference on International Travel and Tourism, Geneva, 1963, p. 14.
26. Raina, A.K. & Jain, Neelu – "Dynamics of Tourism", Kanishka Publishers, New Delhi, 2004, p. 4.

27. Tourist Statistics, Government of India, Department of Tourism, New Delhi, 1998, p. 118.
28. Jha, S.M. – "Tourism Marketing", Himalaya Publishing House, Bombay, 1995, p. 7.
29. Bhatia A.K. – "Tourism Development", Sterling Publishers, Pvt. Ltd., New Delhi, 1982, p. 95.
30. Bhatia A.K. – "Tourism Development: Principles and Practices", Sterling Publishers Pvt. Ltd., New Delhi, 1982, p. 95.
31. Jha, S.M. – "Tourism Marketing", Himalaya Publishing House, Bombay, 1995, p. 7.
32. OECD Tourism Committee, International Tourism and Tourism Policy in OECD Countries Report Organisation for Economic Co-operation and Development, Paris, July, 1973.
33. WTO Travel and Tourism Barometer, Madrid, May 1993.
34. Tourism Statistics 1997: Development of Tourism, Government of India, New Delhi.
35. Hunziker, W. Grand rises der Aldagemeinen Fremden Vekeshnresklra Zuich Polygraphicsher Veriag, A.G. 1942.
36. Bhatia A.K. – "Tourism Development: Principles and Practices", Sterling Publishers Pvt. Ltd., New Delhi, 1982, p. 76.
37. Jovice, Zivadin – "Articles on Tourism and Geography in the International Travel and Recreation," Journal No. 3, p. 23.
38. Lickorich, L.J. – "An Interim Study of Tourism", Practice Press Ltd., London, 1953, pp. 14-15.
39. Robert, McIntosh, W. Charles and Goldener, – "Tourism Principles Practices, Philosophies", J. Wiley & Sons Inc., New York, 1991, pp. 3-4.
40. Jha, S.M.-"Tourism Marketing", Himalaya Publishing House, Bombay, 1995, p. 6.
41. Tourism Society in Britain, 1999.
42. Foster & Douglas – "Travel & Tourism Management", McMillan, London, 1985, p. 5.
43. Tourism Development and Economic Growth, OECD, 1966, p. 12.
44. Singh, Ratan Deep – "Dynamics of Modern Tourism", Kanishka Pub., New Delhi, 1998, p. 63.
45. Tourism Development and Economic Growth, OECD, 1966, p. 12.
46. Singh, Ratan Deep – "Dynamics of Modern Tourism", Kanishka Pub., New Delhi, 1998, p. 65.
47. Peters, M. – "International Tourism", Hutchison, 1969, p. 145.
48. Robinson, H. – "A Geography of Tourism", McDonnell and Evans, London, 1976, pp. 41-42.
49. Bhatia, A.K. – "International Tourism: Fundamental and Practices", Sterling Pub. Pvt. Ltd., New Delhi, 1991, pp. 37-38.
50. Quoted by H.P. Smolks in forty thousand against the artic, 1937.

51. Sharma, K.C. – "Tourism Policy Planning, Strategy", Pointer Publishers, Jaipur, 1996, p. 39.
52. Bhatia, A.K. – "Tourism Development: Principles and Practices", Sterling Publishers Pvt. Ltd., New Delhi, 1982, p. 38.
53. Singh, Ratan Deep – "Dynamics of Modern Tourism", Kanishka Pub., New Delhi, 1998, p. 67.
54. Sharma, K.C. – "Tourism Policy Planning, Strategy", Pointer Publishers, Jaipur, 1996, p. 40.
55. Bhatia, A.K. – "Tourism Development: Principles and Practices", Sterling Publishers Pvt. Ltd., New Delhi, 1982, p. 40.
56. Robinson, H. – "A Geography of Tourism", McDonnell and Evans, London, 1976, p. 45.
57. Bhatia, A.K. – "Tourism Development: Principles and Practices", Sterling Publishers Pvt. Ltd., New Delhi, 1982, p. 40.
58. Singh, Ratan Deep – "Dynamics of Modern Tourism", Kanishka Pub., New Delhi, 1998, p. 69.
59. Bhatia A.K. – "Tourism Development: Principles and Practices", Sterling Publishers Pvt. Ltd., New Delhi, 1982, pp. 30-32.
60. Jha, S.M. – "Tourism Marketing", Himalaya Publishing House, Bombay, 1995, p. 55.
61. Raina, A.K. & Jain, Neelu – "Dynamics of Tourism", Kanishka Publishers, New Delhi, 2004, pp. 7-8.
62. Raina, A.K. and S.K. Agarwal – "The Essence of Tourism Development", Sarup & Sons, New Delhi, 2004, p. 13.
63. Ghosh, Biswanath – "Tourism and Travel Management", Vikas Publishing House, Delhi, 1998, p. 8.
64. Annual Report – Department of Tourism, Government of India, New Delhi, 2004-05.
65. Rajuvedi, V.P. – "Tourism in India", Yojna, Vol. 46, Ministry of Information and Broadcasting, New Delhi, 2003, p. 21.
66. Raina, A.K. & Agarwal, S.K. – "The Essence of Tourism Development: Dynamics Philosophy and Strategies", Sarup & Sons, New Delhi, 2004, p. 18.

2

Travel Motivators and Destination Lifecycle

An Introduction of Travel Motivators

There must be a degree of understanding on the part of travel sellers and suppliers about the motivating factors that leads to travel judgment and consumption behaviour. Travel is motivated by factors that are dependent on specific objectives involving business, education, health, religion, politics and family purposes. The motivations for these types of travel usually can be more readily pinpointed than motivations for pleasure travel. Pleasure travel is surrounded by a wide range of human emotions and motivators that even modern science has difficulty in measuring and to understanding fully. One of the pioneering attempts in motivational theory was Maslow's development of a hierarchy of human needs ranging from a base level of physiological needs such as food, shelter and clothing to self-fulfilment needs at the highest level.[1]

Maslow's Needs and Motivations Listed in Travel Literature

Needs	*Motive*	*Tourism Literature References*
Physiological	Relaxation	Escape Relaxation Relief of tension Sun lust Physical Mental relaxation of tension
Safety	Security	Health Recreation

Contd...

Needs	*Motive*	*Tourism Literature References*
		Keep oneself active and healthy for the future
Belonging	Love	Family togetherness Enhancement of kinship relationships Companionship Facilitation of social interaction Maintenance of personal ties Interpersonal relations Roots Ethnic Show one's affection for family members
		Maintain social contacts
Esteem	Achievement and status	Convince oneself of one's achievement Show one's importance to others prestige Social recognition Ego-enhancement Professional/business Personal development Status and prestige
Self-actualization	Be true to one's own nature	Exploration and evaluation of self Self-discovery Satisfaction of inner desires
To know and understand	Knowledge	Cultural Education Wonder lust Interest in foreign areas
Aesthetics	Appreciation of beauty	Environmental Scenery

Source: Robert Christie Mill & Alastair Morrison "The Tourism System" New Jersey, 1985, p. 7.

Figure No. 2.1: The Tourism System

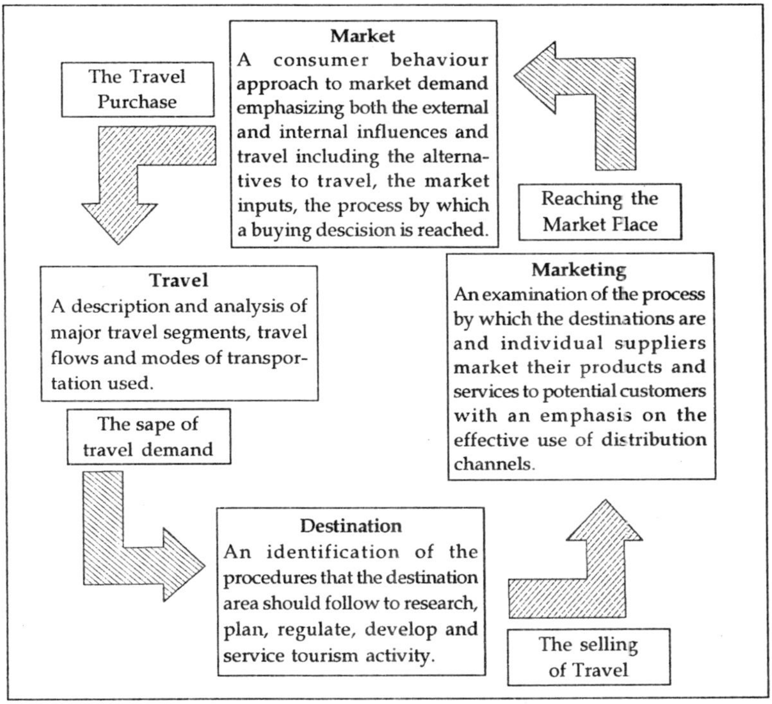

Source: Robert Christie Mill and Alastair Morrison, The Tourism Systems, New Jersey, 1985, p. 2.

The variety of modes in which these needs are satisfied however makes it difficult to construct an operational basis for relating "pleasure travel" to "specific motivators" that can be generalized to all individuals. For some people pleasure is shopping, gambling, romance, others find it more enjoyable to watch television, play tennis or go back-packing in the mountains. In formal identification of motivational differences of individuals "SRI International" a research firm located in Menlo Park. California, USA has developed a new system for categorizing consumers according to their value and life styles rather than just demographics. The system refers to as VALS (Value and life styles) which isolates and identifies different types of consumer each sufficiently distinctive in its behaviour and emotional makeup that constitutes a market segment.[2]

Figure No. 2.2: Relationship among Types of Tourists, Travel Motivations and Types of Destinations

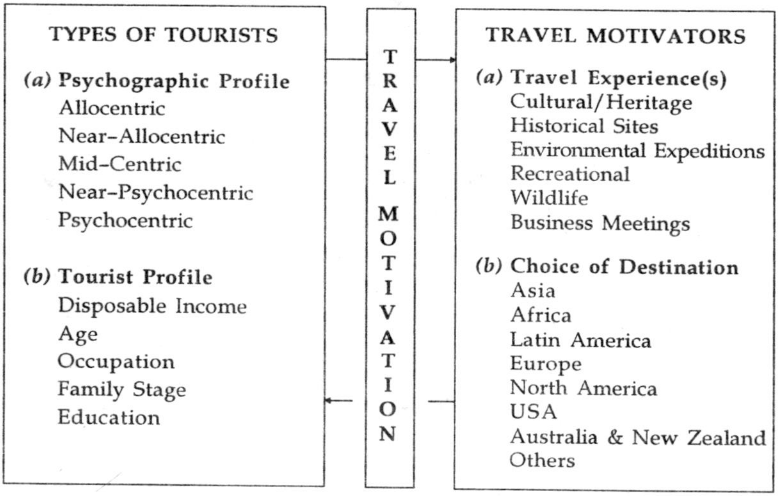

________*Primary Link:* Tourist Flow, Customer Satisfaction.

– – – –*Secondary Link:* Development, Promotion, Marketing.

Source: McIntosh/Goeldner, Sixth Edition, p. 145.

VALS is not the first attempt to view consumers in psychological patterns as a substitute of demographical terms. Over the years, many companies all over the world have conducted studies called Psychographic research to define the Psychological attributes of the buyers and of their products. For the sellers of travel product it is essentially an experience. Motivations values and life style information is becoming increasingly important in successful travel marketing.[3] Travel motivations are basically those factors that create a person's desire to travel. They can be divided into two categories "not primarily related to the actual destination" and "those that are primarily related to the actual destinations."[4] Attraction in the pleasure travels is itself deeply read behaviour. Thus, as tourism promoters, we have to persuade people to travel for pleasure. Once they have tried it, they are likely to travel more. Travel brings about satisfactions to acquire only by such experiences. Viewing pictures of a particular place is only a fragment as satisfying as an actual visit. Satisfactions often include a relaxation of tension as well.

Basic Travel Motivators

Basic travel motivations can be divided into four categories as put by McIntosh/Goeldner:

(a) *Physical motivations* are related to physical rest sports participation, beach recreation, relaxing entertainment and other motivations directly connected with health. Additional motivators might be a doctor's recommendations and the use of health spas curing baths, and health treatment activities. These motivations all have one feature in common namely the diminution of tension through physical activities.

(b) *Cultural motivators* are identifying by the wish to know about other areas—their food, music, art, folklore, dances, paintings and religion.

(c) *Interpersonal motivators* include requests to meet new people. Visit friends or relatives, escape from routine or make new friendships.

(d) *Status and prestige motivators* are ego needs with personal development. Within this category are trips related to business, conventions, study and the pursuit of hobbies and education. The desire for recognition, attention, estimation, knowledge and good reputation can be fulfilled through travel.[5]

There are many more specific reasons as to why more and more people engage in tourism These include:

1. ***Industrialisation***—Industrialisation, urbanization, motorization, the "rat-race" etc. have created great affliction in modern life. Speed, stress and strain have made it more necessary than ever before for people to relax and to undergo refreshment of body and mind. Refreshment varies with an individual to individual.[6] To some, it is secured by a change in the environment. Others seek sunshine and stimulation at seaside or other resorts. Some seek relaxation in seeing new places. Meeting an unknown person and seeking new experiences whatever form the holiday taker, relaxation is always sought in a certain measure by the holiday-maker.[7]
2. ***Health***—Such peculiar diet resorts and similar places have taken the place of spas, motivating people to travel all over the world for health reasons. Even the earliest health

travellers went to spas, because the water was thought to help cure such indisposition as arthritis and rheumatism.

3. ***Pleasure***—Getting away from all the deception of everyday life is perhaps the most important motive these days. An individual likes to have fun, stimulation and good time whenever possible.[8] Various brochures and folders emphasize on the pleasure aspect of the holiday and the travel.[9] It should be borne in mind that the anticipation of and planning for, a holiday may be just as enjoyable as the actual holiday itself and forms part of the total pleasurable experience. Thus, while pleasure and romance are primary attributes of the holidays, travel experience, they are also very powerful motivators.[10]
4. ***Business and Profession***—Large numbers of people travel for business or professional reasons. People increasingly have to travel around in connection with their occupational or professional interests.[11] For many operators in the tourism industry business travel is skilful to success on a year round basis, about 85 per cent of all air travel is business related and many hotels are oriented towards business travellers. Convention centres are built to attract business travellers. Auto rental companies, particularly at airports, are almost completely dependent on business persons. An important aspect of business travel is that its demand changes relatively little in regard to variations in airfares, hotel room rates, restaurant meal prices, and other travel costs.[12] Attending conventions and conferences related to the professions, industry or commerce has become very popular. The convention travel has made great strides in recent times. In order to attract more tourists many countries have established grand convention complexes where all kinds of modern facilities are provided for business meetings. Large hotels also provide facilities for conventions as a large number of people travel for business and professional reasons.[13]
5. ***Sports***—One of the interesting modern developments in tourism and holiday making is a wide variety of sporting activities such as mountaineering, walking, skiing, sailing, fishing, sun-bathing, trekking, boating, surf-riding etc. Large numbers of people these days are taking holidays involving physical activities. In recent years there has been a great

increase in sporting holidays. The visitors go to places primarily to entertain in a sporting activity to which all their energies are directed.[14]

6. ***Education*** – Some people do not perceive students studying in another country as tourists but they fit the definition of a "tourist" as their motivation to travel is to study and not to work at a job. Students spending is important to the airlines but less important to hotels, restaurants and some other branches of the tourism business, as students generally stay in dormitories or apartments and do not heavily patronize the hotels and restaurants at their destination.
7. ***Visit Friends and Relatives*** – Visiting friends and relatives is probably the most important of all travel. The mode of travel is usually the automobile, which benefits motels and camp-grounds on the way with little destination effect on hotels and restaurants.[15] This also includes visiting one's relatives and friends, meeting new people and seeking new friendship. A large number of people make travel for interpersonal reasons. A large number of Americans visit European countries in order to see their families or because they feel they are visiting their homeland. Many friendships have been made as a result of holiday familiarity.
8. ***Pilgrimage*** – Travel for pilgrimage has been taking place since ancient times.[16] This practice is widespread in many parts of the world. In India, there are many pilgrimage centres and holy places of all the major religions of the world where every year a large number of pilgrims from all over the world come and contribute for pilgrimage tourism.[17]
9. ***Curiosity and Culture*** – Curiosity has been one of the major reasons for tourism. There has always been curiosity in man about foreign lands, people and places. People are visiting different lands specially those places, having important historical or cultural associations with the ancient past or those places holding special art festivals, music festivals, theatre and other cultural event of importance. In the present day world technological developments in the area of mass media have made it possible for people to read, see and hear about different places. Thus, creating more curiosity about new places and culture.[18] The increased interest shown by many in the art, architecture, music, literature, dance, folklore,

sports, cultures, historical remains and monuments, is another aspect of curiosity among the tourists.[19]

Destination Lifecycle

Destination lifecycle is divided into three parts: (1) Short-term (2) Medium and (3) Long-term destination life cycle.

1. *Short-term cycles*—Short-term cycles are those that occurred within a time of a year or less. A good example: these cycles being the seasonal cycle at resort, such as the peak summer season at a sea-side destination or the peak winter season at a ski resorts, with little to sustain business in six months or longer off season. Sometimes tourist destination is divided into two cycles in a year: first is summer and second is winter season. Many tourist destinations can provide year round facilities many of them still have a seasonal annual business. For example, the major tourist destinations may operate at capacity for vacationing tourists during the summer season and try to fill its accommodation during the balance year. In May-June is traditionally the vacation month when all persons want to be away on vacation. The strains on the superstructure (road) and infrastructure (hotels, restaurants) of tourist destination during this month remain in full demand. This type of seasonal demand also causes important strain on the tourist industry and its labour force there by creating another problem. In highly seasonal destination because such business must maximize their revenue in order to survive through the holidays, there may be price differentials between the "peak demand" and the "off season" periods and these can affect even local residents who may wish to use a tourist facility. For example a resident using a local restaurant may pay a higher price for the same menu item in the peak season than the off season. Traffic inflow and the lack of parking space during the peak tourist season can cause similar disappointment and even opposition towards tourism and tourists.
2. ***Long-term Cycles***—Long-term life cycle is often described as having four stages: Discovery, development, maturity and decline in their life.

Figure No. 2.3: Long Term Cycles

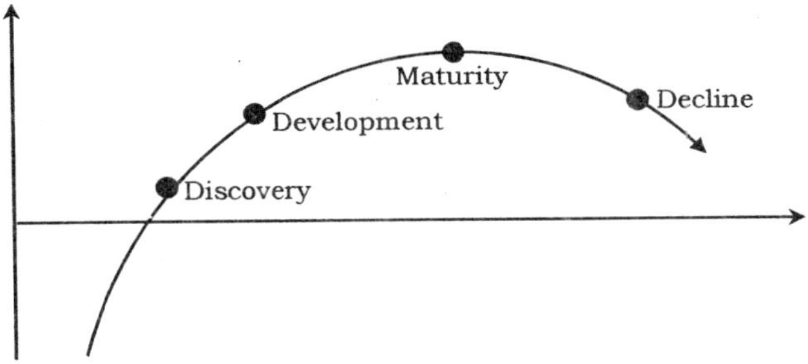

During Discovery, tourists are generally welcome by the residents and their visits are viewed in a positive manner.[20] Growth and development means number of tourists increase. The tourist continues to adapt to the local culture, although there are signs that the tourist industry is also beginning to adapt to the need of the tourist. Increased attention may be paid to sanitation and guest comfort ever if the change is nothing more than the addition of screened doors and windows.The increase interaction between tourists and residents begins to create a reassessment of thinking among residents as to life goals and the means to attain them. This may result in a desire for better education, a realisation of the availability of different occupations; an increased awareness of the outsides world, and perhaps a shift away from traditional vocations. Toward the end of this stage contact between tourists and resident becomes more impersonal and formal tourism continues to grow, but local tourist services and local resources, such as administrative, economic and organisation skills, are no longer able to keep up with the volume of tourists.[21]

Maturity is characterized by a large number of tourists and formalization of service, itineraries and roles. There may be a loss of local decision-making power and control over the tourism industry. During the Maturity institutionalisation stage, procedures and facilities become standardized. This leads to greater efficiency, but may also create resentment against the loss of culture through the franchized appearance of structures and services. On the positive side, the diets of local resident improve as they are exposed the new foods and increased income opportunities. A revival of native crafts may occur since these items are in demand by travellers. Increased production of native craft to meet the demand generates income and provides in-home employment, usually referred to as a 'Cottage Industry'. The availability of jobs creates population growth in the area intensifying social pressures, particularly when an illiterate peasant class suddenly finds itself in an urban or semi-urban environment. It also leads to a decline in the concept of natural help of cooperation among individuals and within a family. Decline is the final stage, the destination has become saturated and residents have become disenchanted that tourism has not produced all of the promised benefits. For the visitor, the factors that were responsible for the destination's earlier success—the hospitality and enthusiasm of the residents, the appeal of the new destination, the clean and uncongested environment, and lack of gross commercialisation—have disappeared, and travellers begin to seek other unspoiled destinations the key to orderly development of a destination, then, would seem to lie in good planning for controlled development, awareness and concern on the part of host communities and government and careful monitoring of actions.

Introduction and Application of Tourism Behaviour

Understanding the behavioural aspects of man is significant to the tourist industry. Man is a social animal and gregariousness is a feature of human society; he is dependent as an individual upon social membership. One of the instinctive emotional tendencies of the individual is to seek the company of his fellow men. This may help to explain why families persist in going to crowded seaside resorts, why they will put up with crowed beaches, restaurants, places of amusement etc. and why they will tolerate queuing in traffic jams to get to a holiday resort. It helps to explain also the success of "holiday camps" which carry socialization to an exertive. Many tourists participate in such holidays as much because they enjoy being members of the organized group as because they enjoy meeting people. Social stratification also still tends to exert a strong influence upon tourism. Formally, the upper classes titled as the wealthy and the leisured, went to the winter centres and holidayed in the off seasons. Social attitude reflects the natural tendency of individuals to display and assert themselves among their fellow men and to find satisfaction in gaining their admiration. Associated with these attitudes is the element of fantasy, escapism. A holiday is, very often, simply an escape from the routine existence of everyday working life. Curiosity is a human attribute of great significance to tourism. Many individuals are motivated by an urge to experience sometime new.

Another aspect of particular relevance to tourism is social communication: social organization is only made possible and maintained by communication people are very prone to be influenced by advertisements and tourist agents and operations are not slow to press psychology into service. We have just mentioned the significance of curiosity as a motivating factor, but the most powerful incentives are not the unknown, but the partially known, hence the advertiser titillates the potential tourist with glossy, brightly coloured brochures or films and television pictures which are highly selective and flattering. Such advertisements are specially designed to entice the tourist and they do so with remarkable success. Man's physiological needs: fresh food, air, drink, rest, comfort etc. necessary for the maintenance of general bodily well being, are equally important as a motivating factor. Hence the stress which is so often laid by hoteliers and tour operators upon such items as cuisine, lounges, bathing pools etc. There are indeed many tourists who are drawn to a particular place simply because of the guarantee of good food and comfortable environment.[22]

Market Segmentation and Tourist Research

Market Segmentation

Market segmentation states that in tourism few vacation destination areas are universally acceptable and desired. Therefore rather than dissipate promotion resources by trying to please all travellers, 'AIM' should be to promote specifically to the wants and needs of likely prospects.[23] An effective marketing strategy will determine the target market and then attempt to reach only those markets. The selection of particular segment as "target market" depends on competition cost of developing a destination for them and managerial capacity of handling that market along with its sales potential. The process of selection and corresponding decision to develop a marketing programme suitable to meet the needs of those segments is known as "positioning". Market segmentation refers to a process by which people with similar needs and wants are grouped together for the purpose of better focusing on and securing the market.[24] "Marketing segmentation consists of taking the total heterogeneous market for a product and dividing it into several sub-market or segment each of which tend to be homogeneous in all significant aspects."[25] "Market segmentation is the process by which an organization attempts to match the total marketing programme to the unique manner in which one or more customer behaves in the marketplace."[26] "Segmentation is an act of dividing a market into distinct group or buyers who might require separate products and/or marketing mixes."[27]

"A market segment is a group of buyers who share qualities that make marketing significance. Existence of a group of individual with common characteristics does not itself constitute a market segment only when they have. Common characteristics as buyer do they form market segment?"[28] In view of the above, it is right to mention that market segmentation is the grouping or division of markets with a more pragmatic approach, is a game of divide and rule. When we talk about the tourism market segmentation, our emphasis is on dividing or grouping the tourist market. The division is grounded in different groups or users, requiring separate tourism product and/or marketing mixes. The market segmentation is supposed to be a device to concentrate on a particular segment or a group of tourists and to design the marketing mix accordingly. We all are well aware of the fact that tourism is a multi-segment industry and so. It is natural that market segmentation for the tourism industry covers in its purview almost all the products and buyers or users concerned with central or peripheral services. When we call tourism market that actual and potential demand for the tourism product, its segmentation is naturally meant the division or grouping of all actual and potential tourists who tour or bear the capacity to tour. While segmenting tourism market our emphasis is on all categories of users of services using or buying the intangible or tangible elements. This is a natural way that makes segmentation of tourism market a descriptive concept in which different bases are found applicable.[29] The tourist generating areas are also including in the concept of tourism market and so while practicing segmentation of the tourist sites in actual use and the tourist sites to be used are also found significant. We all call tourist market segmentation process of creating sub-market in which all categories of users and potential users are including. We may further support the fact that segmentation of tourism market is a device to identify the potential tourists. The most sensitive aspect in the marketing process is the identification of potential tourist. In view of the diversity of tourist demand, it is important to relate the needs and preferences of particular segments of the market to specific destination or products.

Bases for Segmentation

According to Engel (marketing segmentation) marketing managers usually divide consumers into three classes for the purpose of marketing strategy,

1. *Similarity*—All consumers are basically similar although differences exist among consumers. These differences are not thought to be important in affecting the purchase of their specific product class. A standard product will essentially satisfy the large majority of consumers.
2. *Unique*—All consumers are unique. The differences among consumers make a standardized product or service unacceptable. Market offering must be tailored specifically to the needs of each individual consumer.
3. *Differences/Similarities*—Consumer differences and similarities exist and are important sources of influences in market demand. Such difference can be regarded as differences in consumer needs and wants. Differences and similarities facilitate the grouping of consumers into aggregates of segment according to their needs and wants and the degree to which they are present. Marketers using a segmentation approach adopt marketing programmes to match the peculiar need combination of each of some market segment.[30]

   (a) *Holiday base:* Generally the holiday is of two or three weeks but there are some long distance tours where even six weeks are found in usual duration. The travelling decisions are influenced holidays. The holiday market is classified in terms of demand.[31] First is the mass market which involver the largest number of vacations who generally travel in large group. They prefer all-inclusive tour. The user generally belongs to the conservatives group. The skilled and semi-skilled workers, blue–collar employees are the bulk of the potential users. Another in this segment is popular market involving smaller groups going on inclusive or semi–inclusive tour the customers are usually from class one and class two groups, pensioners and retired people. Finally we find individual, holiday market where the tourists prefer to travel independently and stay at hotels of their own choice. Thus, travelling decisions are influenced by the duration of holidays.

(b) *Purpose base:* Another base for segmenting the market is purpose of travel. We find different categories are in this segment. In the business travel, we find generally the executives influenced by the quality of services. They are motivated by the world class services made available to them in the hotels and at tourist sites. In the culture tourism, the tourists are influenced by new cultural events. The availability of new cultural events attracts the potential tourists. The members of a religious society are the customers or belonging to the club, association, temples, churches, marquee mainly figure this group.

(c) *Demand base:* The demand base segment tourists can be classified into different categories like primary, secondary and opportunity markets. Primary markets are those tourist generating areas which are providing the main portion of the tourist traffic to a destination or resort. The customers are generally aware of the destination. The secondary markets are those providing some tourist traffic having much greater potentials. The opportunity markets are areas distinct from the destination country. Thus, this base of segmentation assigns due weightage to the demand generated by the tourists.

(d) *Geography as a base:* In this category the segmentation is based on geographical considerations. The cities, provinces, regions, countries are the main segment. The base of classification is the area and so, it is natural that tourists are grouped on the basis of regional consideration.

(e) *Psychograph as a base:* In this segment, the life style, personality, motives, product and knowledge are important consideration. To be more specific the life style proves to be an important aspect in this category of segmentation. It is advocated by the psychologists that the potential tourists are influenced by their life style.

(f) *Demography as a base:* In this group, we consider age, sex, occupation class and religion as important consideration for segmenting the tourism market.

(g) *Socio-economy base:* This base of segmenting the tourism market classifies tourists on the basis of economic status, development of area and education.

(h) *Age as base:* Age is an important basis for segmenting the tourism market. It is significant for tour operators since the people of different ages have different interests and habits. In a natural way, the travel needs are also different; younger people are restricted by their low income. The young married with young children have also financial constraints but they give priority to the safety of their family and make travel decisions accordingly. The older people generally wish to avail better quality hotels and luxury transportation facilities.[32]

Need and Importance of Segmentation in Tourism

Tourism market is the actual and potential demand of the tourism product and segmentation means division or grouping of all. Segmentation is the process of identifying potential tourist having positive attitude towards travelling and creating sub-markets of all types of users. Segmentation simplifies the task of persons associated with tourism industry. Two tourists are never identical in their preferences, habits, choices etc. hence, their expectation levels are also different that is why segmentation is needed. If we can offer the services to the expectation of a particular group then industry will be able to transform potential tourists into actual tourists. Segmentation helps in the simplification of accomplishment of organization goal and is needed:

- For establishing leadership, locating the potential tourists.
- For designing market strategy, identifying the habit, lifestyles and preference of tourists.

Figure No. 2.4: Effective Tourism Market Segmentation

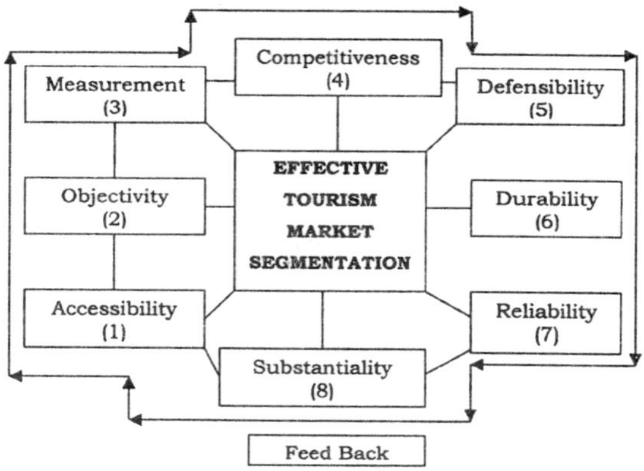

- Gauging the levels of expectations.
- For identifying the opportunities in the marketplace.
- Bringing creativeness in marketing decision, optimum allocation of resources, search of new markets and new products.
- For excelling in competition by differentiating its own products from others and matching it to the requirement of particular segment.
- Simplification of the task of marketers. Tourism market segmentation to be effective must have the following qualities like measurability, accessibility, substantiality, defensibility, durability, competitiveness, reliability and objectivity as shown in the figure.
- Developing marketing programmes and budgets on the basis of a clearer idea of the response and characteristics of specific segment.
- One can attain greater ability to tailor his behaviour, promotion, logistics, distribution channels and marketing mix to the marketers.

Assumptions of market segmentation in tourism as perceived by Dr. Abhinav Kamal Raina.

Market segmentation can be based on following assumptions:

- It assumes that tourists can be grouped into different market segment.

- People having different vacations, travel needs and preference thus, can form particular market segment of their own.
- A specific destination or tourist experience will appeal to some segments of the market more than others.
- It assumes that tourism supplier can improve their marketing efforts by developing products and services that appeal to specific market segment.[33]

Segmentation model involves seven stages:

- Selection of the basis of segmentation.
- Selection of a set of segment descriptions.
- Sample design mostly stratified and occasionally a quota sample according to the various classes of the dependent variable.
- Data collection.
- Formation of the segments based on a sorting of respondents into categories.
- Translation of the findings about the segments estimated size and profile into specific marketing strategies including the selection of target segments and the design or modification of specific marketing strategy.[34]

Figure No. 2.5: Segmentation Decision Process

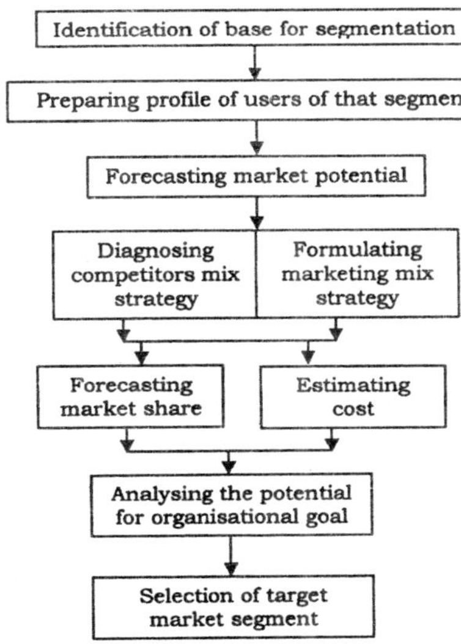

Figure No. 2.6: Hierarchy of Segments Approach to International Market Segmentation

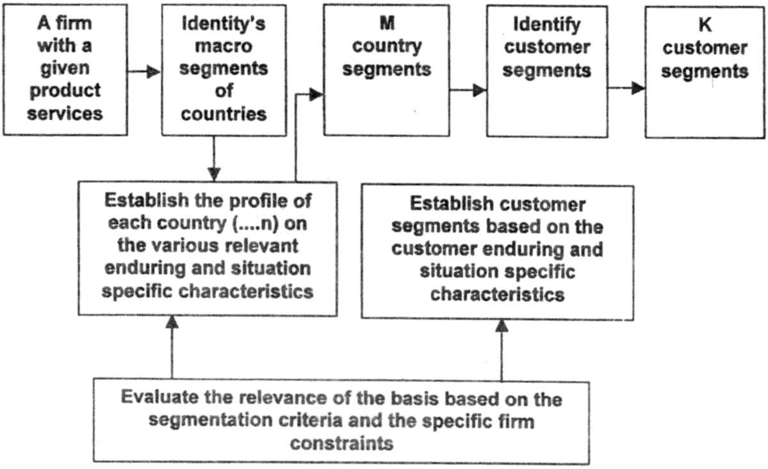

Source: Wind and Douglas. International Market Segmentation; *European Journal of Marketing*, Vol. 5, No. 1, 1972.

Tourist Decision Making Process

Tourist Demand

The generation of wants and their conversion can be treated as "BEHAVIOUR" in psychological terms. Environmental factors generate a number of contradictory wants. Some of these wants materialize into the effective demand. Thus, the core problem is to recognize how these wants are converted into demand in general and tourism demand in particular. In other words, how does a tourist decide upon a particular destination? Conversion of wants into demands is not automatic and in most cases they are mediated by various processing factors. These factors may be other individuals, groups of persons or organisations such as tourist bureaus, travel agents, airlines etc. In the decision-making process the visitor is unprotected to a number of stimuli, most of which reach him already pre-processed by opinion leaders. The various elements of the decision-making model of modern tourist areas as put by Dr. A.K. Raina (2006): *(i)* Desire, *(ii)* Leaders opinion, *(iii)* Methodology of selection, *(iv)* Functional transformation, *(v)* Feedback.

Figure No. 2.7: Elements of Decision-Making Model

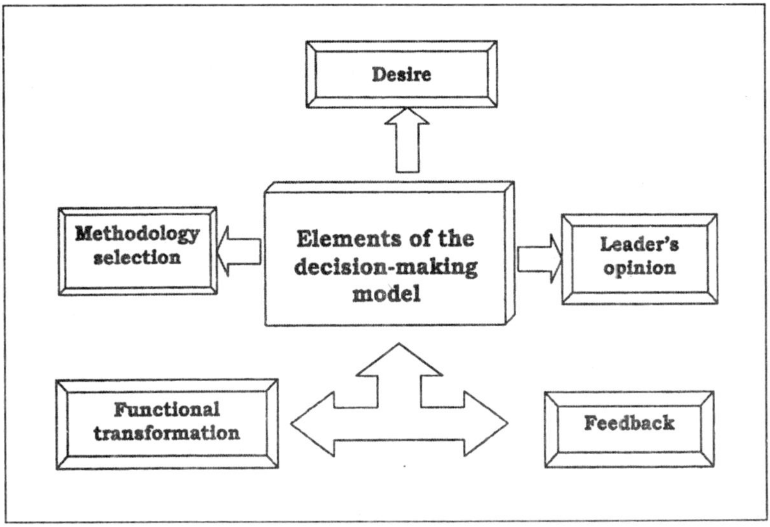

Desire

Desire to travel is like a gatekeeper that lets only some of the stimuli enter the selector's mind. In the stimuli process complexity of individual needs and wants of the potential visitor is faced with the two-fold problem i.e. choosing travel against other competing attractions and selection of a destination. A visitor is exposed to a number of stimuli which are often contradictory such as holidaying in the neighbourhood, or going on an international trip. He is, thus, faced with the two-fold problem of deciding on travel rather than spending his money on other goods as well as the selection of a particular holiday destination.

Leader's Opinion

The effect of opinions and attitude of friends and family members who have already been to particular destinations is more important than that of printed message. Interpersonal relationship seems to influence the individual opinions, attitude, habits and values. The communications made by the opinion leaders do not enter the selector's system automatically. How exactly messages are integrated depends upon the pre-dispositional structure of an individual.

Selection Methodology

An individual is the sum total of his attitudes, beliefs, values, goods, personality traits, self-image and group influence. It is largely determined by his cultural, sociological and psychological background. These can account for the behaviour of a tourist who is attracted to areas situated unfavourable. The kind of response a stimulus would evoke depends upon the nature of each person's pre-disposition. With knowledge of the pre-disposition of a tourist the advertiser can be in a better position to tailor the message to the tourist's needs and wants. Another dimension of the multiple men is the "Psychological Frame" which in turn is greatly influenced by economic, cultural and sociological factors. The same message can be interpreted differently by the various groups within a culture. A tourist is most likely to hold on to beliefs that he has grown up with. If a message is not in keeping with his beliefs about a particular destination he might ignore or distort it, especially if it involves changes in the affective elements of the attitude.

Process of Transformation

At this stage the information process is the conversion of attitudes into action. Once a visitor is mentally prepared for the final act of undertaking a tour of a certain country or region he requires the help of an organisation that must ensure that his favourable attitude does not get destroyed along the way. The existence of efficient organisations is essential in the case of tourism particularly because a visitor must face a number of competitive demands on his limited time and budget.[35] What is interesting is the fact that favourable attitudes are quickly converted into action. In the transformation process the two most relevant factors are:

1. Situational factors and
2. Organisational factors.

In the area of situational factors in certain cases the decision to go to a particular destination may arrive at the demand stage unprocessed, as shown by the joining attitude and behaviour. As far as organisational factors are concerned, it has been noticed that most of the tourist makes use of the offices of the processing agents whose job is to provide the necessary information and make all the arrangements. Advice given by the transforming agent can greatly bring the attitude into action.

Figure No. 2.8: Transforming Process

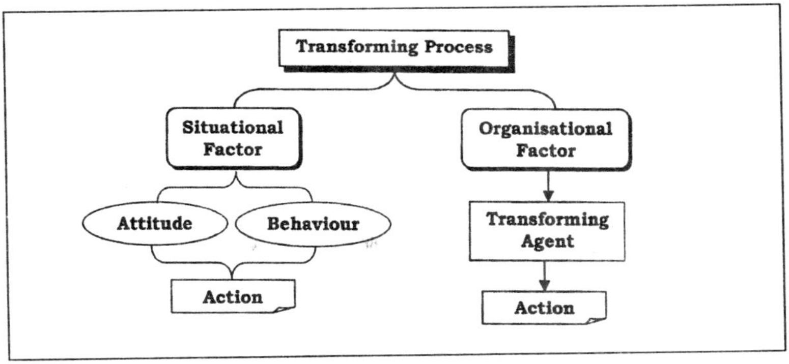

Figure No. 2.9: Tourist Decision Making Process Final Decision

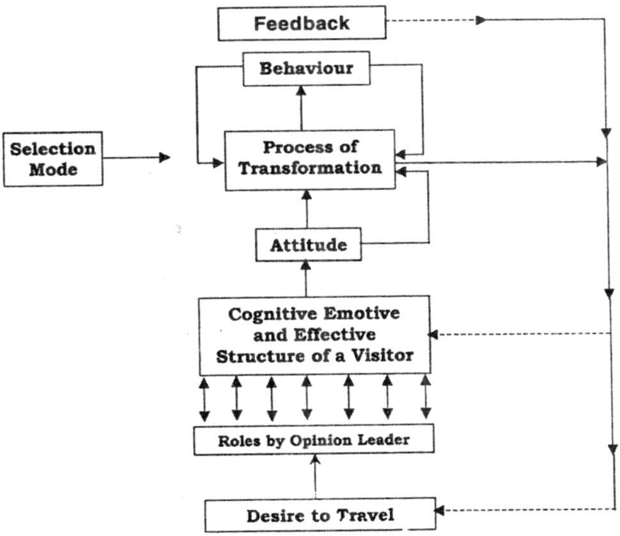

Feedback

The last link in the decision-making model is the feedback from various sources. It carries valuable information about the visitor's satisfaction or dissatisfaction. Depending upon the nature of his experiences during his trip, the visitor generates what is called 'word of mouth' information which is the most important factor in the decision-making process. Since the visitor comes into contact with many people; his opinions are important. One must not overlook the role of such visitors as opinion's leaders. If these visitors are dissatisfied with a visit to a particular destination, they can put to naught all the advertising efforts of the tourist organisation of that destination. Since experience gained is fed into the cognitive structure of a visitor, they will either reinforce previous attitude or bring about certain changes, depending on the nature of his experience and attitude.

Society and Tourist Behaviour

Horner and Swarbrook (1996: 4) opted for a simple form of definition, setting for defining consumer behaviour as the study of why people buy the product they do, and how they make the decision. There is a construction on the term 'customer' which implies a simple economic relationship between a business and a buyer, i.e., that the relationship is based on monetary exchange. Gabbott and Hogg (1998: 9). Wiklie (1994: 132) defines consumer behaviour as "the mental emotional and physical activities that people engage in when selecting, purchasing, using and disposing to products and services so as to satisfy needs and desires."[36]

Tourism Behaviour

Tourist is unique in nature and this inquisitive is reflected in the consumption behaviour and in tourism as well. Tourist behaviour analysis is seen helpful for tourist developers, government agencies and for others who involve in tourist promotion and supply of tourist products. Understanding tourist behaviour is to know the reason why tourist differs from one another in purchase and in services. Tourist behaviour is an analysis of tourist mind regarding what products and services tourist is willing to buy and also how often do they buy. Tourist behaviour can be defined as a 'decision process of tourists' that helps to understand how tourist involvement is used for depositing of tourist services. It is helpful to understand the preference of different tourists.

Over the years it has been observed that different groups of tourists buy different products and represent the different market segments. In order to provide the best possible choices of different tourists, tourism supplier has to be constantly innovative and has to prepare the marketing strategies to satisfy the verities of tourists, needs and preferences. Tourist behaviour provides a valuable clue and guidelines to marketers in the tourism sector on new frontiers which they should explore. Tourist behaviour is a process and a system. Various factors and influences play an important role on tourist consumption behaviour. Tourist behaviour can be affected by a host of variables, ranging from personal motivations, needs, attitudes, values, personal characteristics, socio-economic and cultural background, professional status, recommendation of various friends and relatives. The combination of various factors produces in different set of processes in the purchasing behaviour. Therefore, each tourist has his or her role on standards of judgment and distinct behaviour in every aspect. The role of consumer underlying tourist similarities can help us explain the behaviour of specific type or groups of people. It is these similarities and analysis by which the behaviour of tourists can be understood. Sociological needs, motivation, personality characteristics are same of the similarities which have an influence on different type of peoples and their behaviour. As a tourist, the decision to purchase and use certain products and services is not only influenced by sociological factors and life style but also by the people around you with whom tourists interact. Over the years it has been analysed that the group with whom the tourists interact directly or indirectly influence the purchasing decision and, thus, act as an important tool for marketers to classify and understand the various behavioural patterns. Tourist behaviour has been seen influenced by two groups: 1. Primary and Secondary Groups; 2. Formal and Informal Groups.

Among primary group neighbours, friends, co-workers, colleagues interact on regular basis with tourist. Therefore the opinion of such groups remains important for the marketers. Among the formal informal groups like social clubs, societies, rotary clubs, lions clubs can play specific role in influencing the tourist towards purchasing processes. All the above two groups directly or indirectly influence the attitude and behaviour of tourists and their application while making decision for purchasing. Culture is also considered most pervasive influence on all the aspects of behaviour including purchasing behaviour. Tourist operators within the cultural framework of society and purchase within each culture there exist many sub-cultures and these sub-cultures represent unique values, life style and purchasing patterns. The marketers must understand that the people of different culture and sub-culture, their social background has different inclination towards different tourist's products and brands and therefore tourist's products and marketing strategies have to be formulated keeping in view the culture considerations as well. It is very important for the marketers to understand how tourists make different choices. Human behaviour is seen quite rational and he makes use of information available to them. The modern tourists evaluate the available alternatives of the tourist's products and select the best among then. His or her decisions involve a degree of active reasoning. There are two factors which have an influence on the degree of active reasoning and is undertaken by the tourist in his or her decision making.

1. *Differentiation*

This type of reasoning is found when the tourist perceives that various alternatives differ to each other in different forms and patterns. But on other hand if the alternative is not available to the tourists then they are bound to buy the first available product and brand and will not spend more time in evaluating various alternatives.

2. *Time Pressure*

Time pressure makes the decision quickly. In this situation the tourists probably buy whatever is ready to avail to him. Therefore, the marketers must know how the tourist arrives the decision to purchase a tourist product so that he can design and effect the marketing strategies. Over the years the marketers are trying to understand tourist decision making process with techniques known as the input process and output model. Input refers to the marketing and non-marketing stimuli received from the various characteristics of an individual of groups based upon need reorganization, pre-purchase information and evaluation of alternatives which are available in the market. The output of this model comprises of actual purchase and other purchase behaviours. Therefore, the study of this model is important for better decision making process.

Consumer behaviour concerns the way in which tourists, as purchasers of products and services, behave in terms of spending, and their attitudes and values towards what they buy. Their age, sex, marital status, educational background, amount of disposable income, where they live and other factors such as their interest in travel is affected directly. For marketers who sell and promote tourism products and services, these factors are crucial to know how they divide tourists into groups as consumer so that they can provide specific products that appeal to each group. One frequent approach used by tourism marketers is to achieve this goal in market segmentation. There is a range of approaches that can be used in market segmentation but the most commonly used is demographic or socio-economic segmentation, which occurs where statistical data such as those provided by the census are used together with other statistical information to identify the scale and volume of potential tourists who like to visit a destination. Key factors such as age and income are significant to determine the demand—for example, the amount of paid holiday and an individual's or family's income both has an important bearing of demand.

Figure No. 2.10: Kotler's Consumer Behaviour Model

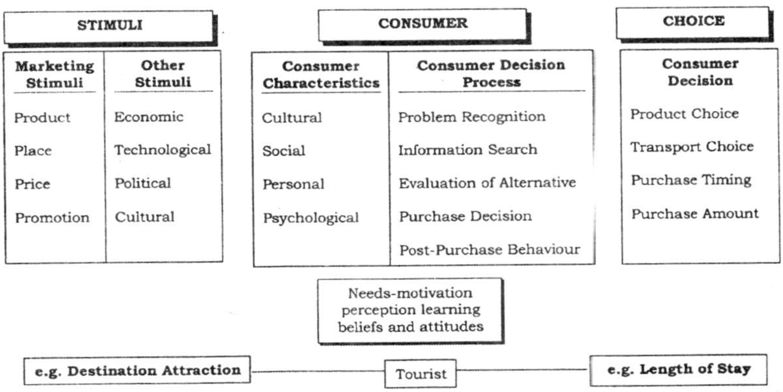

One powerful factor shaping demand in a demographic context is social class, which is related to income, social standard, and the way status evolves from these factors. Social class is widely used by marketers as a way of identifying the spending potential of tourists.

Tourist Destination Marketing

Marketing in the Service Sector—A Study

Tourism is considered a very important industry by many countries mainly on account of the vast potential it has for canalizing the inflow of foreign exchange thereby, making a substantial contribution to the balance of payments position of the country. Many countries like China, Nepal, Sri Lanka, and other South East Asian countries like Thailand, Singapore and Korea, have realized that a methodical approach to marketing their tourist attractions can ensure valuable in-flows of Yens, Dollars, Pounds and other stable currencies. Accepting the basic guidelines of marketing and the prescriptions of market segmentation, the development of various types of tourist attractions catering to the different range of customer requirements is viewed in different parts of the Globe. Some positive evidence in this regard can be seen in the Indian context. Rajasthan Tourism Development Corporation is actively developing new places and attracting tourists to visit locations not very popular till very recently. The large development of the north and southern beaches of Sri Lanka as a product likely to cater to the needs of the vacationers is another case in point. Tourism distribution requires considerable planning *vis-à-vis* the means and speed of travel and the level of comfort. Based on this, it is possible to define an exhaustive distribution spectra ranging from travelling in a tourist bus at one end to air travel at the other end. Another aspect relating to distribution is the concept of chain marketing of varied destinations. The hospitality sector provides interesting application of this new concept of chain marketing. Often a tourist choice of destinations is guided by the presence or location of a hotel unit belonging to the chain which is his or her particular choice. This element of the marketing mix has to be closely linked to the other elements of the mix especially product and distribution. The popular package tours with a mix of different means of transport could be placed somewhere in the middle which is the most popular tourist preference. An illustrative case which reflects the understanding of relating the pricing strategy to the chosen consumer segment is the latest attempt of Jammu and Kashmir tourism to offer offbeat holiday sport in Kashmir at a price around Rs. 50 per person and advertised as for a price little over what it costs to stay at home. Now tourists can experience Kashmir at differential price levels ranging from over Rs. 50 per day to Rs. 1500 per day. Although the pricing element in the domestic scene by and large reflects the understanding of the marketing principles of "what the market can bear" it appears to have gone overboard in relation to attracting foreign tourists.

In tourism the human factor determines the extent of satisfaction of a tourist since his interface with a particular country is through its people, the officials of the airlines, customs, hotels, railways and even the common man. It is remarked that one of the key factors which have enabled Philippines to achieve a million tourists in the year 2006 is the spontaneous warmth and the heart warming friendliness of Philippines that no amount of money can buy contrast.

One of the management practices which has paid rich dividends in the recent past regarding selling tourist destinations is the case of two or three related agencies pooling their resources to market complementary services under "one roof." A classic illustration is that of promoting Nepal under the holiday Nepal campaign. Royal Nepal Air Corporation and Indian Airlines offered a 30 per cent discount on air travel hotels provided rock bottom rates to increase their occupancy rates and the casino provided free coupons to attract the travellers. The tourists thus get a package deal at an attractive rate making them to think in enthusiastic terms about visiting Nepal which in twin is highly congruent with the business objectives of the airlines, hotels travel agencies and the casino. In order to increase the inflow of tourists to India, Department of Tourism, Government of India must pool resources of various agencies and offer so as to develop strong tourism footings for the state.[37]

Ethical Consideration and Tourist Protection

Safety and security in major areas of concern of international tourism with the past facts of bad experience like kidnapping, rape, theft, terrorist activities at many tourist places all around the world, thus, disturbing international peace and understanding. Safety and security in tourism referred to the protection of life, health and the physical, physiological and economic honesty and soundness of many visitors, tourism staff and people constituting the communities. Safety and security at the tourist places mostly affects the decision making behaviour of tourists. The major problem of the visitors' satisfaction level, destination image and the conflict between private and public sector regarding responsibility of safety and security are some of the guiding factors to formulize strategic marketing to compete with other international tourist destinations. A co-ordinated effort is required by different sectors of tourism as to ensure safety and security to tourists at the destinations. The safety and security of tourists should be taken in broad perspective like:

1. To develop the extensive policies and strategy with regard to tourism safety by collecting information from other countries and learning from their experiences.
2. To collect process and disseminate statistics and other information relevant to the safety of tourists and to ensure that all stakeholders are informed of trends and developments impacting on tourism safety.
3. To combat eliminate and prevent crime. by developing mechanisms to maximize co-operation and collaboration between the various bodies involved in crime prevention.
4. To mobilize and channel the energy of the tourism business community to participate in activities that will reduce crime.
5. To monitor the press for any publicity on crime against tourists and ensure that reporting on such events is done responsibly by developing a clear and trusting relationship with the media.

REFERENCES

1. Maslow, A.H.—"Motivation and Personality," Harper and Row, New York, 1954, p. 74.
2. Howard, N.—"A New Way to View Consumers", Dun's Review, No. 2, August, 1981, p. 118.
3. Gee, Chucky, Choy, Dexter J.L., Makens, James C.—"The Travel Industry", The AVI Publishing Company Inc., West Part, Connecticut, 1984, pp. 40-41.
4. Michael, Coltman—"Travel and Tourism", Van Nostrand Reinhold, New York, 1989, p. 42.
5. McIntosh, Goeldner—"Tourism Principles, Practices, Philosophies", John Willey & Sons, Inc, Canada, 1990, pp. 131-32.
6. Robinson, H.—"Geography of Tourism", McDonald & Evans, London, 1976, p. 32.
7. Bhatia, A.K.—"Tourism Development: Principles and Practices", Sterling Publication Pvt. Ltd., New Delhi, 1982, p. 47.
8. Coltman, Michael—"Travel and Tourism", Van Nostrand Reinhold, New York, 1989, pp. 43-44.
9. Robinson, H.—"Geography of Tourism", McDonald & Evans, London, 1976, p. 34.
10. Sharma, Vivek—"Tourism in India", Arihant Publisher, Jaipur, 1991, p. 17.

11. Robinson, H. – "Geography of Tourism", McDonald & Evans, London, 1976, p. 36.
12. Coltman, Michael – "Travel and Tourism", Van Nostrand Reinhold, New York, 1989, p. 35.
13. Bhatia, A.K. – "Tourism Development: Principles and Practices", Sterling Publication Pvt. Ltd., New Delhi, 1982, p. 49.
14. Bhatia, A.K. – "Tourism Development: Principles and Practices", Sterling Publication Pvt. Ltd., New Delhi, 1982, p. 34.
15. Coltman, Michael – "Travel and Tourism", Van Nostrand Reinhold, New York, 1989, pp. 43-44.
16. Micheal Peters – "International Tourism: The Economics and Development of the International Tourist Trade", London, 1999, p. 80.
17. Kaul, R.N. – "Dynamics of Tourism", Sterling Publication, New Delhi, 1985, p. 8.
18. Bhatia, A.K. – "Tourism Development: Principles and Practices", Sterling Publication Pvt. Ltd., New Delhi, 1982, p. 48.
19. Robinson, H. – "Geography of Tourism", McDonald & Evans, London, 1976, p. 35.
20. R. Naronha – "Social and Culture Dimensions of Tourism: A Review of the Literature in English", Tourism Projects Dept., World Bank, May 18, 1977.
21. Chuck, V. Gees, Dexter J.L. Choy, James C. Makers – "The Travel Industry", The AVI Publishing Company, Inc. Westport, Connecticut, 1984, p. 101.
22. Robinson H. – "A Geography of Tourism", MacDonnell and Evans, London, 1976, p. 31.
23. Maslow, A.H. – "Motivation and Personality," Harper and Row, New York, 1954, p. 120.
24. Howard, N. – "A New Way to View Consumers", Dun's Review, No. 2, August, 1981, p. 118.
25. Gee, Chucky, Choy, Dexter J.L, Makens, James C. – "The Travel Industry", The AVI Publishing Company Inc. Westport, Connecticut, 1984, pp. 40-41.
26. Coltman, Michael – "Travel and Tourism", Van Nostrand Reinhold, New York 1989, p. 42.
27. McIntosh, Goeldner – "Tourism Principles, Practices, Philosophies", John Willey & Sons, Inc, Canada, 1990, pp. 131-132.
28. Bhatia, A.K. – "Tourism Development: Principles and Practices", Sterling Publication Pvt. Ltd., New Delhi, 1982, p. 47.
29. Robinson H. – "A Geography of Tourism", MacDonnell and Evans, London, 1976, p. 32.
30. Baker, Michael J. – "Marketing", Fourthly Edition English Language Book Society, McMillan, 1985, p. 110.

31. Bhatia, A.K.—"Tourism Development: Principles and Practices", Sterling Publication Pvt. Ltd., New Delhi, 1982, p. 47.
32. Sharma, Vivek—"Tourism in India", Arihant Publisher, Jaipur, 1991, p. 17.
33. Raina, A.K and Agrawal, S.K.—"The Essence of Tourism Development", Sarup and Sons, New Delhi, 2004, p. 161.
34. Coltman, Michael—"Travel and Tourism", Van Nostrand Reinhold, New York, 1989, p. 72.
35. Anand, M.M.—"Tourism and Hotel Industry in India", Prentice Hall of India, New Delhi, 1976, p. 35.
36. Raheja, Banwari Lal—"Tourism and Hospitality Services", Arises Publishers and Distributors, New Delhi, 2004, p. 6.
37. Managing Business Enterprises, Module-V, p. 209.

3

Impaçt Assessment and Feasibility Study

There are many ways to bring money and business into various sectors of economy like in agricultural, industrial and tourism sector for overall growth and development. Development by the tourism sector is the quickest and least difficult method of the three. The economic impact of tourism has for reaching significance both in magnitude and direction due to the vertical and horizontal expansion of the market.[1] Tourism is used by many national and local governments as a medium for the development and re-generation of economics. There are several arguments for this. Firstly, the demand for international travel continues to grow in developed countries. Secondly, as income in the developed countries increases, the income elasticity of demand for international travel also increased even at faster rate. Thirdly, developing nations need foreign exchange earnings to aid their own economic development to satisfy expectations of their growing population.[2]

Economic impact of tourism varies according to the type of visitors attracted to an area and their activities. The impact of tourism on any destination is influenced indeed, by a wide variety of factors like:

- The volume of tourist arrivals;
- The structure of the host economy;
- The type of tourism activity;
- The different and social cultural characteristics between the host and the guest;
- The fragility of the local environment.

The greater the economic and social diversity of the destination, and more the facilities it has for visitors, the more easily it will accommodate additional tourists.[3]

In seeking to understand the extent of the consequences of tourism on the economics of countries and destinations, a range of analytical methods have been developed by economists. These usually involve collecting data regarding expenditure patterns from the tourism and its impacts by identifying.

- Direct expenditure by tourist on goods and services consumed (hotels, restaurants and tourist transport services), although this is not a definitive account of expenditure owing to the leakage of tourist spending to areas and corporations outside the local economy.
- Indirect expenditure by visitors, which is often estimated by identifying how many tourism enterprises use the income derived from tourist's spending and pay for services, taxes and even employees and then recirculates it in the urban economy.
- Calculating the impact of expenditure from those employed in tourism and its effect on the local economy.

(a) Tourism Expenditure

The overall structure of tourism expenditure is of crucial economic importance, since there is an economic mechanism of interaction between tourism expenditure and national income, tourism expenditure and tax revenue, tourism expenditure and employment. Over the years, it has been seen that expenditure on international tourism, which were once an unnoticed residual item in a country's balance of payment, now the tourist account balance has become an important item of considerable significance which the government may seek to manipulate. The tourism expenditure is more pervasive in its economic implication for it acts as a stimulant to numerous sections of the economy. The spending behaviour of tourist as founded by Peter and Checchi:

Table No.–3.1
Typical Pattern of Tourism Expenditure

S. No.	*Item of Expenditure*	*Peter Michael's % Classification*	*Checchi & Co's % Classification*
1.	Accommodation	30	25
2.	Food and Drinks	25	32
3.	Internal Transportation	05	05
4.	Recreation and Entertainment	10	10
5.	Purchase	25	25
6.	Sundry Expenditure	05	03
	Total	**100**	**100**

Source: (1) Peter Michael's "International Tourism" Economics and Development of International Tourist Trade, London 1969. (2) Report Prepared by Checchi and Co. for V.S. Department of Commerce entitled "Future of Tourism in Pacific and Far East", by Harry G. Clewent.

Table depicting expenditure pattern of tourists has identified accommodation, food, and purchase as the major items of tourism expenditure.

Destination of Tourism Expenditure

Visitors	*Travel Industry*	*Ultimate*
Spend for	Spend for	Beneficiaries
		Accountants
		Advertising Relations and Public
		Appliance Stores
		Architects
Lodging		Arts and Crafts Producers
	Wages and Salaries	Attorneys
		Automobile Agencies
	Tips Gravities	Bankers
		Banks
Food		Beach Accessories
	Payroll Taxes	Butchers
		Carpenters

Contd...

Visitors	*Travel Industry*	*Ultimate*
	Commissions	Cashiers
		Charities
		Chemists
Beverages	Music & Entertainment	Clerks
		Clothing Stores
	Administrative and General Expenses	Clubs
		Confectioners
		Contractors
		Cooks
Entertainment	Legal and Professional Services	Cultural Organisation
		Dairies
		Dentists
		Department Stores
	Purchase of Food, Beverages etc.	Doctors
		Dry Cleaning
		Electricians
Clothing etc.	Purchase of Goods Sold	Engineers
		Farmers
		Fisherman
	Purchase of Materials and Suppliers	Freight Forwarders
		Garages and Auto Repairs
Gifts and Souvenirs		Gardeners
		Gift Shops
	Repairs and Maintenance	Government
		Education
	Advertising, Promotion and Publicity	Health
		Roads & Rail Roads
Photography		Utilities
		Development & others
		Greengrocers
	Utilities – Electric Gas, Water etc.	Grocery Stores
		Financiers
		Furniture Stores
		Importers
Personal Care Drugs and Cosmetics	Transportation	Insurance Agencies
		Landlords
	Licenses	Laundries

Source: McIntosh, R.W. – "Tourism Principles, Practices and Philosophies", John Willey, New York, 1986, p. 284.

The expenditure incurred by the tourists has their ramification on different sectors of the economy in varying degrees. It also has a wide dispersal effect as against other economic pursuits owing to the complex and multifaceted structure of tourism industry. The tourism expenditure is distributed in the form of salaries and wages to persons employed and as the profit to management engaged in tourist agencies, hotels, cafes, transport companies. Moreover persons engaged in recreation activities, handicrafts also get a due share of tourism expenditure. Apart from these direct beneficiaries tourism expenditure puts an expansion in demand for the products required by tourist servicing sectors. Thus, through a backward linkage the suppliers of food, raw materials etc. also stand benefited. As a result of successive chain of income and expenditure, the ultimate increase in income exceeds the initial outlay. The first round of tourist expenditure or the income earned by the tourist serving sectors is thus multiplied through the subsequent rounds of expenditure and thereby raising it to higher level. This growth coefficient of step by step magnification of the impact of tourism expenditure which gets subsequently multiplied and spread over other sectors is called Tourism Multiplier.[4]

(b) Tourism Multiplier

The concept of a multiplier was first put forward in another connection by Prof. J.M. Keynes in 1936. The actual world "multiplier" expresses the numerical co-efficient showing the actual change in income brought about by some change in input or investment. It is the numbcr r by which a change in input must be multiplied in order to determine the resulting change in income most excluding the turnover of initial expenditure. Thus, as an example, if there is a multiplier co-efficient of 3 for a tourist expenditure of Rs. 18,000 for a particular trip to Jaipur the economic impact of this would amount to Rs. 54,000. A correlation between tourist spending and multiplied income can be demonstrated through a formula:

$$K = \frac{1}{1 - \frac{\Delta C}{\Delta Y}}$$

The formula, in effect, says that the multiplier K is dependent on the relationship between a change in consumption C and a change

Figure No. 3.1: Tourism Multiplier

Multiplier Effect

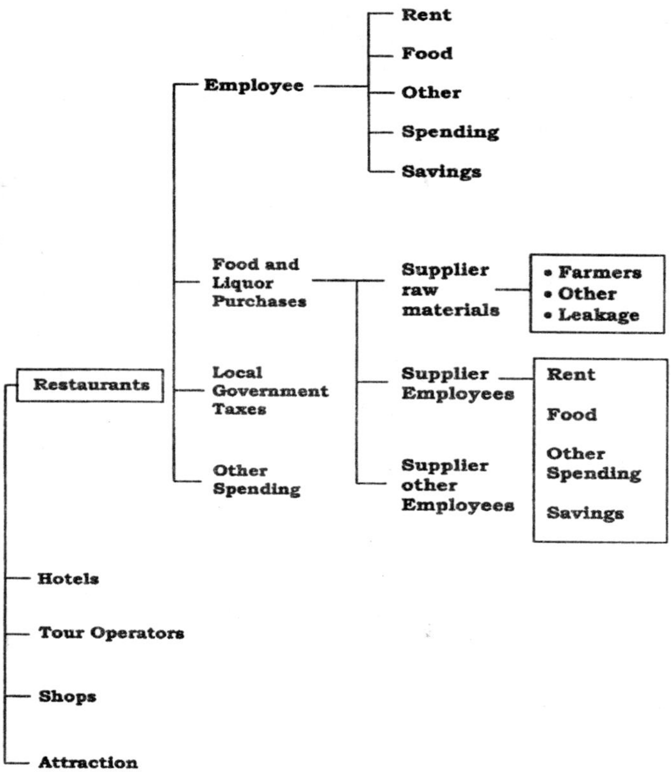

Source: A.K. Raina and Neelu Jain, "Dynamics of Tourism", Kanishka Pub., New Delhi, 2004, p. 77.

in income Y. Thus, for example for Rs. 1000 of tourist expenditure, the change in income (Y) may amount to Rs. 3275.50 and the change in consumption (C) Rs. 2272.50, then the multiplier (K) would equal 3.27.[5]

$$\frac{1}{1-\dfrac{2272.50}{3275.50}} = 3.27$$

The term "multiplier", which comes from macroeconomics, is used to describe the total effect that is both direct and secondary, of an external source of income introduced into an economy. The concept of the multiplier typically is used in the travel industry to encompass the direct and secondary effects of visitor expenditure on an economy.[6]

Multiplier Effect

The "multiplier" impact comes into play as visitor spending circulates and recalculates. The direct effects are the easiest to understand as they result from the visitor spending money in tourist enterprise and providing a living for the owners and managers and creating jobs for employees. This visitor expenditure gives rise to an income that, in turn, leads to a chain of expenditure-income-expenditure and so on, until leakages bring the chain to a halt. Consequently, the impact of the initial income derived from the tourist's expenditure is usually greater than the initial income, because subsequent rounds of spending are related to it.

The effects of an expenditure pattern determine the impact produced in a typical situation, not all of the income generated in each round of expenditure is spent. Some portion tends to be saved, and some portion tends to be spent outside the local economy. The greater the proportion of income spent locally, the greater will be the multiplier. *If the local economy is able to produce the goods and services that tourists buy, the greater will be the multiplier effect. The more goods that have to be imported from outside the region, the smaller the multiplier.*[7]

Multiplier Equation

Lundberg (1976-P.157) provides the following equation for calculating tourism income multiplier (TIM)

$$T = \frac{1 - TPI}{MPS - MPI}$$

T = Tourist Spending; TPI = Tourist's Propensity to import (or buy imported goods or services); MPS = Marginal Propensity to save (by residents); MPI = Marginal Propensity to import (by residents).

Estimated Tourism Multiplier

S. No.	*Country*	*Multiplier*	*Research Conducted by*
1.	Greece	1.2-1.4	David B. Suits, An econometric Model of the Greek Economy 1964, pp. 119-121, Centre of Economic Research, Athens.
2.	Ireland	2.7	Study of Economics of Tourism in Ireland, 1966.
3.	Lebanon	1.2-1.4	Pierre Gorra, Department Nouve le etude, Prospective Sur J.' apport, du Toursisme a development Economiquedu Lebanon 1967, Department Researches etc. documentation, O.N.T., Lebanon.
4.	Pacific and far east	3.4-4.3	Harry G Dement. The future of Tourism on the Pacific and far East 1961, Washington D.C.
5.	Balemas	1.36	Checchi & Co., Washington D.C.
6.	Pakistan	3.3	Master Plan for Development of Tourism in Pakistan, 1965.
7.	Hawai	0.9-1.3	Paul G. Graig, The future growth of Hawaiian Tourism and its impact on the state and Neighbour Islands 1963, p. 105-107, University of Hawaii ECO Research Centre.
8.	New Hampshire	1.6-1.7	Vacation Travel Business in New Hampshire 1962, State of New Hampshire Division of Eco Development.
9.	India	3.2-3.6	Cost Benefit Study of Tourism.

Source: Raina, A.K. & Jain, Neelu – "Dynamics of Tourism", Kanishka Publishers, New Delhi, 2004, p. 80.

Types of Multiplier

1. *Income Multiplier*—Jobs mean income which stimulates the economy of the area in which the development occurs. Stimulation depends on several factors? Using a hotel as an example, the management takes one of two actions concerning the revenue earned, it either spends the money on goods and services, or it saves part of such funds. Economists refer to such action as MPC *(Marginal Propensity to Consumer) or MPS (Marginal Propensity to Save, removing funds from the local economy)*. Such removal of these marginal funds can be made in two ways:

1. They can be saved and thus not loaned to another spender or
2. They can be used to purchase imports. In either case, so doing removes the funds and thus, does not stimulate the local economy.

$$\text{Multiplier} = \frac{1}{1 - \text{MPC}}$$

M= Marginal, P = Propensity, C = Consumers, S = Savings

For example suppose 1000 Rs. of tourist expenditure and an MPC of ½ then :

1000	
+	
500	$\frac{1}{2} \times 1000$
+	+
250	$(\frac{1}{2})^2 \times 1000$
+	+
125	$(\frac{1}{2})^3 \times 1000$
+	+
62.50	$(\frac{1}{2})^4 \times 1000$
+	+
31.50	$(\frac{1}{2})^5 \times 1000$
+	+
15.63	$(\frac{1}{2})^6 \times 1000$
+	+
7.81	$(\frac{1}{2})^7 \times 1000$
2000 (approx)	

$$\text{Multiply } \frac{1}{1 - \frac{1}{2}} \times 1000 = 2000$$

The original Rs. 1000 of tourist expenditure becomes Rs. 2000 of income to the community.[8]

Figure No. 3.2: Basis for Tourism Multiplier

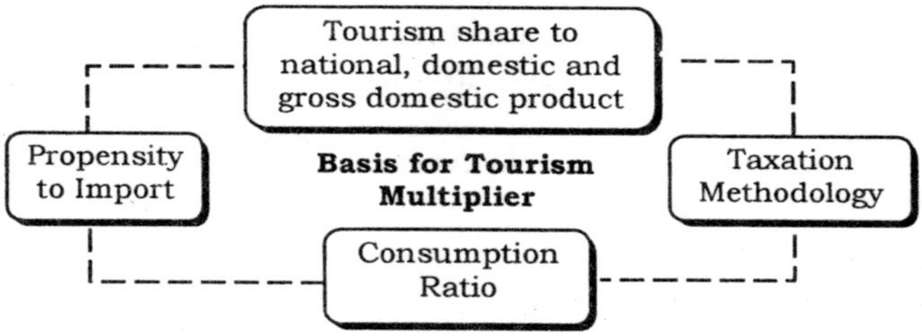

2. ***An Output Multiplier***—This measures the size of added output produced in primary and all the second rounds in an economy due to an increase in tourist spending. An output multiplier is different from a similar transactions multiplier in the sense that an output multiplier considers changes in actual level of production within the timeframe of the processes while a sales multiplier is concerned with the change in total volume and value of sales irrespective of the sales from inventories. Thereby, the value of an output multiplier may vary from the parallel transactions multiplier. An output multiplier (k) can be put as:

$$K_o \frac{\text{Additional output generated in an economy}}{\text{Increase in tourist expenditure}}$$

Whereas, a transaction (or sales) multiplier (k) can be depicted as:

$$K_s \frac{\text{Size of additional business revenue}}{\text{Increase in tourist expenditure}}$$

3. ***An Employment Multiplier***—This is a measurement of either the total level of employment created in the economy during the full course of multiplier process i.e. first round and the successive rounds by an addition unit of visitor spending or the rate of 'total level of employment generated by increased tourist expenditure to the direct employment i.e., employment generated during first round in the direct tourism related sectors. An employment multiplier (K) can be described as:

$$K_n \frac{\text{Total level of employment generated into the economy}}{\text{Direct employment}}$$

Employment multipliers are conspicuous as they explain the secondary effects of tourism.

4. ***A Government Revenue Multiplier*** — A government revenue multiplier is a measure of the impact of an increase in tourism expenditure on government. Public revenue in all forms and from all sources, such a measure has two aspects in gross terms and in net terms. In gross terms it implies total increase in government revenue emerging from an increase in visitor spending while in net terms it measures the net increase in public revenue i.e., revenue increase in public spending resulting from an increase in tourist expenditure.[9]

In gross terms, a government revenue multiplier is:

$$K_{gr} \quad \frac{\text{Total increase in government revenue}}{\text{Increase in visitor spending}}$$

In net term a government revenue multiplier:

$$K_{gm} \quad \frac{\text{Net increase in public revenue}}{\text{Increase in visitor spending}}$$

Employment Generation in Tourism

Tourism is highly labour or employment intensive. This employment is either primary or secondary. Primary, or direct employment refers to those employees directly involved in tourism businesses such as hotels, restaurants and sight seeing. Secondary, or indirect employment is the employment created in the construction of tourist infrastructure and superstructure or in agriculture as a result of tourist's demand for food. This indirect employment depends on how closely the tourism is linked to the local economy. The closed the link is, the more secondary or indirect jobs will be created.[10] It is agreed that tourism is more labour intensive than other industries and for this reason it deserves development support. The degree of labour intensive can be measured in term of the cost per job created or the employment/output ratio.[11] Travel and tourism is the largest industry in the world in terms of employment in almost every country of the world.

Tourism is considered as a job creator with maximum degree of multiplier effects. The jobs are mainly in small, medium size and family owned enterprises. The employment creation in tourism industry is growing faster than any other industries.

Revenue Yielding Effect

Tourism industry provides governments' huge tax revenues through the taxes levied on accommodation, restaurant and various forms of fees etc. Tax revenues generated by tourism could be used to improve community facilities like hospitals, roads, schools and watershed management and energy requirements etc. Improvements in infrastructure could open new opportunity for local residents and improve standard of living. Tourism industry is an important source of tax revenue and total revenue of the state government of Rajasthan besides the income creation and employment generation. The revenue yielding effect of tourism receipts has been estimated with the help of following equation—

$$T = E_t . K_t . P$$

where

- T = Tax Revenue
- E_t = Expenditure by Tourists (National and International both)
- K_t = Tourism Multiplier
- P = Proportion of State Income accruing the Government, through Direct and Indirect Taxes.

Destination Site Analysis

Although not all tourism related projects require physical site locations, a very large proportion do. An economic feasibility study can either specify a site, or determine if an appropriate site exists within a given geographic area. A tourism project site normally requires certain specific characteristics for it to be successful. This is not true of all industry sectors in an economy, as there are many "footloose" enterprises that are not location dependent. In tourism, location has an extremely important bearing upon financial viability. The first step in the site analysis must, therefore, be to identify the criteria that are crucial to the project being considered. Tourism project site criteria or characteristics can be divided into three parts:

- Market related site criteria.
- Criteria related to the physical characteristics of sites.
- Other criteria.

The market related site criteria encompass the site's proximity to potential markets, transportation facilities/routes, essential support facilities, and competitive facilities. When the site analysis is not site specific, it is a common practice to first identify a "long list" of potentially suitable sites and then to rank these sites on the basis of their compatibility with the project. This is often accomplished by attaching a weighting factor to each site selection criterion/characteristic and by then giving each site under consideration a numerical score for that criterion/characteristic. The evaluation of sites for some forms of recreational and tourism project requires a high degree of specific technical expertise. Generally these cases occur when the project is highly dependent for its ultimate success on the characteristic of the natural resource base and when also the construction costs are high.[12]

SWOT Analysis of a Destination

The condition confronting a destination can be analysed by a comprehensive deliberation of the strength and weakness of its current operations and from examining the different socio-cultural-economical and environmental impact for prospective threats or opportunities.

The reaction is a methodical SWOT analysis.

Strength	*Weakness*
Attraction	Pollution/Congestion
Infrastructure and Superstructure Safety and Security	Area prone to natural calamities Local residents
Opportunities	*Threats*
Emerging	Attraction being
Tourism Paradigms Newer Markets	Development in neighbouring regions increasing competition

Master List of Tourism Site Selection

1. *Market-Related Site Criteria*	
Proximity of site to potential markets	Proximity of site to essential support service (such as accommodation)
Proximity and ease to accessibility to transportation facilities and modes:	Restaurants, and shopping centres
Highways and roads	Proximity of site to other major
Airports	Tourism demand generators
Railroad services	Visibility of site to passing vehicular traffic
Marina and harbour facilities	Proximity to major competitive facilities
Trail systems (liking, cross-country/ Alpine skiing, snowmobiling, bicycling etc.)	
Bus services	
Ferry services	
2. *Criteria Related to the Physical Characteristics of Sites*	
Aesthetics of adjoining lands and land uses natural conditions	Site aesthetics
	Scale
Climate and microclimate	Views
Temperature	Focal points
Precipitation	Variety (feature, form, colour)
Sunshine and clouds	Noise
Humidity	Smells
Winds	Vegetation
Seasons	Tree types
Purity of air	Ground cover type

Water supply	Visual and physical condition
Natural springs	Clearing problems
Waterfalls and cascades	Wildlife and fish
Rivers and streams	Species and type
Lakes and seas	Effects of development on these
Drainage patterns	Available infrastructure
Flooding problems	Source of energy
Geology and geomorphology	Water supply
Bedrock type	Sewer system and waste disposal
Water table level, well depths	Services
Quality	Transportation facilities
Geologic history	Other needed services
Soils and topography	Other site characteristics
Soil types	Dimensions and shape
Slopes	Existing rights of way and easements
Depths	Lengths of shoreline available Height above sea level Geographical orientation Ability of land to support various types of recreation activities
	3. Other Criteria
Manpower availability	Social and economic characteristics of host area
Availability of staff accommodation	Source and types of financial assistance in host area
Availability of suitable quality of land for project	Labour laws and labour relations history
Cost of land	
Zoning laws and other legal regulations	

Source:

(*i*) Checklist of factors determining the selection of Site for Tourism Development (Madrid, Spain, World Tourism organization, undated) pp. 1-16.

(*ii*) Manual for the preparation of industrial feasibility studies (New York, united national, 1978) pp. 94-97.

(*iii*) Project investigation/recreation facility site evaluation.

(*iv*) Wisconsin Department of Local Affairs and Development: Bureau of Recreation, undated) pp. 4.2-4, 9.

Destination Market Analysis

The goal of a market analysis is to determine the attractiveness of a market and to understand its evolving opportunities and threats as they relate to the strengths and weaknesses of the industry. David A. Aaker outlined the following dimensions of a market analysis:

- Market size (current and future)
- Market growth rate
- Market profitability
- Industry cost structure
- Distribution channels
- Market trends
- Key success factors

Market Size

The size of the market can be evaluated based on present sales and on potential sales if the use of the product is expanded. The following are some information

Source for Determining Market Size

- Government data
- Trade associations
- Financial data from major players
- Customer surveys

Market Profitability

While different firms in a market will have different levels of profitability, the average profit potential for a market can be used as a guideline for knowing how difficult it is to make money in the market. Michael Porter devised a useful framework for evaluating the attractiveness of an industry or market. This framework, known as Porter's five forces, identifies five factors that influence the market profitability:

- Buyer power.
- Supplier power.
- Barriers of entry.
- Threat of substitute products.
- Rivalry among firms in the industry.

Industry Cost Structure

The cost structure is important for identifying key factors for success. To this end, Porter's value chain model is useful for determining where value is added and for isolating the costs. The cost structure also is helpful for formulating strategies to develop a competitive advantage.

Distribution Channels

The following aspects of the distribution system are useful in a market analysis:

- Existing distribution channels - can be described by how direct they are to the customer.
- Trends and emerging channels - new channels can offer the opportunity to develop a competitive advantage.
- Channel power structure - for example, in the case of the product having little brand equity, retailers have negotiating power over manufacturers and can capture more margin.

Market Trends

Changes in the market are important because they often are the source of new opportunities and threats. The relevant trends are industry-dependent, but some examples include changes in price sensitivity, demand for variety, and level of emphasis on service and support regional trends also may be relevant.

Key Success Factors

The key success factors are those elements that are necessary in order for the firm to achieve its marketing objective. A few examples of such factors include:

- Access to essential unique resources
- Ability to achieve economics of scale
- Access to distribution channels
- Technological progress

It is important to consider that key success factors may change over time, especially as the product progresses through its life cycle.

Peters says that the majority of analysis undertaken show that the tourist market to be made up on three elements: recreational travellers, business travellers and travellers for purposes other than pure recreation or business. Recreational travellers probably make up two-third or even more of the total travel for holiday or pleasure purposes. In recreational travel the choice of destination lies in the hands of the travellers. Subject to certain contingencies or restrictions such as political constraints currency, restrictions, availability of time etc; and secondly the costs involved in transportation and at the destination are borne by the individual or his parents or perhaps a friend. The amount of income, and especially discretionary income, the amount of time at the travellers, disposal and the length of paid holiday and the social and educational background of the travellers, will all influence the choice of destination and the demand for foreign holiday travel, but the current fashion in a holiday destination or national controls designed to restrict travel abroad or even the marketing activities of other countries within the traveller's homeland may also exert an influence. Cost may well be the main factor and the opportunity of a cut-price "inclusive tour" may decide the holiday traveller's destination.[13] Business travel differs from recreational travel in three principal ways: *(i)* the destination of the business travellers is determined for him and is normally not influenced by personal considerations; *(ii)* the costs incurred in the business trip are borne by the company or firm; *(iii)* business travel, which is regarded as an essential part of the business process, is not greatly affected by travel cost. In contrast to the recreational component of the travel market, the business component is usually considered to be relatively price-inelastic: reductions in the cost of travel would be unlikely to affect material increase in business travel. Any increase in the volume of business travel is related essentially to expending trade relationship. The business component of the travel market is expanding although its numerical growth rate does not show the spectacular increase which have occurred in recreational travel, particularly as a result of the developments in inclusive tour holidays. Business travel is a valuable part of the tourism industry however since the business traveller tends to be a higher spender than the holiday maker. The business end of the travel market is highly specialized and is becoming move so; this whole complex industry is now geared to providing what the businessman wants quickly and smoothly. Indeed, so specialized is business travel today that it has developed its own service industry.[14]

The third sector of the travel market comprises those who travel for other purely holiday or business reasons and into this category fall those who travel for the purpose of visiting relatives or friends, for personal health reasons, for educational purposes, for attending international conferences when the cost is borne by the individual. There is no satisfactory all-embracing definition for this third group of travellers and so it is usual to categorize them as travellers for other purposes. These three groups of travellers are not mutually exclusive, for the private individual visiting friend or relative frequently combines this with a holiday while the business traveller often includes a holiday break in his journey. For such reasons, statistics based on purpose of visit may be misleading and caution must be taken in their interpretation.[15]

Cost Benefit Analysis

The cost benefit analysis is a useful technique for understanding the viability of new investments or expenditure projects. This analysis was initially developed as a decision making technique in commercial and public sector organizations. The use of cost benefit analysis helps appraising the estimated cost in investment programme for each year or for the project life. This technique balances the cost against benefits to show the estimated net effect of the project life. Under this analysis all types of the costs like initial and replace investment, all operating costs, working capital and also the estimated benefits accruing from such investment are grouped for each year of project life. The benefits of cost benefit analysis is to find out the feasibility of the project to evaluate by weighing the net gross benefits over the years and comparing it with that of the total life period of the project. Over the years, this technique proves advantageous in different manners as it acts as an examination of all the cost and benefit from investment and the proper timing of it. This analysis is not confined to only commercial decisions rather it is more extendable from a wider prospective. This analysis can also be employed to evaluate the investment by different players of the industry and at different levels by the developers/financiers/lenders/management and even by the government. As far as social cost benefit analysis is concerned it helps policy makers a framework for arriving at rational decision on the use of the public resources. This analysis also describes the behaviour of any decision maker who weighs the expected gains against expected costs prior to making a decision. Social cost benefit analysis when applied in public policy helps in obtaining the information about all positive and negative impacts that a proposed policy will have and to evaluate the impacts so as to indicate the optimal social choice. Cost benefit analysis is seen also useful for private investors which expect maximum returns in their investment. For this purpose the benefits and cost over the economic life of the investment are normally valued at a set of constant prices i.e. the price prevailing at the time of appraisal of investment and the period of time for which the investment can remain blocked. This analysis helps such investors to know the financial liquidity of the project at actual costs and thus, it leads the investors to take the methodological decision regarding their investments. As far as the tourist industry is concerned cost benefit methodology enables planners to evaluated the non-market impact together with the economic costs and benefits of tourism proposals to determine the desirability of alternative developmental strategies. Cost benefit analysis methodology in tourism also lends itself to easy integrations with other analytical models if any. Such touristical intertwined matrix model is outlined by Mueller.

The following formula is used in decision criterion to express the Cost Benefit Analysis of any organization:

$$Is \quad \sum_{t=0}^{n} \frac{(B_t - C_t)}{(I - d)^t} \geq 0$$

Is = Investment

B_t = Annual Benefit in Period, t,

C_t = Annual Cost in Period, t,

d = Specified Discount Rate

n = Life Period of the Project (in number of years)

Social cost benefit in tourism renders the framework of economic and social evaluation. General cost benefit analysis is more focused only in economic evaluation. In social cost benefit analysis, socio-economic impact and other proposals of the activities are being evaluated by employing major attributes of the destination under study.

Under this methodology costs are determined in terms of 'opportunity costs' on the benefit aspect. Over and above the benefits and costs are quantifiable. In economic terms there are non-quantifiable benefits and costs beyond economic values, cultures, traditions, acquisition of specialized knowledge through interaction with the tourists' incommensurables and intangibles. These may involve qualitative judgments and may prove significant to the project as well as to the society and therefore, are to be highlighted in the activity. For instance, the economic benefit of tourism-related hotel project can be identified as follows:

- Tourist spending on food, accommodation, local transportation, souvenirs, entertainment etc. within and outside hotel.
- External benefits such as international transportation benefits, particularly where a national carrier is concerned. These are called external benefits as they arise because of the activity, but are not included in the direct benefits of the project.
- Additional external benefits accruing from the linkages created in agricultural and for industrial sector besides environmental conservation because of the project and consumer surplus.

In wider perspective the benefits of tourism project to the economy as a whole, cannot be contemplated as benefit since resources will be consumed in furnishing tourist facilities. The counted value of such activity is the difference between revenue and costs accounted at shadow prices and expressed in terms of accounting ratio. To compute this, visitor spending has to be classified into economic groups and accounting ratios determined for each sector. For analytical purpose, visitor spending is normally divided into two broad classes, namely accommodation, food and beverage and shopping. Nevertheless, other specific elements may be incorporated in these categories as per the nature of the project. Today social cost-benefit analysis has more relevance as in these both economic as well as social aspects are generalized and measured.

REFERENCES

1. Raina, A.K. and Jain, Neelu—"Dynamics of Tourism: Concepts, Philosophy and Strategies", Kanishka Publishers, Distributors, New Delhi, 2004, p. 73.
2. Mill, Robert Christie and Morrison, Alastair M.—"The Tourism System: An Introductory Text", Prentice Hall Inc., Englewood Cliffs, New Jersey, 1985, p. 222.
3. Makhan, Dileep—"Tourism as an Economic Enterprise", Adhyayan Publishers and Distributors, New Delhi, 2006, p. 185.
4. Raina, A.K. and Jain, Neelu—"Dynamics of Tourism: Concepts, Philosophy and Strategies", Kanishka Publishers, Distributors, New Delhi, 2004, pp. 76-77.
5. Kaul, R.N.—"Dynamics of Tourism", Sterling Pub. (P) Ltd., Delhi, 1985, p. 82.
6. Chucky Gee, Dexter J. L. Choy and Maker,—"The Travel Industry", AVI Publishing Company, Westport, 1984, p. 109.
7. McIntosh, R.W. and Goeldner—"Tourism: Principles, Practices, Philosophies", Sixth Edition, John Wiley & Sons Inc., Canada 1972, p. 281.
8. McIntosh, R.W. and Goeldner—"Tourism: Principles, Practices, Philosophies", Sixth Edition, John Wiley & Sons Inc., Canada 1972, pp. 282-283.
9. Makhan, Dileep—"Tourism as an Economic Enterprise", Adhyayan Publishers and Distributors, New Delhi, 2006, pp. 209-210.
10. Coltman, Michael M.—"Introduction to Travel and Tourism: An International Approach", Van Nostraid Reinhold, New York, 1989, p. 226.
11. Mill, Robert Christe and Marrison, Alastair M.—"The Tourism System: An Introductory Text", Prentice Hall, Inc, Englewood Cliffs, New Jersey 1985, p. 230.
12. Mill, Robert Christie and Morrison, Alastair M.—"The Tourism System: An Introductory Text", Prentice Hall Inc, Englewood Cliffs, New Jersey, 1985, pp. 323-324.
13. Bhardwaj, D.S., Kamra, K.K., Chaudhary, Majula, Bhushan, Ravi Kumar, Boora, S.S., Chand Mohindar, Taxak, R.H.—"International Tourism: Issues and Challenges", Kanishka Publishers, Distributors, New Delhi, 2006, pp. 16-17.
14. Key part of the Market, Business Travel, Financial Times Survey, Financial Times, 23rd May, 1973.
15. Robinson, H.—"A Geography of Tourism", McDonald and Evans, London, 1976, p. 60.

4

Tourism Operations and Physical Carrying Capacity

Managing Tour Operators

Although tour wholesaling began in the mid-nineteenth century it was not until the 1960's that the packaging of tours increased dramatically.[1] Tour wholesaler put packages of tourism experiences for consumer. A tour package consists of at least transportation and accommodation and may also include some or all meals and even entertainment or attractions entrance fees. Sometimes this tour is sold through the wholesaler's own company, or a retail outlet that controls, or approves retail travel agencies. These packages can be offered to the public at lower prices than the individual tourist could find, because the wholesaler can obtain lower bulk prices from airline and other transportation companies, hotels, restaurants, attractions and others. The wholesaler can package a wide range of different tours at different prices, with different destination choices, different hotels at each destination and different lengths of tours. Tour wholesaler generates a large amount of revenue for the travel industry. Although there are many tour wholesalers, within each country, a few major companies seem to predominate. Most of the sale volume generated in each country is with those larger companies as they can deal more easily with tourist suppliers such as the airlines and the hotels and thus offers the tourist with lower prices.[2]

Wholesaler Activities

The wholesaler in the travel industry is similar to a wholesaler in any other industry. The commonality among most wholesalers is that they purchase and take title to merchandise; however, this is not the same for a travel wholesaler. A travel wholesaler does not necessarily take title to travel services. Instead, travel wholesaler utilizes minimum deposits to secure in advance available space for hotels, airlines and other suppliers. A travel wholesaler or wholesale travel agent does not work on a commission basis or retail travel agents. A wholesaler secures large block of advance reservations for airlines and for ground services such as hotels, restaurants, entertainments and sightseeing tours. A wholesaler usually must put down large deposits with suppliers. These deposits and other prepayments to suppliers can be lost by a wholesaler if he fails to generate sufficient volume to fill the large number of rooms or seats that were reserved for months and sometimes years in advance.

The term, tour operator, can be confusing, since traveller may refer to a local sightseeing company as a tour operator. Wholesalers make their profits by purchasing large volumes of travel services from suppliers. Suppliers are interested in this business since it helps to assure them of advance sales; consequently, wholesalers are able to contract for the space or services from suppliers at substantially reduced prices. The wholesaler must decide what type of tour packages would appeal to travellers, package the services accordingly and sell them. The packaged tours are made attraction to potential travellers through prices lower than what the traveller would pay for these services on an itemized or individual basis and by merchandising attractive and colourful brochures describing the interesting and exciting places and events the traveller will experience. Properly packaged tour merchandising does not simply list the hotels and airlines a traveller will use.[3] The independent tour wholesaling business is very concentrated, with a small number of companies accounting for a large percentage of total revenue generated and passengers carried.

Types of Tours

Escorted Tour

A type of organized tour that includes the services of a tour escort who accompanies an individual or group throughout the tour.

Hosted Tour

A type of organized tour that includes the services of a tour host who meets an individual or group at each destination to make local arrangements, but does not accompany the tour.

Package Tours

A type of organized tour, individual or group that includes airfare and some ground arrangement, but does not necessarily include the services of anyone meeting the individual or group at the destination.[4]

Method of Operation

Wholesalers sell their packages through retail travel agents, not to them. Retail travel agents receive a commission and at times an override based on volume from wholesaler to sell their packages. Wholesalers may also sell through incentive companies, who act as agents in selling packages to corporations and other organizations. These firms use the tours as motivational incentives for employees. Wholesalers as tour operators, also sell tour packages directly to groups of tourists. Wholesalers also serve as retailers when they own travel agencies.[5]

Business Functions

A single tour programme consists of three parts.

Tour Preparation

The preparation of a tour begins with market research. By using the results of research organizations by analysing tourist movements and by surveying retailers and past and potential tourists the wholesaler gets an indication as to which tours will sell. This information is combined with past operating results as to which tours have sold will and have made a profit. The policies made a profit. The policies and tour destinations of competitors are also considered. When preparing the development of a new destination it is likely that the wholesaler will participate in a familiarization visit to determine the tour potential, to evaluate ground services and to solicit government support for tour business. At this point, detailed tour specifications are prepared on such items as departure dates, length of the tour, and types of transportation and ground services that will be used. These activities may take place fourteen to eighteen months before the tour is scheduled to take place.

Tour Marketing

The marketing of a tour is the aspect most crucial to its success. The marketing programme will depend upon the size of the wholesaler and the market segments being targeted. All marketing programmes, however, involve brochure distribution, media advertising, personal selling and contact with other wholesaler. Brochures are usually distributed to all retail outlets. Emphasis may, however, be given to retailers who have worked with the wholesaler before or whose customers have exhibited the characteristics of the target market. Tours are often consolidated into brochures of the airlines providing transportation and distributed by the airline. The reverse is also true. Media advertising consists of advertising to the trade as well as to potential tourists. The messages are of necessity; different advertisements in trade publications describe to tour and give retailers information on how to book the tour. A coupon is often included to allow retailers to order tour brochures, posters and other sales aids. Consumer advertising tends to be more glamorous and oriented toward creating interest in the tour. By completing a coupon, consumers may send for tour brochures with the composition to book the tour through a retail travel agent. Wholesalers will also employ sales representatives who concentrate on personally selling the wholesaler's offerings to those retailers regarding as the best prospects for selling the tours. Because of the high cost of distribution, tour wholesalers from one part of the country may use wholesalers from another part of the country to distribute their tours in that region for a fee.

Tour Administration

The administration of a tour tends to begin six months prior to the tour departure. Detailed schedules or worksheets are prepared describing the tour programme and a reservation system sufficient to detail the documentation and payment status of each passenger is set up. The tour operation part of the administration of the tour may be handled by the tour wholesaler or by ground service operator at many destinations.[6]

Future of Wholesaler

1. *Regulations or Laws by Industry and Government:* Increased regulation is a constant possibility and becomes even more

Figure No. 4.1: The Tour Wholesaler Operating Cycle

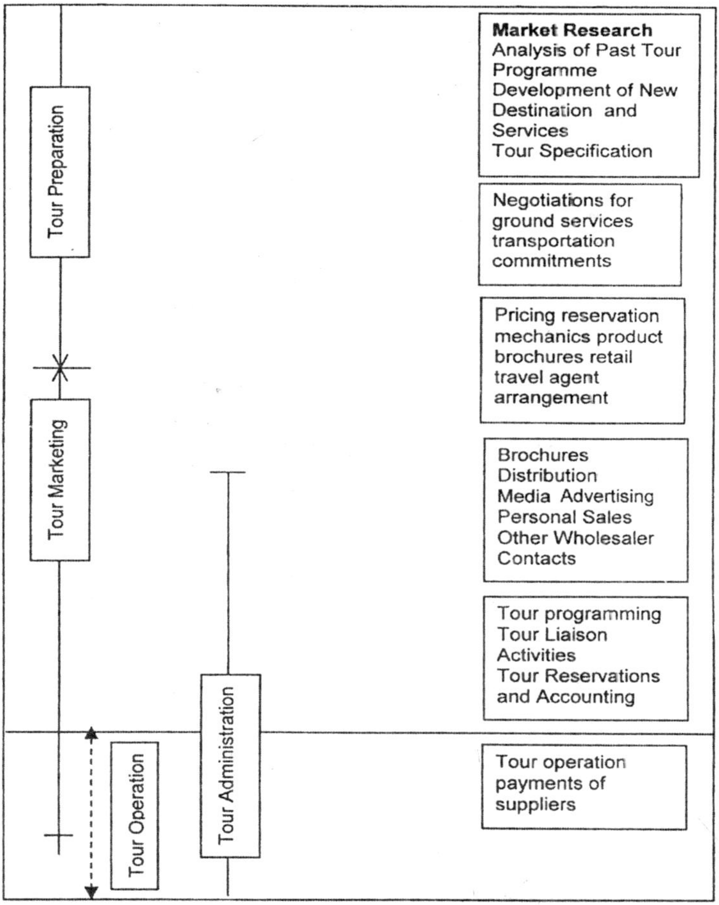

Source: A Study of Tour Wholesaler Industry, Touche Ross & Co. 1976, p. 48.

likely whenever a large wholesaler declares bankruptcy. An increase in the number of inexperienced wholesaler has caused calls for increased regulation of wholesaler.

2. *Restricted Supplies at Discounts:* Suppliers would be unlikely to sell blocks a advance space to wholesaler at discount prices if such space can be sold at higher prices directly to the traveller or through travel agents.

3. *Competitive Packages by Suppliers:* Suppliers have shown a willingness to combine travel services with other complementary suppliers to create air, ground and/or sea packages. These could be sold in greater number directly by suppliers in competition with wholesalers.
4. *Low Individual Prices from Suppliers:* Discount fares and other low prices from suppliers could effectively discourage travellers from purchasing group tours put together by wholesalers.
5. *Changes in Travel Habits:* Changes in travel habits due to energy shortage, high costs, or other reasons could affect the wholesalers positively or negatively. The high cost of gasoline, for instance, has caused increased popularity of short distance vacations at resorts close to traveller's home.
6. *Increased Litigation aimed at Wholesaler:* Many wholesalers have faxed serious lawsuits. As consumers become increasingly sophisticated in travel, a rise in lawsuits directed against wholesalers could seriously affect their future.[7]

Physical Carrying Capacity at Tourist Destinations

Carrying capacity consideration is based upon three dimensions: physical – ecological, socio-demographic, political – economic. Each tourist destination differs in one another depending upon social, political economical environment and ecological considerations and also the relationship and interrelationship into each other. Local resource, population size, economic structure, cultural and local heritage are considered the characteristics of the locality and are considered as the basic structure for the tourism development. The dynamism of the host community, their cultural and economic status are considered as an important input for the development of tourism at a particular destination. The tourist development and local economy are also considered important for measuring and implementing for carrying capacity programmes. The above mentioned attributes of destination are seen significant in carrying capacity considerations.

Coastal Areas

Coastal areas are normally associated with mass tourism, large scale construction and infrastructure, intensive land development and extensive urbanization. Carrying capacity issues revolve around considerations about tourist density, the use of beaches and tourist infrastructure, congestion of facilities, sea pollution, etc.

Islands

Island tourism, if not falling within the previous category, is more of the selective type with small and medium scale accommodation, often in (or around) existing settlements, rural local societies, small communities, etc. Carrying capacity considerations focus on the relationship of tourism with the local society/culture. the effects on local production systems and the economy of the island, quality of life but also the demands and impacts on resources such as water and energy, the management of waste, etc.

Protected Areas

Tourism in protected areas is associated with appreciating and observing nature scientific endeavour and education. This type of tourism is associated with minimal development of infrastructure and small scale interventions in areas of normally-strong control and restrictive management. Carrying capacity issues concern the number of tourists, visitor flows and spatial patterns of concentration/dispersion *vis-à-vis* the protection of nature and the functioning of ecosystems but also the quality of experience of visitors.

Rural Areas

Tourism in rural areas covers a wide range of purposes (motivations) and is usually associated with visiting areas of special beauty, being in nature, low intensity activities but widely dispersed around low density—often remote—rural communities. In some areas agro-tourism falls within this category. Carrying capacity issues involve questions about visitor flows, impacts on local society and culture, effects on rural economies, the spatial patterns of visitor flows, etc.

Mountain Resorts

These are likely to resemble the intensive development, mass tourism category, often centred around winter sports. Carrying capacity issues include environmental impacts from large scale infrastructure or access roads on natural ecosystems, microclimate change from artificial snow, vegetation cover losses and soil erosion, landscape deterioration, but also congestion of facilities and waste management.

Historical Settlements and Towns

Tourism is attracted to historic towns as a result of the built cultural heritage, urban amenities, lifestyle and cultural traditions, cultural events, etc. There can be several types of tourism in this category. The dominant mass tourism associated with large numbers of visitors centring on monuments, museums, etc. often of a short stay (even daily visits) in which case carrying capacity issues centre around congestion of facilities, traffic, urban land-use change, waste management etc. At the other end of the spectrum in some other cases tourism in historic settlements could be more of the selective type associated with small groups of visitors, low pressures for development, etc. in which case carrying capacity considerations could be limited to urban fabric change, etc.

Tourist Carrying Capacity—An Assessment Methodology

The Approach: tourism carrying capacity as part of a planning process— The definition of assessment and implementation of tourism carrying capacity needs to be considered as a process within a planning process for tourism development. We consider some steps of a planning process.

1. The process of defining and implementing tourism carrying capacity and a broader process of planning for sustainable tourism, which are parallel and complementary processes, can provide a general framework which could guide the local community, planners and decision-makers. This framework consists of principles, goals, objectives and policy measures in regard to tourist development in an area on the basis of the area's distinctive characteristics/features respecting local capacities to sustain tourism.
2. Setting capacity limits for sustaining tourism activity in a place involves a vision about local development and decisions about managing tourism. These should be carried in the context of democratic community strategic planning, which requires participation of all major actors and the community at large. Consultation with relevant stakeholders

is a key issue at all stages. The whole process is dynamic and cyclical.

3. Overall measuring Tourism Carrying Capacity does not have to lead to a single number (threshold), like the number of visitors. Even when this is achieved this limit does not necessarily obey to objectively, unchangeable, ever lasting criteria. An upper and a lower limit of tourism carrying capacity can be of more use than a fixed value. Tourism carrying capacity assessment should provide not only the maximum but also the minimum level of development that is the lowest level, necessary for sustaining local communities. In addition, tourism carrying capacity may contain various carrying capacity limits in respect to the three components: physical-ecological, social-demographic and political-economic. "Carrying capacity is not a scientific concept or formula of obtaining a number, beyond which development should cease. The eventual limits must be considered as guidance. They should be carefully assessed and monitored, complemented with other standards, etc. Carrying capacity is not fixed. It develops with time and the growth of tourism and can be affected by management techniques and controls."
4. The process of defining tourism carrying capacity is composed of two parts. Within this context of particular importance is the identification of:

   - *Constraints:* limiting factors that cannot be easily managed. They are not flexible, in the sense that the application of organisational, planning, and management approaches, or the development of appropriate infrastructure does not alter the thresholds associated with such constraints.

   - *Bottlenecks:* limiting factors of the system, which managers can manipulate (number of visitors at a particular place).

   - *Impacts:* elements of the system affected by the intensity and type of use. The type of impact determines the type of capacity (ecological-physical, social, etc.). Emphasis should be placed on significant impacts.

Figure No. 4.2

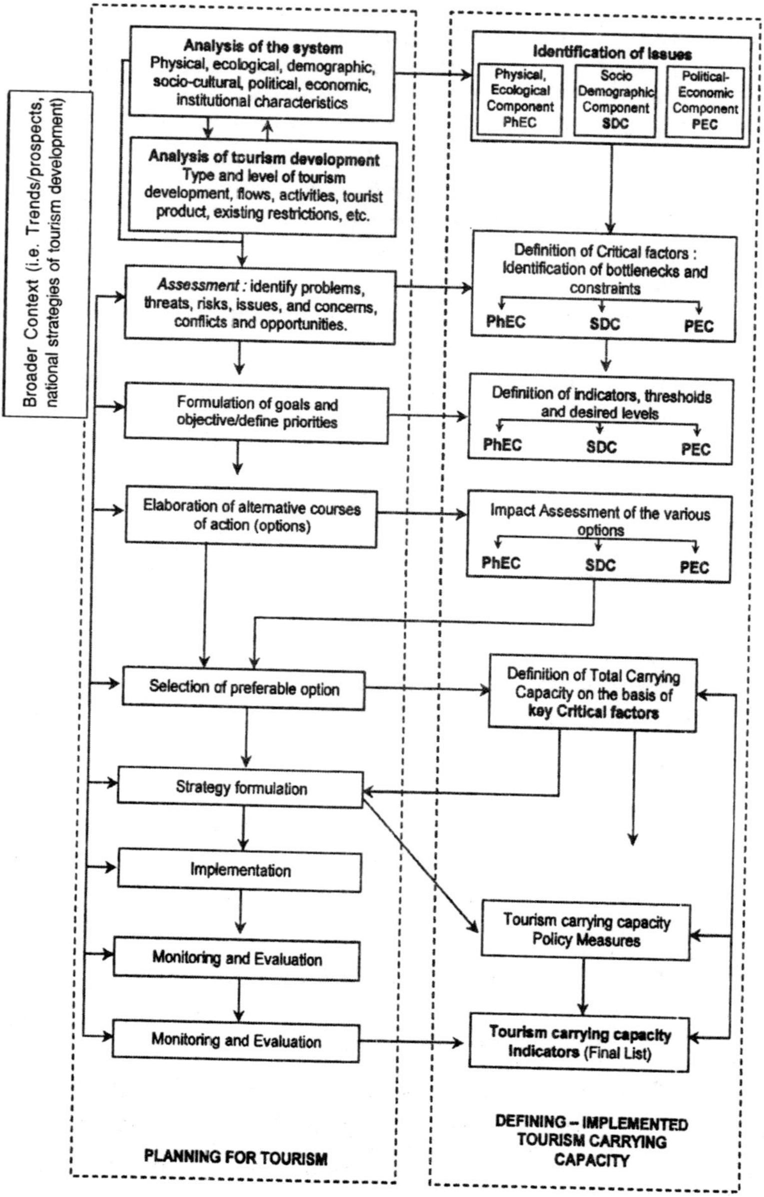
Broader Context (i.e. Trends/prospects, national strategies of tourism development)
Analysis of the system
Physical, ecological, demographic, socio-cultural, political, economic, institutional characteristics
Analysis of tourism development
Type and level of tourism development, flows, activities, tourist product, existing restrictions, etc.
Assessment : identify problems, threats, risks, issues, and concerns, conflicts and opportunities.
Formulation of goals and objective/define priorities
Elaboration of alternative courses of action (options)
Selection of preferable option
Strategy formulation
Implementation
Monitoring and Evaluation
Monitoring and Evaluation
PLANNING FOR TOURISM
Identification of issues
Physical, Ecological Component PhEC
Socio Demographic Component SDC
Political-Economic Component PEC
Definition of Critical factors : Identification of bottlenecks and constraints
PhEC SDC PEC
Definition of indicators, thresholds and desired levels
PhEC SDC PEC
Impact Assessment of the various options
PhEC SDC PEC
Definition of Total Carrying Capacity on the basis of key Critical factors
Tourism carrying capacity Policy Measures
Tourism carrying capacity Indicators (Final List)
DEFINING – IMPLEMENTED TOURISM CARRYING CAPACITY

Tourist Carrying Capacity

Evaluative Part (B) describes how an area should be managed and the level of acceptable impacts. This part of the process starts with the identification (if it does not exist already) of the desirable condition/preferable type of development. Within this context goals and management objectives need to be defined, alternative fields of actions evaluated and a strategy for tourist development formulated. On the basis of this Tourism Carrying Capacity can be defined. Within this context of particular importance is the identification of:

- *Goals/objectives:* (i.e. define the type of experience or other outcomes that a recreation setting should provide)
- *Evaluative criteria:* specify acceptable levels of change (impacts).

The Components

On the basis of the main dimensions of development/environment interface, following a systemic analysis, the impacts of tourism in an area can be analysed in terms of three major axes: physical environment (natural and man-made including infrastructure), social (population and social structure and dynamics) and economic (including institutional and organizational). These can provide also the basis for analysing and assessing tourism carrying capacity in terms of main and distinct, but interrelated, components.

Physical-ecological Component

The *physical-ecological* set comprises all *fixed* and *flexible* components of the natural and built-cultural environment, as well as infrastructure. The "fixed" components refer to the capacity of natural systems expressed occasionally as ecological capacity, assimilative capacity, etc. They cannot be manipulated easily by human action and to the extent these limits can be estimated, they should be carefully observed and respected as such. The "flexible" components refer primarily to infrastructure systems (and their characteristics) like water supply, sewerage, electricity, transportation, social amenities (postal and telecommunication services, health services, law and order services, banks, shops and other services). The capacity limits of the infrastructure components can rise through investments in infrastructure, taxes, organizational-regulatory measures, etc. For this reason their values cannot be used as a basis for determining carrying capacity, but rather as a framework for orientation and decision on management/action options. Levels of capacity for the components can be set, for example, in terms of:

- Acceptable level of congestion or density in key areas/spatial units such as parks, museums, city streets, etc.
- Maximum acceptable loss of natural resources (i.e. water or land) without significant degradation of ecosystem functions or biodiversity or loss of species
- Acceptable level of air, water and noise pollution on the basis of tolerance or the assimilative capacity of local ecosystems
- Intensity of use of transport infrastructure, facilities and services
- Use and congestion of utility facilities and services of water supply, electric power waste management of sewage and solid waste collection, treatment and disposal and telecommunications
- Adequate availability of other community facilities and services such as those related to public health and safety, housing and community services, etc.

Socio-demographic Component

The *socio-demographic* set refers to those social aspects, which are important to local communities, as they relate to the presence and growth of tourism. Social and demographic issues, such as available manpower or trained personnel, etc. including also socio-cultural issues, such as the sense of identity of the local community or the tourist experience etc. Some of these can be expressed in quantitative terms but most required suitable socio-psychological research. Social capability thresholds are perhaps the most difficult to evaluate as opposed to physical-ecological and economic, since they depend on a great extent on value judgments. Political and economic decisions may affect some of the socio-demographic parameters such as, for example, migration policies. Social carrying capacity is used as a generic term to include both the levels of tolerance of the host population, as well as the quality of the experience of visitors to the area. Levels of capacity for the components may be expressed in terms of:

- Number of tourists and tourist/recreation activity types which can be absorbed without affecting the sense of identity, life style and social patterns and activities of host communities.
- Level and type of tourism which does not alter significantly local culture in direct or indirect ways in terms of arts, crafts, belief systems, ceremonies, customs and traditions.
- Level of tourism that will not be resented by local population or pre-empt their use of services and amenities.
- Level of tourism (number of visitors and compatibility of types of activities) in an area without unacceptable decline of experience of visitors.

Political-economic Component

The *political-economic* set refers to the impacts of tourism on local economic structure, activities, etc. including competition to other sectors. Institutional issues are also included to the extent they involve local capacities to manage the presence of tourism. Considerations of political-economic parameters may be also necessary to express divergence in values, attitudes within the local community *vis-à-vis* tourism. Levels of capacity for the components may be expressed in terms of:

- Level of specialization in tourism
- Loss of human labour in other sectors due to tourism attraction
- Revenue from tourism and distribution issues at local level
- Level of tourism employment in relation to local human resources.

Application of Tourism Carrying Capacity

Issues to be Considered

Dairying capacity is a powerful concept for policy making although from a scientific perspective it has met with considerable controversy due to the analytical difficulties in arriving at a "calculated" capacity (threshold or limit). This difficulty stems from the multiple dimensions of the concept and the inherent constraints in estimating limits in natural and human ecosystems. Getz (1987) identified six different approaches of interpretations or methods of determining carrying capacity Tangible Resource Limits, Tolerance by the Host Population, Satisfaction of Visitors, Excessive Rate of Growth of Change, Capacity based on the evaluation of costs and benefits, the role of capacity in a systems approach. In recent literature the interest of carrying capacity has shifted from an "objectively" assessed threshold to 'policy useful' *desired conditions* providing more advantages to planning and decision making. Alternative concepts have been also suggested in the spirit of *management-by-objective approaches* such as Visitor Impact Management, Limits of Acceptable Change, Visitor Experience Resource Protection framework, instead of tourism carrying capacity. There is a growing concern for developing and utilizing tools that could facilitate planners and decision-makers in their efforts to control tourism development. However, there is limited, almost non-existent, experience not only in implementing tourism carrying capacity but also in measuring it. Within this context the following should be taken into account.

Spatial Considerations

Carrying capacity is easier to be defined in limited well-defined areas. In addition tourism carrying capacity could vary among the different parts of an area (ex. centre of the town vs. surrounding areas, or in various sub-areas within ecologically sensitive areas, etc.). In some cases it could be that entire regions can be considered as for example in the case of islands or river valleys, etc. Through planning tools, such as zoning, and management techniques, such as visitor flow management, the impacts of tourism (therefore the capacity of an area to sustain tourism: tourism carrying capacity) can be mitigated.

The Role of Actors

- Effective implementation depends on the political will to impose rules on the way tourism develops, as for example, to control access to a destination in order to protect it. Within this context the development of appropriate institutions measures/mechanisms is absolutely essential. An effective legal framework could help to reduce/mitigate the negative impacts from tourism.
- Consensus of key stakeholders over the definition of tourism carrying capacity is critical. An agreement on the goals of tourism development will be necessary. The results of the

tourism carrying capacity study should be communicated to stakeholders, local people and users who will have to support the implementation of envisaged measures.

- The participation of tour operators is essential too in those cases where they may have a prominent role (i.e. mass tourism destinations, as coastal zones).
- The implementation of carrying capacity needs to take into consideration *cultural elements.*

Integrating Tourism Carrying Capacity in Planning Process and Institutional Context

- Carrying capacity studies have to be incorporated in a plan for sustainable development although this is not a prerequisite in order to employ tourism carrying capacity. Consensus among various stakeholders over a strategic vision of the area could be helpful.
- Tourism carrying capacity should be incorporated in the institutional framework.

Evaluation-Monitoring

- Carrying capacity needs to be flexible and reflect the particularities of the area under study. Systems are dynamic, therefore are subjected to continuous changes. Visitors and local communities, for example, tend to alter their behaviour over time and often adapt to worsening or different conditions, resulting to a different social response.
- There is a need for monitoring but also for credible data and information in order to assess and implement carrying capacity. In that sense significant resources will be required in the initial stage but also during implementation. *Demand* needs to be monitored as well.

Constraints and Common Pitfalls in Implementing Tourism Carrying Capacity

- The changing role of the state. In a market economy, the private sector is expected to undertake increasingly the responsibility or *initiative* of nature/environmental protection or local identity enhancement. In some countries for example forests are privatized. This may probably lead to an increase in pressure, since recreational activities may grow and expand in order to increase profits.

- Action is generally encouraged at local and national level, while several environmental problems are translational. Managing pressures at local level often require policies at a higher level.
- Synergies are often overlooked as a result of fragmentation of responsibilities. An integrated approach in planning and management could provide a good basis.
- Several rather sophisticated systems have been developed in order to measure carrying capacity. However the final number provided does not prove to be always useful and the confusion over alternative measures might discourage managers and policy makers. Furthermore limited effort and resources have been given for the implementation of tourism carrying capacity assessments. The promotion of more pilot projects at European level is necessary including the dissemination of experiences over the use in managing tourism.

Institutional Tools to Implement Tourism Carrying Capacity

At European level there are several instruments that may encourage and facilitate the application of tourism carrying capacity. There are opportunities to include tourism carrying capacity (as guidelines) in existing interventions and tools which are well accepted:

- *Natural 2000*, the *Habitat Directive* and the *Red Lists* are valuable instruments for nature protection and for defining CC levels for ecological sensitive sites so as to limit tourist development. Of significant value can be corresponding institutional approaches like *Emerald Network, UNESCO World Heritage* and *Biosphere Reserve, Ramsar Convention,* which set as a priority the protection of these areas.
- Rely on the *Compensation Principle.* It is one of the ways to put priorities on capacity considerations, as for example in the case of TGV construction in France, by assigning nature a price in order to protect it.
- Tourism carrying capacity as a required concern in *Environmental Impact Assessment.* It should be applied to proposed development projects and programmes in order to evaluate the potential impacts in light of forecast tourism

growth and peak demand. Alternative sites for development should be considered, taking into account local constraints and carrying capacity limits.

- Tourism carrying capacity could be a central concern required in *SEA* (Strategic Environmental Assessment) since this reflects anticipating development on the basis of the capacity of local systems to support it.

Management Tools for Implementing Tourism Carrying Capacity

Regulatory

- *Zoning* is a rather useful tool, easy to be applied. It is applied mainly in protected areas, since their special status allows the definition and delimitation of zones where protection, conservation and limitations in various uses are imposed. A typical division in zones is the following:
    - Zone A—Most valuable and vulnerable. Entry only to authorized scientific teams
    - Zone B—Highly sensitive. Escorted visits in small groups
    - Zone C—Considerable natural interest. Some traditional and tourism activities, limited car access
    - Zone D—Mild development and buffer: Tourism and visitor facilities, car access and parking, compatible activities.
- *Limits to free access.* It could help significant environmental protection. However, many European laws protect free access. It is not possible to discriminate people on the basis of various factors (ex. cartavenezia). Imposing limits to accessibility is allowed only in certain cases like the application of International Conventions.
- *Limits to specific activities.* All kinds of tourist activities have to be evaluated in order to prevent impacts on the environment or conflicts among different users. Special permits or the application of EIA are not foreseen in the case of new forms of activities as in the case of infrastructure development. Some activities may be forbidden given particular conditions, while others may be just limited to certain periods of the year or to a limited number of users. For example, paragliding is forbidden in some French National Parks because it disturbs fowls.

- *Eco-labels.* The use of eco-labels in tourist hotels and other public establishments has a little overall effect on resource consumption and waste production.
- *Concentration or dispersion of development pressures and tourist flows.* From an environmental point of view concentration is not always the best approach to manage tourist flows. Dispersal is preferable, because externalities appear only when the system reaches certain levels of thresholds. However it is also a matter of choice: it is better to concentrate tourists or to disperse them? Alternatively, could it be better to promote the creation of several poles of tourist development? The concept of carrying capacity can be applied in all three cases. However even in cases where a plan for tourism dispersion exists, it would be difficult to manage and guide tourist's flows.
- *Land use/spatial planning* is a process par excellence to implement carrying capacity assessment in the case of islands and coastal areas, while for the areas with ecologies value institutional mechanisms seem to be a more appropriate way in order to ensure protection. As far as historical centres, where the pressure is not from land development, the management of flows could prove to be a more suitable way to go. However, attention needs to be placed on the changes of the functions/ uses within the cities.

Economic

- *Pricing.* It is not always the most appropriate tool to use in order to limit/ centre tourism development/ growth. In the case of Venice, such a policy is expected to penalize tourists and not excursionists, who do not consist a preferable target group. Imposing such a policy selectively to certain groups (i.e. lower prices for residence) is against European laws, since it implies discrimination. However, there are occasions when pricing for parking and entry to major attractions should be imposed in order to discourage visitors. Although pricing is considered as the least desirable solution, remains the most effective at least in the short-term.
- *Taxes* may be used as a way to incorporate in prices various externalities like environmental destruction. Increased prices can discourage tourists and entrepreneur as well.

- *Cost-benefits analysis* should be conducted in different phases of the life-cycle of a tourist destination. Costs are always higher in the earlier phases of tourist development.
- *Incentive schemes* should be applied in both public and private sectors in order to spread tourism demand over time and space and optimizes the use of accommodation.

Organisational

- *Reservation and booking systems.* They facilitate management of both tourists and excursionists' flows. In Venice, for example, the promotion of the Venice card, which corresponds to a package of services, facilitates management of tourist's flows. In this case it is also possible to introduce taxes in a more equitable way, because the Venice card is available to everyone. People who use this card can also benefit from discounts on local transportation, and entry fees to museums and other facilities. The only condition is advance booking. However the use of such system may encourage social inequalities since the cost for visiting such places would be affordable only to specific groups. One should also be aware of the possibility of the creation of a "black market." The possibility of introducing a corresponding package for excursionists should also be explored.
- *Information management.* In Venice information in respect to congestion, peaks, traffic, etc is constantly provided through the web site. This is a way to discourage tourists from visiting Venice and avoid as a result overcrowding.
- *Education* of local community in order to gain their support for implementing tourism carrying capacity is essential.
- *Training* of local planners-managers in the use of various techniques, etc.
- *Market control.* At present, there is little co-ordination between management, planning and tourism marketing. Sophisticated marketing and communication allows marketers to pursue particular market segments and to undertake promotions for periods in which carrying capacity is available. Tour operators could play an important role in managing environmental impacts and maintaining the sustainability of tourism through promoting activities and other actions.

REFERENCES

1. Mill, Robert Christie – "The Tourism System", Prentice Hall Inc. New Jersey, 1985, p. 406.
2. Coltman, Michael – "Introduction of Travel and Tourism", Van Nostrand Reinhold, New York, 1989, p. 325.
3. Gee, C.Y. and Dexter, Choy, J.L. – "The Travel Industry", AVI Publishing Company, Westport, Connecticut, 1984, p. 150.
4. Page, Stephen J. – "Tourism Management System", Butterworth-Heinemann, 2003, p. 407.
5. Gee, C.Y. and Dexter, Choy, J.L. – "The Travel Industry", AVI Publishing Company, Westport, Connecticut, 1984, p. 151.
6. Mill, Robert Christie – "The Tourism System", Prentice Hall Inc. New Jersey, 1985, pp. 412-413.
7. Gee, C.Y. and Dexter, Choy, J.L. – "The Travel Industry", AVI Publishing Company, Westport, Connecticut, 1984, p. 151.

5

Human Resource Development in Service Industry

There are a number of factors that contribute towards the success of an enterprise. These factors include capital, equipment and manpower. All these factors are important but the human factor is the most significant one, since it is the people who have to use all other resources. Without the productive efforts of its workers, the material resources would be of no use. The human resource development function has become increasingly important in today's fast changing world. Several trends, such as global competition, technological dynamics, increasingly knowledgeable and sophisticated customers and more educated workforce, all forcing companies to organize more responsively.[1]

Some Definitions

"Human resource development is a series of organized activities, conducted within a specified time and designed to produce behavioral changes. More specifically it refers to three activities: first training, second is education and third is development. The training is focused on present job, education is future job and development is concerned with providing learning experiences to employees, so that they may be ready to move in new directions that organization change may require." —*(Nadler 1969)*

"Human resource is the energies and the skills, talent and knowledge of people, which potentially can and should be applied to the production of goods and services. Development means all formal and informal processes by which the individual learns."

—***Harbison (1973)***

Human resource development is a development oriented planning effort in the personnel area, which is basically concerned with the development of human resources in the organizations for improving the existing capabilities and acquiring the new capabilities for achievement of the corporate and the individual goals.

*– **Samker (1989)***

Human resource development in the organizational context is a process by which the employees of an organization are helped in a continuous and planned way to:

- Acquire or sharpen capabilities required to perform various functions associated with their present or expected future roles.
- Develop their general capabilities as individuals and discover their own inner potential for their own or organizational development purpose and
- Develop an organizational culture in which supervisor subordinate relationship, collaboration among sub-units are strong and contribute to the professional well being, motivation and pride to the employees.

Human Resource Development can be seen as building knowledge base within the organization and dissemination of knowledge information to the people at the right time. It will expand their capacity to create the results they truly desire, broaden their pattern of thinking, mould their attitude, nurture a conducive learning environment and above all will develop a shared understanding of procedures and systems.

*– **T.V. Rao (1991)***

Human Resource Development v/s Tourism Industry

Since the end of the Second World War, the whole world has seen many important developments and changes in society. Our major development is the considerable improvement in the standard of living of the vast majority of working people. These improvements have come about as a result of many different factors including greater national productivity, the improved welfare facilities, more enlightened management and pressure from trade union. The contribution made by the tourism industry to this general rise in living standard is varied and considerable. Many type of behaviour, demand, decision making and responses of the tourists cannot be predictable or anticipated. Comparing with many other labour intensive service based industry, the tourism product is meant for people. It involves the human factor more to deal with the basic needs of tourist. Many tourism products include people as an integral part of the experience of their visit. It is a contact with people who contribute to the actual experience, whether they being an integral part of the location city dweller in Mumbai, vendors in Gujarat, traditional dancers in Rajasthan etc. or as direct contributors to the actual product delivery and experience or other professions and activities that collectively run the global tourism industry. It is important to note that development of packaging; marketing and deliveries of tourism products strongly depend on human factor in the attainment of service quality in the tourism sectors.

Human Resource Development Process is a set of mechanisms and a technique comprises of placement, training and development, career management, compensation management and quality of work life, performance appraisal and organizational development etc. It is a process, which helps each individual employee to grow, develop and acquire right type of skill and knowledge at the right time to perform efficiently in his current position and prepare him for the future assignments. Human resource development may be used as a tool to eradicate the poverty and unemployment by providing adequate opportunity to the employees to acquire new knowledge and skill to work efficiently in the tourism and hospitality industry. The development and growth of tourism demands a large number of manpower to work in different Job Categories. There is lack of well trained and skilled manpower in tourism sector. It requires proper strategic planning to acquire, motivate, retain, and perform with human touch. This can be only possible by proper management of the compensation package and reward management. Human resource is an inseparable functionary of the tourism industry. It is a greatest labour intensive industry in the whole world. The key to the successful management of tourism and hospitality industry requires better Human Resource Management. Tourism is a service oriented industry. It requires proper knowledge. Most of countries are facing the shortage of skilled and trained manpower for tourism industry. Most of countries are lagging behind the development of tourism due to the non-availability and adequate financial support to conduct training programmes. People are not interested to work in the industry due to its unsociable working hours, poor salary, uncertain employment condition and undignified job. The concept of human resource development was not prevalent in the tourism and hospitality sector in the past, as it is being given much importance today. Tourism is a labour-intensive sector. It provides employment to the skilled, semi-skilled and unskilled people in different units of the tourism and hospitality sector.

Group and Mass Tourism

The tourism benefit can better be incurred through the movement of group tourist i.e. normally pre-arranged tour. This will have a tremendous impact on the host country in the form of giving revenue, infrastructure development and employment.[2]

Social Tourism

Social tourism is a type of tourism practiced by low income groups and which is rendered possible and facilitated by entirely separate and therefore easily recognizable service.[3] From this definition of social tourism the following elements become clear. The first is the idea of the limited means. Manual workers are thus included in the scope of social tourism. Secondly social tourism is subsidized. Thirdly it involves travel outside the normal place of residence preferable to a different environment.[4]

Different Occupations in Tourism Sector

Providers of Direct Traveller Activities	*Providers of Travellers Support Activities*	*Manufacturers of Travellers Equipments / Products*
Night Clubs,	Hotels and Motels,	Automobiles,
Sports Centre,	Park and Recreation	Sporting Goods,
Race Tracks,	Concessions,	Foods and Beverages,
Theme Parks,	Food and	Airplane,
Convention	Beverage Machines,	Boats,
Centres, Cruise	Restaurants and Bars,	Buses,
Ships, Motor	Airlines and Railways,	Camping Equipment,

Contd...

Providers of Direct Traveller Activities	*Providers of Travellers Support Activities*	*Manufacturers of Travellers Equipments / Products*
Coach Tour, Museums, Vacation Homes, Theatres, Eco Tours, Public Parks, Camps, Golf Courses, Resorts, Health Spas, Chatter Fishing, River Rafting, Festivals and Events, Casino, Adventure Tours, Visitor Interpretation.	Car Rentals, Bus Lines, Advertising Firms, Car Services, Travel Agencies, Shops, Sales Business for Motor Cycles, Sports Equipments, Boats Aircraft, Photo Supplies, Crafts.	Photo Equipment and Supplies, Motor Cycle, Rvs Crafts.

Recruitment Process

The following steps are given for carrying out the recruitment process in the tourism and hospitality sector. Recruitment is a process designed to attract a qualified pool of job applications to the organization. These requirements can be established by job analysis, job descriptions and job specifications. Job analysis is an orderly study of job requirement and involves systematic investigation relating to the operation and responsibilities including knowledge, skills and abilities required for the successful performance of a job. The information collection includes work activity as to what is being done, nature of the physical environment, type of equipment and tools used performance standards and personal attributes of the worker such as skills, training, experience and so on. Job analysis forms the basis for job description and job specifications.[5]

Figure No. 5.1: Job Descriptions: The Job of Personnel Management

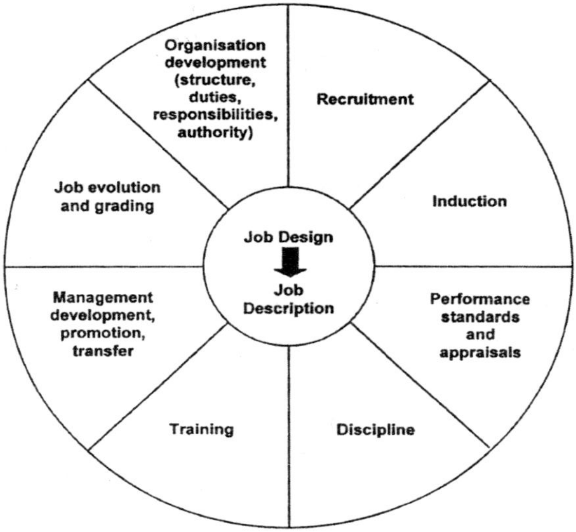

Source: Sharma, Hemant–HRM Hospitality Industry, ABD Publishers, Jaipur, 2006, p. 55.

Job descriptions have following purposes to perform:

- Give employees an understanding of their jobs and standards of performance
- Clarify duties, responsibilities and authority in order to design the organization structure
- Assist in assessing employees, performance
- Assist in the recruitment and placement of employees
- Evaluate jobs for grading and salary administration
- Provide information for training and management development.

There are two distinct but equally important parts to the full description of jobs. The first is the statement of conditions for which employees contract to do work. The second part of describing jobs requires the provision of information to employees which specifies clearly what results are expected of them and indicates how their performance will be measured. Job descriptions should contain the following main elements:

Job Identification

This section identifies the job title, department and level in the hierarchy. The following is the important element in the job identifications:

Content

It describes the detailed statement and normally includes a list of duties and how these are performed and what standard of performance is required.

Conditions

This section describes any particular conditions that make the job more and less difficult.

Authority

This describes any limits to the employee's authority such as cash limits; authority to make contracts on behalf of the employer authority to engage or dismiss subordinates.[6]

Job Specification

In many cases, more detail that is normally contained in a brief job description may be necessary for a job to be performed satisfactorily. A detailed statement of the job may be required specifying the precise skills and knowledge needed to carry out the various components of the job. This information may be contained in a document, often referred to as a Job Specifications. Alternatively, the information may be contained in such documents as manuals of operations, operating instructions and the like for the last few years' job descriptions and specifications have become much more highly developed in the service industry.[7]

Internal Recruitment Process in Tourism

Tourism sector gives priority to the internal source of recruitment for utilizing the internal workforce effectively. Organization improves the morale of the promoted employees. It is easy for an organization to evaluate the performance of the employee for the internal recruitment. It also fills in vacancies on the basis of giving promotion to the seniors or other employees within the organization. The internal recruitment method also reduces training cost, recruitment formality cost etc. There are also some drawbacks within the process of internal recruitment in the tourism sector. It promotes a sense of inbreeding and inflow of idea diminishes. Some employees attribute promotions to friendship and relations with managers and supervisors.[8]

External Recruitment

If no existing staff is suitable, is to go on the open market. This is where most problems arise and where most money and effort can be wasted. The numerous and varied means of recruitment include:[9]

- Newspapers: National, local and trade
- Agencies, including the department for education and employment and the youth employment offices
- Executive selection and management consultants
- Colleges
- The internet.

External Recruiting in Tourism

The external recruitment process is also practiced in the tourism sector. It brings new blood and new ideas into the company. It also gives recruiter an opportunity to overlook applications from both direct and indirect sources. It is sometimes cheaper than training. It serves as a form of advertising for the company. The external method of recruitment has also certain drawbacks like:

- It is more difficult to adjust with the culture and management philosophy through external recruiting.
- It will stop current employees to advance their career.
- It takes long time for the job orientation in the external recruitment.
- External recruiting can lower the productivity over the short run.[10]

Selection

McMurray has listed some comprehensive steps that can be taken in the selection process.

First Step: First step for the selection is to be thoroughly familiar with the requirements of the job as well as the qualifications and expectations of the candidate.

Second Step: is to conduct a preliminary screening interview to have an initial assessment of the candidate's abilities and aspirations. This interview would generally establish a candidate's goals and interests and general attitude towards the organization.

Third Step: is the completion of a formal application from which summarily lists a person's background, education, experience and special skills.

Fourth Step: is to check the candidate's reference and seek opinions from his previous employers or instructors if the candidate is fresh out of college. This should be done prior to the comprehensive interview so as to get a better idea about the candidate, especially in the area of those characteristics that do not show upon application forms. These characteristics include leadership qualities, ability to act assertively, ability to communicate well and attitudes towards subordinates as well as superiors.

Fifth Step: is to give certain tests to the candidate, if necessary, to make judgments about certain specific aspects of the candidate. These tests may be classified in many ways and the type of test given to the candidate would depend upon the type of job required to be filled.

Sixth Step: is the in-depth interview which is conducted to evaluate the applicant's acceptability in terms of his ability to fit into the company's culture and his "motive" in joining the company.

Seventh Step: is to establish the applicant's physical health. This can be checked from his medical records as well as a thorough physical examination conducted by the company physician. This will ensure that the candidate is physically fit and capable to exercise his duties and responsibilities.

Final Step: is the process of hiring for some responsible executive positions, the management may want to get socially acquainted with the candidate before the final decision is made.[11]

Training and Development

Training and development is the process of developing knowledge, skills and behaviours in people that will enable them to better perform their current and future job. In order to design effective training programmes the following principles should be known and understood:

1. Training can only be successful if it is recognized that learning is a voluntary process; that individuals must be keen to learn and consequently they must be properly motivated.
2. People learn at different rates and particularly in the case of adults, often start from different levels of knowledge and skill and with different motives and attitudes.
3. Learning is hindered by feelings of nervousness, fear, inferiority and by lack of confidence.
4. Instruction must be given in short frequent sessions rather than a few long stints.
5. Trainees must play active roles-they must participate.
6. Training must make full use of appropriate and varied techniques and of all the senses, not just one, such as the sense of hearing.
7. Trainees need clear targets and progress must be checked frequently.
8. Confidence has to be built up by praise not broken down by reprimand. Learning has to rewarding.
9. Skills and knowledge are acquired in stages marked by periods of progress. Standstill and even a degeneration of the skill or knowledge so far acquired. Instructors must know about this phenomenon, as it can be a cause of disappointment and frustration for many trainees.[12]

Training Techniques

On-the-Job-Training

This method is the most widely used method and it simply means putting the worker on the job under close supervision of a trained instructor. In support, there may be a variety of training aids and techniques such as lecture manuals, procedure charts, sample problems, demonstrations and so on. This training continues until the supervisor is satisfied that the employee can adequately perform the job without supervision. In order to train employees in a variety of jobs, some trainers will move employees from job to job. This process is known as job rotation and the employee learns a variety of skills. It helps the organization to have a pad of multi-job trained workers in case of absences, vacations or resignations of some workers.[13]

On-the-Job-Methods

On-the-job-methods are usually preferred in management development programmes because it saves production hours and the programme can be more conveniently tailored to the individual. This training is achieved in any of the following ways:

- *Coaching:* In this technique the manager (the trainer) and the subordinate (trainee) work together in a student-tutor relationship in which the trainer coaches and guides the trainee and the purpose is to explain the "whys" and "hows" of particular job functions, and provides feedback to the trainee regarding his/her performance and any grounds for improvement.
- *Job Rotation:* This refers to the movement of trainee executive from one job to another within the organization on some planned basis. This would help the trainee to be familiar with different aspects of the organizational operations which results in broadening of outlook and exposure to a variety of management skills.
- *Junior board meetings and committees:* This method involves participation in junior board meetings and decision making committees where the information is shared and discussed involving real life organizational problems. It helps the trainee in widening his perspective and he is initiated to the managerial process of understanding comprehension, analysis and decision-making.
- *Planned work activities:* This involves giving assignments to develop their experience and ability. Trainees may be asked to head a taskforce so that they can acquire leadership and managerial skill.[14]

'Off the Job' Training

'Off the job' training takes place away from the working situation. A variety of methods and techniques may be used but the particular choice will depend on what is to be imparted. The main methods are listed below:

1. Talks are best used for imparting knowledge such as company history and policies, legal matters, regulations, recipes and outlines of methods and procedures. In giving a talk, progress must be checked frequently by use of questions and answers.
2. Discussions are best used to elaborate on and to consolidate what has been impacted by other techniques.
3. Lectures often mean little more than talking at trainees and are therefore to be avoided, as there is usually little trainee participation.
4. Case studies, projects and business games are best used to illustrate and to consolidate principles of management such as planning, analytical techniques etc.
5. Role playing is best used to develop social skills such as receiving guests, handling customer complaints, selling, interviewing or instructional techniques. Ideally this should be supported by tape recording and closed circuit television recordings.
6. Films, charts and other visual aids should not normally be used as instructional techniques by themselves, but should support talks, discussions, case studies and role playing. Films on a variety of hotel and catering subjects are obtainable from several training organizations.
7. Programmed texts, interactive videos, CD-ROMs satisfy many of the principles of learning. In addition, they can be used by individuals at any convenient time-not requiring the presence of an instructor. They cannot, of course, be used to teach some things, such as manual skills and they can be very expensive to design.[15]

E-Recruitment

The most well known human resource system today is e-recruitment. This has been frequently practiced to ensure the effectiveness and promptness of the tourism industry across the world. The objective of the e-recruitment is to use maximum corporate websites and external job sites for finding the recruitment information. The benefit of e-recruitment is quick, cost saving and greater interactivity with customers. Training in the hospitality and tourism industry is less advanced and still in the infancy stage of developing e-recruitment.

Drawbacks of e-Recruitment in Tourism Sector

- Insufficient knowledge to anticipate.
- Fear of unsuitable applicants.
- Low marginal cost of providing information to additional users.
- Support of marketing intelligence and product design functions.
- Development of target mailing list through people who actively request information.
- Make interactivity with prospective customers.
- Cost and benefit analysis for developing international presence for small and medium sized tourism enterprises.

Key Human Resource Issues in Global Tourism

- Demographic and the shrinking employment and labour shortages.
- The tourism industry's image as an employer.
- Cultural and traditional perceptions of the industry.
- Inadequate rewards, benefits and compensation.
- Improper recruitment, low retention and high staff turnover.
- Insufficient education and training both within colleges and in industry.
- Skill shortage especially at higher technical management level.
- Linking human resource concern with service and product quality.
- Poor management and planning information about human resource matters in the industry.
- Lacking tendency to develop human resource policies, initiatives and remedial programme.[16]

Performance Appraisal

The evaluation of the performance of employees serves as a basis for judging the contributions and weaknesses of employees. So that continuous efforts can be made to build a stronger and more effective workforce. Performance appraisal constitutes a systematic way of evaluating a worker's performance and his potential for development. This continuing monitoring of the performance and periodic evaluation help in retaining, promotional and retraining policies.

Performances can be evaluated against some set standard. The formal appraisal plans and designed to meet three objectives.

- Performance appraisal provides evidence to justify or validate selections, promotions, transfers or salary increments.
- The workers learn as to where they stand relative to expectations and whether any changes are required in their behaviour, attitudes, skills or job knowledge.
- Performance appraisal helps determines what additional training the employee may need.[17]

Performance Appraisal Methods

- *Narrative Technique*—In this method, the rater simply writes a page or so about the strength and weakness of the employees and makes some personal recommendations. It provides actual description of performance.
- *Ranking Method*—This method simply ranks the person from the 'most valuable' to the 'least valuable'. This is the simplest method of separating the most efficient from the least efficient worker.
- *Graphic Rating Scales*—A commonly used method, it assesses a person on the quality and quantity of his work divided into a number of factors. These factors can be categorized as employee contribution. The employee characteristics include qualities such as initiative, leadership, dependability, cooperativeness, enthusiasm, loyalty, decisiveness, emotional stability, maturity, analytical ability and so on. The employee contribution includes quantity and quality of work, responsibility undertaken, results achieved, devotion to the organization, attitudes towards superiors as well as subordinates and so on. These traits are evaluated on a 'continuous' scale from unsatisfactory to outstanding, wherein the rater puts his mark along this scale based on his judgment of that particular trait.
- *Behaviorally anchored rating scales (BARS)*—In this method the rating process is highly job oriented rather than trait oriented. This makes the method more quantifiable. In this technique, the requirements for effective performance as well

Figure No. 5.2: Policies of Sustainable Tourism

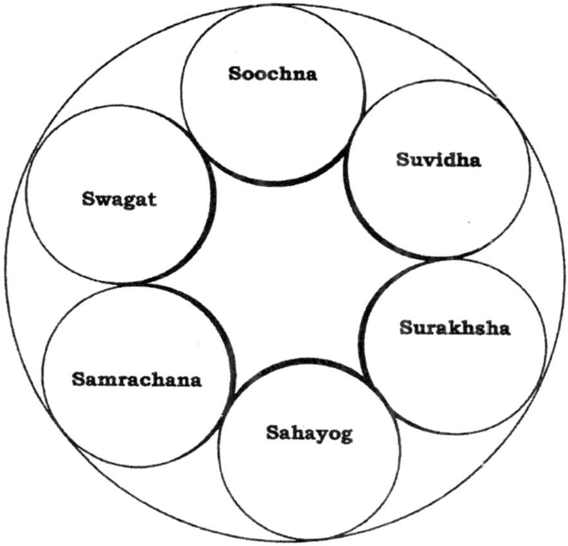

as the requirements for ineffective performance are identified on the basis of judgment by a specialist and these. requirements are 'anchored' at each end of a vertical bar.

The bar consists of a series of vertical scales, each scale identifying each important dimension of job performance. Each bar is scaled, generally from 1 to 9, where 1 is the lowest rating and 9 is the highest rating for most effective performance. The rating is on a continuous basis and identifies specific example of job behaviours. The rater then scores the performance of each behaviour on the appraisal form. This method is designed to reduce the risk and impact of errors that are caused by subjective judgment and personal prejudices.[18]

Sustainable Tourism

According to the Draft National Tourism Policy of India, "Our mission is to promote sustainable tourism as a means of economic growth and social integration and to promote the image of India abroad as a country with a glorious past, a vibrant present and a bright future. Polices to achieve this will be evolved around six broad areas such as *Swagat, Suchana, Suvidha, Suraksha, Sahyog* and *Samrachana*. The objectives of tourism development are to foster understanding between people, to create employment opportunities and bring about socio-economic benefits to the community particularly in the interior and remote areas and to strive towards balanced and sustainable development and preserve enriched and promote cultural heritage."[19]

Issues and Challenges of Sustainable Tourism

There are a myriad of definitions of sustainable tourism, including eco-tourism, green travel, environmentally and culturally responsible tourism, fair trade and ethical travel. The most widely accepted definition is that of the world tourism organization. They define sustainable tourism as "tourism which leads to management of all resources in such a way that all are economic. Social and aesthetic needs can be fulfilled while maintaining cultural integrity, essential ecological process, biological diversity and life support systems." In addition they describe the development of sustainable tourism as a process which meets the needs of present tourists and host communities whilst protecting and enhancing needs in future.[20]

Tourism is one of the world's largest industries. For developing countries it is also one of the biggest income generators. But the huge infrastructural and resource demands of tourism (e.g. water consumption, waste generation and energy use) can have severe impacts upon local communities and the environment if it is not properly managed. To reach this current state, we have witnessed an exponential growth in global tourism over the past half century. 25 million international visitors in 1950 grew to an estimated 844 million people by the year 2006. Several factors have contributed to this rise in consumer demand in recent decades. This includes an increase in the standard of living in the developed countries, greater allowances for holiday entitlements and declining costs of travel. Tourism is an important export for a large number of developing countries and the principal export for about a third of these. Statistics for domestic tourism is not so easily available. However it is certain that domestic tourism is also growing rapidly in many countries.[21]

Key elements of tourism sustainability include:

- Meeting the needs of visitors and host communities.

- Protecting and enhancing the tourism attraction for the future as part of a national economic resource.
- Preserving the current resource base for future generations.
- Maintaining the productivity of the resource base.
- Maintaining biodiversity and avoiding irreversible environmental changes.
- Ensuring equity within and between generations.
- Maintaining and protecting the heritage of the area, region or nation.[22]

Further sustainable tourism has following principle:

1. Tourism planning, development and operation should be part of conservation or sustainable development strategies for a region, a province (state) or the nation.
2. Tourism planning, development and operation should be cross-sectoral and integrated, involving different government agencies, private corporations, citizens, groups and individuals thus providing the widest possible benefits.
3. Agencies, corporations, groups and individuals should follow ethical and other principles, which respect the culture and environment of the host area economy.
4. Tourism should be planned and managed in a sustainable manner, with due regard for the protection and appropriate of the natural and human environment in host areas.
5. Research on the nature of tourism and its effects on the human and cultural environment should be available prior to and during development, especially for the local people, so that they can participate in and influence the direction of development and its effects as much as possible, in the individual and the collective interest.
6. Local people should be encouraged and expected to undertake leadership roles in planning and development with the assistance of government, business, financial and other interests.
7. Integrated environmental, social and economic planning analysis should be undertaken prior to the commencement of any major projects, with careful consideration given to different types of tourism development and the way in which they might link with existing uses, ways of life and environmental considerations.

8. Throughout all stages of tourism development and operation a careful assessment, monitoring and mediation programme should be conducted in order to allow local people and others to take advantage of opportunities or to respond to changes.[23]

Issues: Progress and Challenges

Tourism and the Environment

The natural environment is an important resource for tourism with increasing urbanization, destinations in both industrialized and developing countries with significant natural features, scenery, cultural heritage or biodiversity are becoming increasingly popular sites for tourist destinations. Efforts to preserve and enhance the natural environment should therefore be given a high priority for the industry and for governments. Some of the different kinds of impacts that tourism development and operational activities can have include:

- Threats to ecosystems and biodiversity e.g. loss of wildlife and rare species, habitat loss and degradation.
- Disruption of cost e.g. shoreline erosion and pollution, impact of coral reefs and fish spawning grounds.
- *Deforestation* — loss of forests for fuel wood and timber by the tourist industry also impact on soil and water quality, biodiversity integrity, reducing the collection of forests products by local communities.
- *Water overuse* — as a result of tourism/recreational activities e.g. golf courses, swimming pools and tourist consumption in hotels.
- *Urban problems* — congestion and overcrowding, increased vehicle traffic and resultant environmental impact, including air and noise pollution and health impacts
- *Exacerbate climate change* — from fossil fuel energy consumption for travel, hotel and recreational requirements.
- *Unsustainable and inequitable resource use* — Energy and water consumption, excessive production of waste and garbage are all common impacts.

Financial Leakages

Powerful trans-national corporations continue to dominate the international tourism market. Estimates suggest that about 80 per cent of international mass tourism is controlled by TNC's. These companies have an almost unhindered access to markets and use this to drive down the cost of supplies. The result is high levels of financial leakage, and limited levels of revenue retention in the destination or host countries. Financial leakages tend to occur due to various factors, including importation of foreign building material, skilled labour and luxury products and packaged travel arranged with TNC's. This is as opposed to locally sourcing the necessary resources. It has been estimated that on average, at least 55 per cent of tourism expenditure flows back out of the destination country, rising to 75 per cent in certain cases.[24] During the Seventh UN Commission on Sustainable Development meeting financial leakages was identified as a key area for stakeholders to take action and work together in order to assess the situation, as well as seek solutions to better support local communities in host/developing countries. The CSD called upon the UN and the world tourism organization, in consultation with major groups, as well as other relevant international organization, to jointly facilitate the establishment of an ad-hoc informal open ended working group on tourism to:

- Assess financial leakages and determine how to maximize benefits for indigenous and local communities.
- Prepare a joint initiative to improve information availability and capacity-building for participation and address other matters relevant to the implementation of the international work programme on sustainable tourism development (UN CSD 1999).

Impact on Livelihood in Destination Communities

In most tourist destinations of developing countries, the livelihood impacts of tourism takes various forms. Jobs and wages are only a part of livelihood gains. Tourism can generate for different type of local cash income, involving four distinct categories of people:

- Wages from formal employment
- Earning from selling goods, service or casual labour (e.g. food, crafts, building materials, guide services)
- Dividends and profits arising from locally-owned enterprises
- *Collective income:* this may include profit from a community

run enterprise, dividends from a private sector partnership and land rental paid by an investor.

Waged employment can be sufficient to lift a household from insecure to a secure footing but it may only be available to a minority of people and not the poor. Casual earnings may be very small, but more widely spread, and may be enough for instance to cover school fees for one or more children. Local participation in the industry can be categorized into three different categories: the formal sector (such as hotels), the informal sector (such as vending) and secondary enterprises that are linked to tourism (such as food retail and telecommunications). Experience from Asia suggests that:

- As a destination is developing, accommodation for tourists can be as simple as offering home stays at the early stage with lodges, guest houses and hotels replacing more basic options as tourism grows, and some of these may include foreign companies. Once luxury resorts start to develop, the scenario becomes more complex with international investors beginning to play a much more dominant role.
- Transport tends to fall into a grey area between formal and informal sectors. Most destinations have taxies, jeeps or other motorized forms of transport, often driven by the owners. As things expand organized associations of owners, operating on a rota system become more common.
- Data about employment in the formal sector is scattered and collection is often not very systematic. There are references of cases where high-status jobs in resorts typically go to non-locals, expatriate staff or foreign trained nationals. However there is almost no analysis of who is employed in middle and lower ranking jobs. The potential for employment of local staff seems to improve as one moves away from the luxury resorts into less established areas.
- The informal sector includes activities such as vending, running stalls and collecting fuel wood for the tourist industry. The informal sector often provides an easy entry into the industry for the poor, especially for women. The incomes can be substantial but unreliable as it is often a seasonal activity. However it can still provide a substantial boost to the income of the poor.

- The informal sector tends to get the least attention when interventions are planned, and interventions such as planning permissions are frequently detrimental to this sector.

However there are cases where initiatives such as flexible licensing systems and cooperative and associations have helped the sector. Casual labour and self-employment provide major opportunities for local communities to enhance their livelihood opportunities from tourism. Unlike formal employment, self-employment tends to highlight the entrepreneurial spirit of village communities. Villages are used to stringing together a livelihood from a diverse variety of source, often giving them a knack for enterprise. Causal labour includes porters, cooks, guides, cleaners, caterers and entertainers.

- Significant gains also accrue from economic linkages between tourism and other economic sectors such as agriculture, animal husbandry and handicrafts.

There continues to be fairly poor quantitative data available regarding the economic gains that can be generated from travel and tourism, particularly data that quantifies the impacts to formal, informal and indirect activities as touched upon above. There is a need for a standardized framework and guidelines for the collection and analysis of comparative data sets, to better identify the possible economic impacts for different segments of the market, as well as to develop policies which better reflect the needs of the informal as well as formal tourism ventures.[25]

- Domestic or regional tourists are particularly important clients for self-employed sellers and owners of small establishments.
- Budget and independent tourists, particularly backpackers are also more likely than luxury tourists to use the cheaper guest houses, home-stays, transport and eating services provided by local people. They tend to stay longer at a destination than groups of tourists and interact more with the local economy, but also spend less per day often bargaining over prices.
- Nature-based tourism does not necessarily provide more opportunities for the poor than 'mass tourism'. Nature tourism does offer some potential advantages however. It

takes place in less development area, often involves smaller operators with more local commitment. It involves a higher proportion of independent travellers, and if marketed as 'eco-tourism' can stimulate consumer pressure for ensuring domestic socio-economic benefits but it remains a niche in the market, can be heavily dependent on imports and can spread disruption to less development area.

- Mass tourism is highly competitive, and usually dominated by large suppliers who have little commitment to a destination. They are less likely to use local suppliers. However the segment does generate jobs and negative impacts are not always spread beyond immediate localities. Further knowledge is needed about how local economic opportunities can be expanded under such circumstances, as well as to identify how the negative impacts can be minimized in the mass tourism segment.

Tourism and Society/Culture

Tourism developments often stop people from having the right of access to land, water and natural resources. NGO's such as tourism concern and Rethinking Tourism have reported on examples worldwide where the articles in the UN declaration of Human Rights are flouted and where indigenous rights are lost or exploited. Adverse social impacts also include poor working conditions, low wages, childlabour and sex tourism. The international labour organization and international confederation free trade unions note that some parts of the tourist industry still degrades labour and drives workers to the lowest level, exhibiting the worst side of unsustainable production.

REFERENCES

1. Chandan, J.S.—"Management Concepts and Strategies", Vikas Publishing House Pvt. Ltd., New Delhi, 1997, p. 272.
2. George, B.P. and Swain, Sampad Kumar—"Advancements in Tourism Theory and Practice", Abhijeet Pub., Delhi, 2005, pp. 204-05, 210.
3. Sethi, P.N.—"Successful Tourism Management", Sterling Publishers, New Delhi, 1978, p. 14.
4. Bendra, V.P.—"Tourism in India", Parimal Prakashan, Aurangabad, 1979, p. 25.
5. Chandan, J.S.—"Management Concepts and Strategies", Vikas Publishing House Pvt. Ltd., New Delhi, 1997, p. 277.

6. Sharma, Hemant—"HRM in Hospitality Industry", ABD Publishers, Jaipur, 2006, pp. 55-56.
7. Sharma, Hemant—"HRM in Hospitality Industry", ABD Publishers, Jaipur, 2006, p. 59.
8. George, B.P. and Swain, Sampad Kumar—"Advancements in Tourism Theory and Practice", Abhijeet Publications, Delhi, 2005, p. 216.
9. Sharma, Hemant—"HRM in Hospitality Industry", ABD Publishers, Jaipur, 2006, p. 80.
10. George, B.P. and Swain, Sampad Kumar—"Advancements in Tourism Theory and Practice", Abhijeet Publications, Delhi, 2005, p. 216.
11. McMurray, R.N.—"Avoiding Mistakes in Selecting Executives", *Michigan Business Review*, Vol. 22, No. 4, July 1970, pp. 7-14.
12. Sharma, Hemant—"HRM in Hospitality Industry", ABD Publishers, Jaipur, 2006, p. 142.
13. Chandan, J.S.—"Management Concepts and Strategies", Vikas Publishing House Pvt. Ltd., New Delhi, 1997, p. 283.
14. James Stoner, Edward Freeman and Daviel Gilbert- "Management", Prentice Hall, 1995, pp. 392-393.
15. Sharma, Hemant—"HRM in Hospitality Industry", ABD Publishers, Jaipur, 2006, pp. 145-146.
16. George, B.P. and Swain, Sampad Kumar—"Advancements in Tourism Theory and Practice", Abhijeet Publications, Delhi, 2005, p. 240.
17. Richard, Henderson—"Performance Appraisal", Reston Publishing, 1984, p. 133.
18. Campbell, J., Dunnette, M., Arvey, R. and Holervick, L.- "The Development and Evaluation of Behaviourally Based Rating Scales", *Journal of Applied Psychology*, Vol. 57, No. 1, February 1973, pp. 15-22.
19. Singhal, Ravi Shankar Kumar—"Ecotourism and Sustainable Development", Abhijeet Publications, Delhi, 2003, p. 95.
20. Word Tourism Organisation 1996.
21. Goodwin, H. (2000) Pro-poor Tourism: Opportunities for Sustainable Local Development. D+ C Development and Co-operation, No. 5, September-October 2000, pp. 12-14.
22. Singhal, Ravi Shankar Kumar—"Eco-tourism and Sustainable Development", Abhijeet Publications, Delhi 2003, p. 99.
23. Singhal, Ravi Shankar Kumar—"Eco-tourism and Sustainable Development", Abhijeet Publications, Delhi, 2003, p. 101.
24. Shah, K. and Gupta, G.—"Tourism the Poor and Other Stakeholders: Experience in Asia: Overseas Development Institute (ODI)- Fair Trade in Tourism paper, the Sustainable Livelihood Working Paper Series, ODI London, 2000.
25. Harrison, D. and Price M.—"Fragile Environments, Fragile Communities? An introduction in Price M. (ed.) 'People and Tourism in Fragile Environments, Chichester, 1996.

6

Management Functions and Planning Patterns

Management System and Processes in Tourism

Tourism management is a composite subject and does not necessarily mean the development of only the tourism facilities like hotels, restaurants, recreational activities etc. In fact, creation of tourism infrastructure is like roads, water, electricity, and sewerage and telecommunication facilities. The different components of tourism supply should be so organised that the expectations of the tourist while planning the trip must get converted into full satisfaction and pleasant memories on his/her return. There should be perfect coordination and linkages between the availability and performance of all tourism components. This aspect has given importance in the Tourism 'Synergy' programme and it is the first attempt in this regard. A National Strategy for the Development of Tourism in India was drawn up during 1996 for achieving a greater realisation of the importance of tourism and a consensus on the development needs, higher plan allocations and introduction of new schemes for the accelerated development of tourism.[1] The strategy has been endorsed by the Government and Tourism Industry Leaders. The various information and inputs are useful to ascertain the managerial implications of tourism industry. To achieve our objective various questions have to be addressed and readdressed.

What do we think about tourists?

Tourists

- Are our guest?

- Are our customer?
- Are always cooperative?
- Are well-mannered?
- Spend a lot of money?
- Are likely to return to India in future?
- Are of a high social status?
- Are in India only of pleasure?

Tourism like other activities furnishes best when it fits into context of managerial policies and programmers designed to lead the optimum growth of tourism industry as a whole.[2] *It is an area where opportunity seldom knocks twice.* Management in tourism provides a bridge between the present situation and desires further situation in a destination area.[3] Its goal is to develop objectives of tourism development and ways to achieve the latter by maximizing the overall economic, social, cultural advantage of tourism while respecting the dynamic of balance tourism supply and demand.[4]

Tourism Management

The new approach of tourism development must combine planning (the initial goal and development strategy) with management (day to day seasonal operational decisions) because the ability to adjust changing market or seasonal condition is of paramount importance in such a competitive business. Planning must focus on rate of growth of tourism sector; how tourism sector can be fitted for national, regional and local development; role of domestic and foreign capital investment in its development; whether special treatment be accorded to this sector as an industry; whether it should be developed on short term basis. W.T.O. has suggested that greater attention should be focused on three economic criterions in plans which would be used to expand tourism in development nations: the gestation period of investment, the efficiency of capital investment, capital utilization and labour intensity investment.

"The methodical progression in planning should be adopted with the short listing of sites which have the potential to be part of circuits, aesthetic beauty, existing infrastructure, environmental sensitive, tourists' amenities and no less important connectivity and accessibility. Tourism projects must be made in a way that maximum use is made of local products and material and encouragement is given to auxiliary tourist facilities like handicrafts and entertainment.

Tourism plans should not be designed only on tangible benefits alone but on the ideals and principles of intangible factors like human welfare, happiness, preservation of natural and cultural resources that attract the visitors in the first place. Tourism plans should be flexible so as to adapt to changing conditions and requirements as tourism is an industry that is influenced by subjective consideration like that of economic forces, political and social pressures, psychological attitudes, changes of fashion etc.

Need of Tourism Management

Management is necessary to coordinate and synchronize the development of different sectors, to balance competing and sometimes conflicting claims on the same limited resource base, to maximize the positive impacts of tourism development and to minimize its adverse effect. In long run directive measures will usually prove less experienced than corrective ones. It envisages augmented availability and improved organisation of different components of tourism infrastructure to meet the requirement of tourists. Tourism is a complex and diffused activity. The best solution for any problem is to develop a method or plan to access the present situation, forecast the future situation and select an appropriate course of action to make the most of available opportunities. There are 7 basic stages[5] of internal factors through which effective managerial results can be obtained.

- **Stage 0:** *Assessment*: It helps to discover their present level of ability in and awareness of key competencies by means of self-assessment and self-investigation.
- **Stage 1:** *Learning*: by reading, discussing information, relevant research, practical guidelines by the story of entrepreneurs about their business and their personal development.
- **Stage 2:** *Analysis*: This explores appropriate behaviours by examining relevant cases of new business creation and their entrepreneur as role models.
- **Stage 3:** *Practice*: This makes to apply key competencies to a work like situation while in experimentation and feedback from peers and coaches.
- **Stage 4:** *Application*: This gives the opportunity to transfer the process to a real life situation with assignments to be made by entrepreneurs from business.

Figure No. 6.1: Stages of Internal Factors

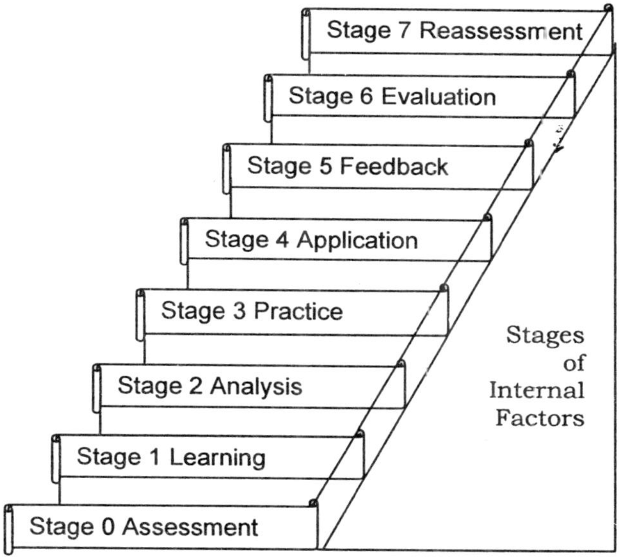

Stage 5: *Feedback*: After each stage there is a presentation of the results with assignments to be made by entrepreneurs from business.

Stage 6: *Evaluation*: One has to evaluate their level of improvement on all competence and has to develop new strategies for the next stage of learning.

Stage 7: *Reassessment*: To reassess their level of improvement on each competence-level, to redesign their personal development strategy, to repeat from zero.

Each stage creates a new level of competence. The zero stage is the core of self-competence service, proper need to start at a level at which they feel comfortable to work developing their present level of competence, each next stage challenging them to perform at a higher level using the onion as a metaphor for the development of competence.

Principles of Tourism Management: A Modern Approach

While drawing out the plans of tourism development in any country the following principles must be kept in mind:

1. ***Basic Principles***—Tourism management must encompass all travel business and pleasure. Planning objectives, process and outcomes vary from macro to micro level, integration at all levels must be done, clustering must be adopted and planning must integrate all components of supply side–urban and rural, traffic and pedestrian planning must be integrated.
2. ***Environment and Resource***—Global environment deterioration demands tourism attention. Sustainable development must be there, resolving of visitor impact management is there, appropriateness and places must be given priority.
3. ***Policies and Goals***—Tourism planning should not focus on economic development but quality and growth. Efforts must be made to attain greater public private cooperation, regional tourism policies must be designed, tourism planning must link government and non-profit organisation.
4. ***Processes***—In tourism management continuous planning needs integration, geography requires destination identification, process technique should be used to identify destination, place making must be there in planning, and side scale design must carefully be planned.
5. ***Future Challenges***—Entrepreneurship, creativity and innovation are essential for future plans. Plans should foster low impact development research and training, proactive environment planning and professional planning.

Factors Involving in Managerial Implications

Overdevelopment in tourism can generate problems like traffic congestion, inadequate parking, hotel dwarfing, displacement of local community, pollution etc. Some of the symptoms of lack of tourism management are:

1. *(a) Tangibles*: Damage or permanent alteration of physical environment, historical, cultural landmarks and resources; overcrowding and congestion; pollution; traffic problems.
   (b) Intangibles: Lack of education and training in this field; lack of awareness of the benefits of tourism to the destination area, loss of cultural identities, dislike of tourists on part of local residents and less accessibility to services and tourism attractions for local residents resulting in local resentment.

2. *(a) External*: Failure to capitalize on new marketing opportunities; erosion of market shares due to the actions of competitive destination area[6]; lack of sufficient awareness in clear markets; cooperative advertising; inadequate capitalization or packaging opportunities.
   (b) Internal: Fragment approach of marketing; lack of cooperation among operators; inadequate representation of tourism industry's identity; lack of support from local public and authorities.[7]

New Dimensions and Synergy Programmes

A well managerial tourism at all levels is essential for achieving successful tourism development and management. Some of the new dimensions of Indian Tourism to be adopted, are as under:

- Establishing the overall tourism development objectives and policies.
- Development tourism in a way that the natural and cultural resources are conserved for future.
- Integrating tourism with the overall developmental policies and establishing linkages between tourism and other economic sectors.
- Optimizing and balancing the economic, environmental and social benefits of tourism with equitable distribution of these benefits to society, while minimizing possible problems of tourism.
- Providing a physical structure, which guides the location types and extent of tourism development of attraction, facilities, services and infrastructure.
- Laying the foundation for effective implementation of the tourism development policy and plan and continuous management of tourism sector, by providing the necessary organizational and other institutional framework.
- Providing the framework for effective coordination of the public and private sector efforts and investment in development tourism.
- Offering a baseline for the continuous marketing of the progress of tourism development and keeping it on the track.

Thus, it can be said that tourism management itself is a powerful integrating factor and management skill is needed for reasons like:

- To coordinate the role of public and private sector.
- To prevent negative impact of tourism.
- To regulate and legislate matters relating to tourism.
- To improve the quality of services.
- To train human resources in this field.
- To market a destination.
- Demarcate the areas of development and types of tourism to be promoted.[8]

In conclusion it can be said that tourism comprises the activities of persons travelling to and staying in places outside their usual environment for leisure, business and other purposes. These persons invariably seek a pleasant and delectable experience on their trips. The most desirable tourism products should consist of environmental peace, stability, assurance of safety/security, an affable host with requisite services, and accessible tourist places with air/internal transport, hotels, restaurants, entertainment/recreation, shopping/communication facility and basic amenities. There should be a perfect coordination in availability of tourism infrastructure. Therefore, it requires managerial skill to provide all the above-mentioned facilities.

Government Initiatives and Tourism Development

In every country Government remain responsible for the promotion and development of tourism. Government has also the responsibilities in connection with its implementation of government policies relating to tourism. Government are inevitably involved for such matter as passport and visas, customs regulation, foreign currency allowances, statutory holidays, the number of weekly working hours and other matters.

A fundamental issue which the government will have to resolve is the division of responsibility between the public and private sectors and it depends upon the degree of development of the country concerned. In a well developed country a thriving private sector is often seen and a lesser measure of direct government intervention but underdeveloped country private sector remains both weak and relatively inactive. Thus, in the underdeveloped countries government have to take over many functions and responsibilities for the development of tourism. It has been generally agreed that if operations are left solely in the hands of the private sector the government could not interfere in the affairs of tourism development and may not proceed at the pace lay down by the national tourism programme. It has also been observed that investment is prone to leg behind the growth in demand since private investors become cautious when it comes to sinking capital in tourism enterprises. Accordingly, if this imbalance between demand and supply is to be corrected state action must be invoked at the earliest. The followings are the basic functions which the government should consider for the development of tourism in any country:

1. Basic market research into future tourism demand.
2. The publicity and promoting the country. This will not only attract the tourism but ensure that when he/she will go away with a good impression and wish to return back again.
3. The regulation and control of the manifold services which make up the industry, i.e. co-ordination of the activities of the numerous private interests concerned. Co-ordination might be best achieved through the liaison machinery of the national tourism organizations and certainly its success would depend upon the mutual co-operation and confidence between the public and private sectors.
4. The economic and social implication of tourism development in relation to the community i.e. the interests of the resident population must not be jeopardized, and appropriate action must be taken to ensure that their welfare is not adversely affected for.
5. Arrangements as deemed necessary for tourism promotion with other governments. This means establishing cordial relationship, facilitating exchange movements or co-operation with neighbouring governments to attract a regional market as well.

The vast array of business interests that are interlinked in the delivery and production of tourism products largely operate for a profit motive, and for them to achieve this objective they need management in order to get things done. Management occurs in a formal sense in organization, and in most cases management is about harnessing the organization resources to create the services, outcomes or products in line with what the tourism requires as a consumer. In practical terms in tourism it involves harnessing the power over resources to bring some degree of order to the tasks necessary to functions and achieve organizational objectives. This requires managers to link with employees to undertake managerial tasks, which comprise managerial work. Most tourism business works towards a set of common objectives.

There is also a debate among tourism researchers, who argue that tourism is a unique sector in that it displays characteristics of partial industrialization where only certain organizations providing goods and services directly to tourists are in the tourism industry.

What Leiper's approach to the tourism sector shows that the management of the broad phenomenon called tourism is a complex activity for a number of reasons:

1. The tourism industry is not a homogeneous sector. It is made up of various organizations that are directly involved in tourism and those that are indirectly involved in tourism and those that are indirectly involved and hence may be described as allied industries.
2. Some of organizations directly involved in tourism are responsible for encouraging and promoting tourism development and marketing.
3. The allied industries do not always see themselves as tourism-related enterprises.
4. The destination or area that the tourist visit is not usually the sole responsibility of one business or group of businesses.
5. The public sector is responsible for trying to plan and manage the diverse group of interests that are associated with tourism, as well as having an underlying responsibility in many cases for the marketing and promoting of the destination.

Thus, it is clear that we identify who is responsible for tourism management at a number to levels:

(a) At the individual business level, it is the manager involved with the functioning and running of the enterprises.

(b) At the destination level, it is often public sector led agency such as the tourism department. In extreme situation where a destination is deluged with tourist due to its popularity, the public sector may lead, with a public-private sector partnership involving business interests to manage the visitors on the ground.

(c) At the country level, national tourism organization sometime, with private sector's members promote and market the country as a place to visit and attempt to manage the diverse interests involved in tourism.

(d) At every level, there is a complex web of interaction and interrelationships that need to be taken into account in the decisions, interests and actions taken to manage tourism.

The managerial process of tourism as being a multilayered process, where the various organizations and stakeholders involved in tourism engage in at different levels through time. These interests and connectivity between management at different levels and between groups mean that in reality these groups also have to be aware of external factors that will impact upon management, like the visitors, the business environment, consumer's trends, the growth of the leisure society and political processes affecting tourism at government level.[9]

Figure No. 6.2: Industrial Business

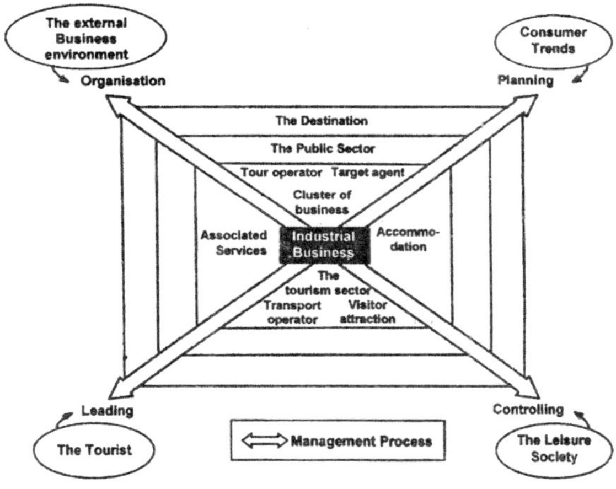

Source: Page, Stephen J.–"Tourism Management System", Butterworth-Heinemann, 2003, p. 23.

Planning

Planning means deciding in advance what actions to take and when and how to take them. Planning is needed, firstly for committing and allocating the organizational limited resources towards achieving its objectives in the best possible manner and secondly for anticipating the future opportunities and problems. Planning is putting down in black and white the action such a manager intends to take. Planning must possess the following characteristics:

- Planning must start from the top as objectives for the entire company are defined by the top management and then they percolate down throughout the organization.
- Planning must be flexible. Planning is needed to anticipate and prepare for the unknown events of the future. To that extent that the future is uncertain and events may or may not occur, planning must be flexible.
- Plans are good only if they are properly implemented by the people down the time. An effective way to ensure this is to involve the people responsible for implementation in the entire process of planning.

Planning Process in Tourism Development

Planning for Tourism

Many countries in the world especially the developing countries have recently realized the importance of tourism planning and the benefits which it brings out. The uses of macro-economic planning techniques for tourism sector are however relatively new. The planning system for national economic development which has been largely utilized since the end of the World War II did not always cover tourism development as a particular field. The increasing importance of tourism as a source of income, employment generation and regional development as a major factor in the balance of payments for many countries has been attracting increasing attention on the part of many governments as well as others with an interest in economic development returns.

In the past, tourism planning was looked at from a simplistic point of view. Planning simply implied that new hotel construction should be encouraged, more airlines should start operation. Promotional campaigns may be launched within the country and abroad and border crossing must be eased. Although it worked to some extent, it was at best an erratic method of planning tourism. Tourism has become a major industry in many countries of the world and has thus a pervasive effect on the economy of the nations as well as their special structure. Unplanned tourism can hamper a nation in getting maximum benefits from its development. The development of the tourism sector is one of the several options before a government, making claims on its resources which in most cases are limited. It is therefore necessary for tourism planners to place their case before the government in justifiable terms listing anticipated contribution through tourism development. The two economic arguments in favour of developing tourism are: *(a)* The contribution in terms of foreign exchange and *(b)* Multiple employment potential of the tourism industry. Tourism development has to be planned in relation to the total development of the country and the available resource.

Planning Process

There are a number of areas where planning may be successful in tapping the resources. Right from the assessment of demand to the formulation of plan and engineering of a sound monitoring mechanism we need a scientific plan. The following steps simplify over task specially while drafting a scientific plan.

Figure No. 6.3: Planning Model

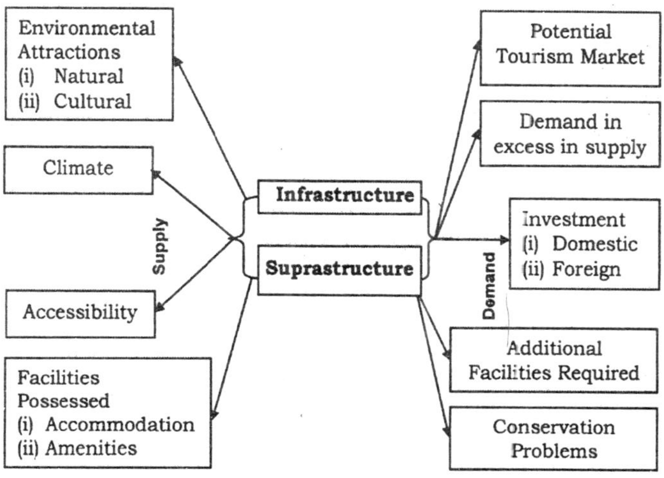

Source: Robinson, H.– "A Geography of Tourism", McDonalds Evans, London, 1996, p. 144.

Assessment of Tourist Demand and Supply

One of the early steps in planning is gathering information on the things the way they are and on the potential available for desirable growth. *Principle 1:* One of the main problems in investigating the potential of tourism can be the simple lack of information. The important initial steps in evaluating a potential for tourism development lies in determining present status. An analysis of the present structure of demand and supply in tourism is a precondition of any other estimate. This information base is a pre-requisite for initiating tourism planning programme. The assessment of demand helps in managing the supply. A careful assessment of physical, cultural and historical attractions gives an idea of the provided capacity to generate services. We find a number of principles for assessment. First principle is optional development of tourist attraction throughout the country. This makes it essential to conduct survey. *Principle 2* is development of a particular area so that cross sections of the society are in a position to visit the spots over the longest possible season. This also helps in minimizing the seasonal pressure. *Principle 3* suggests concentration on such spot which can be developed conveniently and at the minimum possible costs, especially without expanding the infrastructural facilities. *Principle 4* suggests arranging the priority order since it is not possible to develop all tourist spot at the same time. The fifth principle centralizes attention on innovating the tourist spot in time with charging users preferences. All these principles help in assessing the demand and supply of tourist spots which make it convenient to plan for tomorrow.

Controlling and Inter-Department Co-ordination

Control as a method of administration has been in existence from times immemorial. Perhaps the oldest record of managerial activity dealt with what is still a key control problem, the accounting for funds. Controlling helps to ensure that actions proceed according to plans, that proper direction is taken, and that various factors are maintained in their correct inter-relationship so that adequate coordination is attained. Control is greatly concerned with action and remedial actions. It is not just score-keeping. It is not just plotting the course and getting location reports, but rather it is steering the ship.[10] In an organizational setup control can be viewed, (1) as a means of letting members know what is expected from them and (2) as a means for ensuring that they do what is expected. In the real sense control means taking action to correct a condition found to be in error or action to prevent such a condition from arising. It would be wrong to think of controls as purely negative and restrictive meant to prevent action. The essence of control is that it must be positive and constructive, designed to help, rather than hide the achievement of plans. The best kinds of managerial controls are those which correct deviations from plans before they occur.

Definitions of Control

1. *Mary Cushing Niles*, "Control is the maintaining of a balance in activities directed towards a goal or a set of goals."
2. *George R. Terry*, "Controlling is determining what is being accomplished, that is, evaluating the performance accomplished, that is, evaluating the performance and if necessary, applying corrective measures so that the performance takes place according to plans."
3. *Joseph L. Massie*, "Control is the process that measures current performance and guides it towards some pre-determined goals."[11]
4. *Philip Kotler*, "Control is the process of taking steps to bring actual results and desired results closer together."[12]
5. *John G. Glover*, "Managerial control is that personal process which devises and utilizes the determinants that set the pace, govern progress, create coordination, maintain unity of action, provide adequate communication, promote cooperation of personnel and produce the desired results."
6. *Henry Fayol*, "Control consists of verifying whether everything occurs in conformity with the plan adopted, the instructions issued, and principles established. It has for an object to point out weakness and errors in order to rectify and prevent recurrence."

Importance of Controlling

1. Control ensures performance according to predetermined standards and objectives. Vigilant follow up and checking up of the progress for operations brings to light any deviation from the plan, so that timely corrective measures may be taken.

2. Control is forward-looking: It does involve a review of past performances and evaluation of their actual results but only is so far as it is necessary to draw lessons for taking proper measure for the present and future. It is the continuous control process, through follow up that makes long-range planning possible.
3. Coordination is aided by controlling, in that all component activities of the enterprise are regulated by control. Control keeps a continuous check on these functions and steers them to pre-determined common goals through coordinative guidelines.

Figure No. 6.4: Element of Management Control with Feed Loop

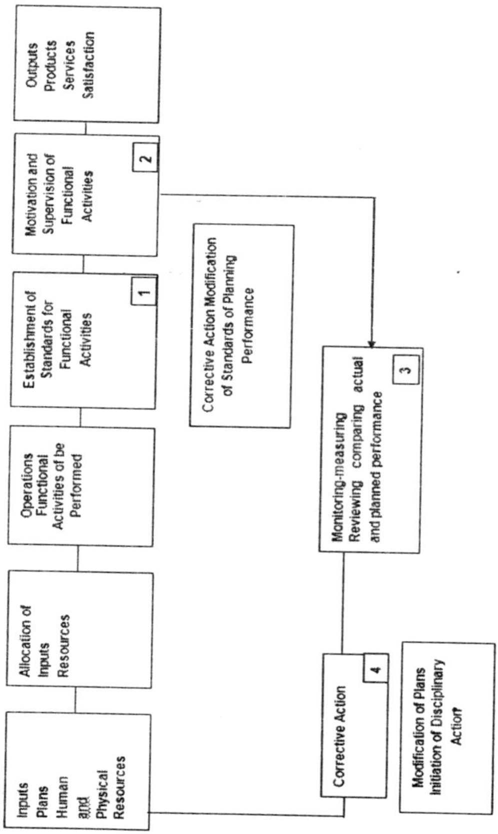

4. If for lack of information, the work performance in any section suffers, control readily comes to the rescue and provides way and means for the necessary information to flow to the section or the person who needs it.
5. Efficient control saves time, money and energy.
6. Good controls in fact lead to greater organizational effectiveness.[13]

The Control Process

1. *Establishment of Goals and Standards*: The first step in control process is to establish goal, plan, policy, standard norm or other yardsticks for the system whose behaviour is to be regulated. These norms and standard form the basis against which the actual operations have to be compared. These standards should be as clear as possible, preferably in quantitative terms and should be understood and accepted by all within the organization quantitative standards are preferred as it would be impossible to evaluate performance against general statement of objectives.
2. *Appraisal of Performance:* The second step in the process of control is to check the actual performance with the pre-determined standards. The objects of comparing the actual performance with the set standard are to detect deviation. Actual performance can be assessed from various types of information gathered by the company. Thus the pattern of information and communication becomes a vital ingredient in the control process.
3. *Determining the Reasons of Deviation:* The next step in process of control is to determine the reasons for variations or deviations. It has to be ascertained whether the error occurred in project design, management and/or in operative performance. The appraiser should find out. *(i)* Cause of deviation, whether it is temporary or permanent, increasing or diminishing *(ii)* the effect of the deviation *(iii)* the size of the deviation and *(iv)* the implications the appraisal has for modification of the standard.
4. *Corrective Action:* The final step in the process of control is to take corrective action when actual performance deviates beyond the accepted range of tolerances. In fact action is the essence of control. Corrective action should include curative

as well as preventive control measure. They may include modification of objectives and plans, provision of positive motivation and reviewing the direction given to the subordinates.

Figure No. 6.5: The Control Process

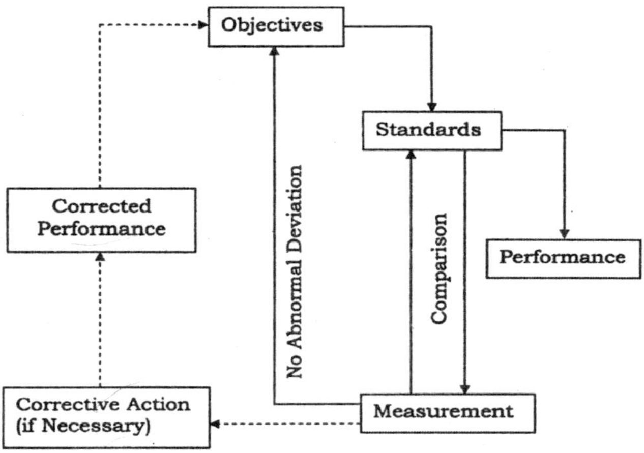

Group Dynamics in Tourism Industry

Group Dynamics

Group dynamics is concerned with the interactions and forces among group members in a social situation. In the context of this course on Management Functions and Behaviour, it is important to understand dynamics of members of formal or informal group in the organization. Group dynamics is a set of techniques. In various group exercises it tries to make the leader as well as the member effective. An attempt is made to make the above members play their roles in a management situation of group discussion, team buildings and finding out various solutions to problems by brainstorming and understanding ourselves in relation to others while we transact or interact with others.

A group is any member of people who:

- Have a common purpose or objective.
- Interact with each other to accomplish their objective.

- Are aware of one another.
- Perceive them to be part of the group.

Types of Groups

1. *Formal Groups:* These groups are established by the organization to accomplish specific tasks. According to Cartwright and Lander (1974) these groups include command groups which consist of managers and their direct subordinates; and committees and task forces which are created to carry out specific organizational assignment or activities.
2. *Informal Groups:* These groups are formed within the structure of the organization but by the members themselves rather than by the organization. Sometimes they do not have the approval of the management. Basically, informal groups are formed to satisfy social needs on the job. Sometimes they are formed to perform a task better; sometimes they are formed to hold production at a certain level. In a rigid system of organization, these informal groups meet fairly regularly to cut short the rigid bureaucratic practices of the management.
3. *Primary Groups:* Cooley defined and analysed primary groups as those characterized by intimate, face to face association and cooperation. They are primary in several senses, but chiefly in that they are fundamental in forming the social nature and ideals of the individuals.
4. *Membership Groups:* These are the ones to which the individual actually belongs.
5. *Reference Groups:* These are the ones with which an individual identifies or to which he would like to belong.
6. *The In-Groups:* The in-groups represent a clustering of individual's holdings prevailing values in a society or at least having a dominant place in social functioning.
7. *The Out-Groups:* The out-groups are the conglomerates looked upon as subordinate or marginal in the future.

Tour Operators and Travel Agents

Operating tours and retailing tourism products to consumers are key elements in the production, selling and distribution of tourism services. Organizations that do this link the supply to the source of demand. However, tourism is not like many other products or services. It is intangible and is often an experience or product that cannot be stored, tried or tested before purchase and so the consumer often buys as an act of faith in the hope that what the tourism industry supplies is in line with their expectations and needs. One of the main ways in which the tourism industry communicates; trades and interacts with the tourist is through the distribution chain using intermediaries – agents that sell products for the industry.[14] Historically tourism products have been retailed through travel agents, who offer products from tour operator, known as principals.

Travel Agents

Distributing tourism products seeks to entice customers into purchasing an offering, linking the supply with demand. In technical terms, the distribution is a system that links the various tourism organizations together with the objective of describing, explaining and confirming the travel arrangements to the consumer. Explaining the tourism offering to the consumer requires retailers to recognize, identify and incorporate the following elements of tourism:

- Tourism in intangible, meaning that it is a speculative investment and an expensive purchase where the product is generally conveyed to the customer via a brochure.
- Tourism is perishable and so can only by sold for the period it is available; this highlights the importance of last minute bookings to sell surplus capacity.
- Tourism is dynamic, meaning that it is forever in a state of flux especially as a product where prices can rise and fall.
- Tourism is heterogeneous, meaning that it is not a standardized product that is produced and delivered in a homogeneous manner.
- Tourism is inseparable, meaning that in the consumer's mind it is purchased and consumed as an overall experience; hence communicating what is being offered, its value and scope is important.[15] Since the consumer is transported to the products.

Tourist Guide

A tourist guide is a person who guides the visitors or tourist visiting places of tourist interest. He should be a person with sound knowledge of various languages and pleasing and attractive personality with historical background and having roads and route map. A tourist guide is available practically at all places of tourist attractions. And because of the language problem they have to keep a good guide to tell them the historical background of the building and its surroundings. A tourist guide is a person who is very helpful to the tourist or groups visiting Rajasthan for sightseeing purpose. There are so many tourist guides in India who have got training in different languages of the affluent society from where lot of tourists are generated. A tourist guide engaged by the group of people, keeps his own mike, transport and loudspeaker so that every one in the group could hear him speaking. He is always at the command of the group and moves with the group from place to place. Government of India has also started providing short term training to the tourist guide in the Department of Tourism of the Ministry of Tourism and Civil Aviation. They have to get themselves registered with the Department and obtain a certificate of proficiency from the Ministry. For a good guide it is quite essential that he should be a qualified person having sound knowledge of English and other Indian languages with sound historical background and complete control over routes and road maps etc.

Tour Operators

A tour operator is responsible for delivering the services specified in a given advertised tour package. He may provide these services himself—some tour operators provide buses, taxies, hotels and other facilities or he may obtain them from a contractor or contractors, such as specific hotels, bus companies, restaurants, attractions, car rental companies or other tour operators. In some cases, tour operators' offerings are developed for and marketed directly to general public. In other cases they are designed to the specification of a wholesale travel agent who markets them under his agency's name through his own retail agents and through airlines. Normally an operator offers a variety of packages in a single season which collectively are known as a "tour programme." Packages may be for individuals or groups and may be independent or escorted. Services that may be included in a package by a tour operator include transportation to the destination or destinations, transfers overnight accommodation, certain meals, sightseeing and/or admissions and car rental. Tour operator referred to as "ground operators" normally provide services at the destination only and do not package or market transportation to or from the destination. The services provided by such operators normally overnight accommodation, sightseeing and transfers and usually collectively referred to as "land arrangements."[16] Ground operators who specialize in services for incoming visitors particularly tourists from foreign countries are called "receiving agents" or sometimes "inbound agents."

REFERENCES

1. George, Young—"Tourism Blessing or Plight", Harmondsworth Penguin Books Ltd., England, 1973, p. 48.
2. Bhatia, A.K.—"International Tourism Fundamentals and Practice", Sterling Publishing House, New Delhi, 1996, p. 108.
3. Pizam, Abraham—"The Social Impact of Tourism", *Recreation Research,* Vol. II, Publication House, Lucknow, 1986, p. 37.
4. Negi, J.M.S.—"Tourism and Travel Concepts and Principles", Gitanjali Publishing House, New Delhi, 1996, p. 112.
5. Piffner and Sherwood—"Administrative Organisation", Prentice Hall, New Delhi, 1964, p. 89.
6. Mill, Robert Christe and Morrison, Alastair M.—"The Tourism System an Introductory Text", Prentice Hall Inc. Englewood Cliffs, New Jersey, 1985, p. 288.
7. Harold, Koontz and Cyril J.O. Connell—"Principles of Managements", 3rd Edition, McGraw Hill Book Co., New York, p. 208.
8. Ogilive, F.W.—"Tourism Movement: An Economic Study", Staples Press Ltd., London, 1980, p. 157.
9. Alex W. Rathe—"Management Control in Business in Management Control System" (ed.) Donald G. Malcolm, John Wiley and Sons, 1960, p. 28.
10. Franklin G. Moore—"Management Organisation and Practice", Harper Row, 1965, p. 139.
11. Joseph L. Massie, Essentials of Management, Prentice Hall of India, 1964, p. 64.
12. Kotler, Philip—"Marketing Management", Prentice Hall of India, 1968, p. 559.
13. Agrawal, Dharma Vir—"Management Principles, Practices and Techniques", Deep and Deep Publications, 1984, p. 327.
14. Page, Stephen J.—"Tourism Management System", Butterworth-Heinemann, 2003, p. 185.
15. Page, Stephen J.—"Tourism Management System", Butterworth-Heinemann, 2003, p. 208.
16. Gee, Chuck Y. Choy Dexter J. L., Makens James C. "The Travel Industry", The AVI Publishing Company, 1984, p. 128.

7

Tourism Marketing Components and Positioning

Strategy for Effective Marketing

Market is an exciting, fast-paced and contemporary field. It influences us daily in both our roles as providers of goods and services and as consumers. As goods and service providers, we make such marketing-related decisions as choosing who our customers are, what goods and services to offer, where to sell these goods and services, the features to stress in advertising, and the prices to change. Marketing-related activities are not limited to industrial firms, to large corporation, or to people called "marketers." These activities are undertaken by all types of companies and individuals. Marketing practices of goods and service providers impact on many of the decisions made by our parents, spouses, other family members, friends and associates. The marketing process affects whom we patronize; the assortment of models and styles offered in the market place, where we shop the availability of knowledgeable sales personnel, the prices we pay and other factors. Marketing practices are in play when we are born, while we grow and ever, while we conduct our everyday lives.[1]

1. *According to WTO:* "Marketing is a management philosophy which, in light of tourist demand, makes it possible through research, forecasting and selection to place tourism products on the market most in line with the organization's purpose for the greatest benefit."[2]
2. *According to Evans, R. Joel*: "The process in a society by which the demand structure for economic goods and services is

anticipated or enlarged and satisfied through the conception, promotion and physical distribution of such goods and services."[3]

3. *According to Alexander*: "The performance of business activities that direct the flow of goods and services from producer to consumer or user."[4]
4. *According to Philip Kotler:* "Marketing is a social and managerial process by which individuals and groups obtain what they need and want through creating and exchanging products and value with others."[5]
5. *According to Bukart and Medik:* "Tourism marketing activities are systematic and coordinated efforts extended by National Tourist organization and/or tourist enterprises or international, national and local levels to optimize the satisfaction of tourist groups and individual in view of sustained tourism growth."[6]
6. *According to J. Krippendorf* : "Marketing in tourism is to be understood as the systematic and coordinated execution of business policy by tourist undertaking whether private or state orient at local, regional, national or international levels to achieve the optimum satisfaction of the needs of identifiable consumer groups and in doing so achieve an appropriate return."[7] Thus, Krippendorf stresses that marketing in tourism involves coordination of several organizations at several levels and is concerned with the needs of identifiable consumer groups. On the basis of above definitions tourism market can be summed as under:

- Tourism marketing is an integrated effort to satisfy tourists by making available to them the best possible services.
- It is a device to transform the potential tourists into actual tourists.
- It is the safest way to generate demand and expand market.
- It is also supposed to be an effort to make possible harmony between the social interests and interaction of tourist organization.
- It is the approach to promote business and to feed the organizations necessary information for framing and revamping the marketing decisions.

- Marketing is a management philosophy which in light of tourist demand makes it possible through research forecasting and selection, to place tourism products on the market most in line with the organization's purpose for the greatest benefit.[8]

Figure No. 7.1: The Marketing Concept

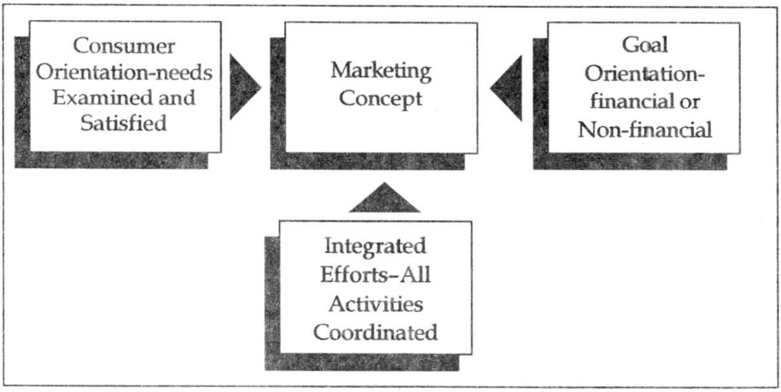

Source: Evans R. Joel & Berman Barry, "Marketing", Prentice Hall, New Jersey 1994, p. 21.

Thus, that marketing is a way of thinking about a situation that balances the need of the tourist with the needs of the organization or destination. It stresses the tourist research that helps in the selection of tourist demand. The concept of the product life cycle and positioning is useful to underscore the proper placement of tourism product on the market and suggest the appropriate marketing policy and strategies resulting from that decision. Thus the tourism marketing comprises the following:

- Fact finding, data gathering and analysis *(Market Research).*
- Communication to inform and promote *(Promotion).*
- Entrusting and facilitating sales, selection of market planning *(Distribution).*
- Coordination, control and evaluation *(Marketing planning and auditing).*

There are eight basic marketing functions:

- *Environmental analysis and marketing research:* It comprises of monitoring and adapting to external factors that affect success or failure. Such as the economy and competition; and collecting data to resolve specific marketing issues.

- *Broadening an organization's/individual's marketing scope:* It helps in deciding on the emphasis to place, as well as the approach to take, on societal issues and international marketing.
- *Consumer Analysis:* Comprises of examining and evaluating consumer characteristic needs and purchase processes; and selecting the group of consumers at which to aim marketing efforts.
- *Product Planning:* Helps in developing and maintaining products, product assortments, product image brands, packaging and optional features; and deleting faltering products.
- *Distribution Planning*: It is based on the establishing relations with distribution channel intermediaries physical distribution, inventory management, warehousing and retailing.
- *Promotion Planning*: Helps in communicating with customer, the general public, and other through some form of

Figure No. 7.2: The Basic Functions of Marketing

Source: Evans R. Joel & Berman Barry, "Marketing", Prentice Hall, New Jersey, 1994 , p. 21.

advertising, public relations, personal selling and/or sales promotion.

- *Price Planning:* Helps in determining price levels and ranging pricing techniques terms of purchase, price adjustments and the use of price as an active or passive factor.
- *Marketing Management*: It is necessary for planning, implementing and controlling the marketing programme and individual marketing functions; appraising the risks and benefits in decision making; and focusing on total quality.[9]

Tourism Marketing

A clear perception of tourism marketing requires a brief analysis of marketing. We are well aware of the fact that there have been some fundamental changes in the traditional concept of marketing which have been influenced by the changing environmental conditions such as social, cultural, political, legal and economic conditions. While clarifying the perception of tourism marketing, it is essential that we assign due weightage to the social considerations as well. The *British Institute of Marketing* finds it as the management function which organizes and directs all those activities involved in assessing and converting customer purchasing power into effective demand for a specific product or service and to achieve the profit motive in moving the product to the final customers or users.[10] The important decisions in the marketing concept are customer orientation where the tourist organization think and plan in terms of the benefits sold rather than the products.

Marketing Uniqueness

The problems of marketing in tourism are somewhat different from the problems of traditional product marketing. The differences are the result of the characteristics of tourism supply and demand. Tourism, first of all, is a service. An intangible experience is being sold not a physical good that can be impacted prior to purchase. In tourism, production and consumption take place at the same time. In manufacturing, goods are produced, stored and sold. The inventory process serves as a way to linking these stages of production and consumption. Tourism supply cannot be stored. A second important factor that makes tourism different from other industries is that the service provided—a vacation—is in fact an amalgam of several products and services. A vacation has a transportation component, accommodation component, a food and beverage component, an attractions component, an activities component and an amenities component. These components are usually offered by different firms, and they may be marketed directly to the tourist or combined into a package in which they are offered as one vacation but the services are supplied by different firms. This lack of control over the entire vacation means a great deal of interdependence of results. From many independent businesses providing a satisfying part of the total vacation results a satisfied tourist. The marketing efforts of each of the parts are thus affected by the efforts of the others providing a part of the vacation. The satisfaction provided is also a function of the human element providing the service. This also is very difficult to control in terms of the consistent quality of service provided. A third factor that makes tourism different from other industries concerns is the role of the travel intermediaries. Because most tourist services are located at distances far from their potential customers, specialized intermediaries-organizations that operate between the producer and the tourist are often necessary to bridge the gap. Also, the fact that many tourism producers are relatively small means that they cannot afford to set up their own retail outlets. Thus, while in most industries, the producer exerts much control over every stage in the development and delivery of the product, in tourism the travels intermediaries can influence if not determine which services should be offered, to whom, when and at what price.[11] The last factor that makes tourism different from other industries related to demand. Tourism demand is highly elastic, seasonal in nature and subject to subjective factors such as taste and fashion as well as the more objective factors of demand such as price. In many cases, the "Product" sought can be satisfied by any number of destinations, with particular on number one in particular.

Tourism Marketing Components

The three basic components of tourism marketing are:

1. ***Orientation***: Before embarking on programme to market tourism it is essential to develop a philosophy that will guide marketing efforts. Some of these philosophies are:
   (a) *Product Orientation:* Product-oriented tourism emphasizes the products and services of tourism supply, based on

physical, cultural, historic attributes or a combination of several of them. This approach to tourism marketing does not take into account the desire of the potential tourist particularly if the marketing is totally product oriented. Theoretically, this marketing approach can be successful if demand exceeds supply but competition among tourism sellers normally does not allow this.

(b) *Market Orientation:* A market-oriented approach emphasizes the needs and wants of potential tourists. It asks what will satisfy those needs and wants and when those needs and wants will occur and then tries to fulfil them. This marketing approach runs the risk of ignoring such things as local natural resources and culture and for that reason, may alienate the local population.

(c) *Societal Orientation:* Societal Orientation[12] a third approach, combines the best of both product and market orientation. It considers the needs and wants of the tourists but does not ignore the long term interests of the local population in such matters as economic, environmental and social/cultural impacts.

Marketing Research

Marketing research, as defined by the American Marketing Association consists of the systematic gathering, recording and analysing of data about problems relating to the marketing of goods and services.[13] If a firm is to succeed in its objects it will need to access information which adds value to decision making and which when analysed enhance competitive advantages. The tourist organization also feels the urgency of making effective marketing decision so as to match their decision with the changing needs.[14]

Scope of Market Research

Investigation of the market may be qualitative and quantitative. Some of the important aspects are as under:

A. Studies on Influences of Uncontrollable

1. General business or economic forecasting concerned primarily with general business climate rather than a single industry.

2. Studies of economic factors affecting sales volume and opportunities.
3. Studies of shifts in the nature of the market (e.g. sectional changes, age-distribution trends, income-distribution trends).
4. Motivational research (e.g. studies of consumer and customer buying motivations).

Figure No. 7.3: The Marketing Research Process

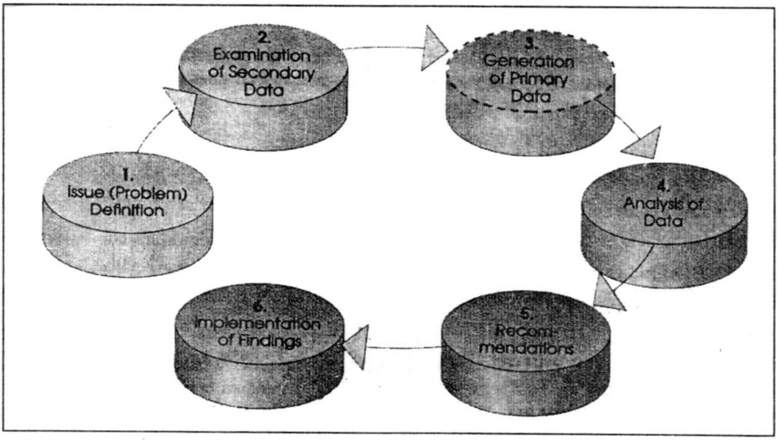

Source: Evans R. Joel & Berman Barry, "Marketing", Prentice Hall, New Jersey, 1994, p. 106.

B. Studies on Competitive Situation

1. Studies on competitive position of company products.
2. Comparative studies of competitive products.
3. Evaluation of new competitive products or competitive new product developments.
4. Studies of price policies, discount structures etc. of competitors.
5. Studies of advertising and selling practices of competitors.

C. Studies on Influences of Controllable

1. Determination of consumer or customer acceptance of proposed new products or services.
2. Establishment or revision of sales territories.
3. Evaluation of existing sales methods.

4. Analysis of salesman's activities.
5. Studies of advertising effectiveness.
6. Determining present uses or application of existing products.
7. Price studies.
8. Appraisals of proposed changes in sales methods.
9. Evaluation of advantages or limitations of proposed new products or services.
10. Measurement of the effectiveness of individual salesman.
11. Studies of dissatisfaction with existing products or services among present or former consumers.
12. Determining or exploring new uses or applications of existing products.
13. Studies aimed at product simplifications or at length or completeness of line of products.
14. Studies of distribution costs.
15. Development of standards of sales performance.
16. Studies of sales compensation-evaluation, review or revision.
17. Selection of advertising media.
18. Packaging research.
19. Studies of the effectiveness of promotional devices.

D. Studies Focusing on Market Measurement and Planning

1. Analysis of market size.
2. Estimation of demand for new or proposed new products.
3. Sales forecasting for the industry or company.
4. Analysis of the characteristics of the market for specific product.
5. Analysis of territorial potentials or sales opportunities.
6. Studies of trends on market size by products.
7. Measurement of territorial variations in sales yield.
8. Studies of the relative profitability of different markets.
9. Market test or test-market operations on new or improved products.
10. Studies of changes in the importance of different types of customers.[15]

The Marketing Research Process

The marketing research process consists of a series of activities defining the issue or problem to be studied, examining secondary data, generating primary data, analysis information making recommendations and implementing findings.[16]

Figure No. 7.4: Tourist Centred Marketing Research

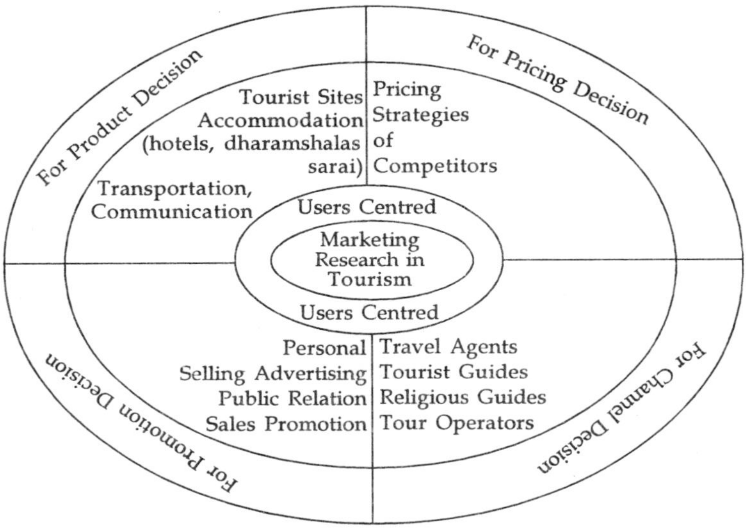

Source: A.K. Raina & Neelu Jain – Dynamics of Tourism Concepts: Philosophy and Strategies, Kanishka Publishers and Distributors, New Delhi, 2004, p. 142.

Method of Research

Market research is a continuous process and there are various ways for collection data for the research they are as:

(a) ***Secondary data:*** It consists of information not gathered for the immediate study at hand but for some other purpose. Secondary data are useful as they are inexpensive. Data collection is quick, frequently available, high credibility and is important for exploratory research. The internal secondary data can be collected by budget, sales, figures, profit and loss statement, customer billings, inventory records, prior research reports, written reports etc. External secondary data can be collected from regular publications, books,

monographs, commercial research houses, government publications etc. In the tourism sector desk research method is an important tool for the collection of secondary data.

Desk research

This involves a secondary research technique. Information is collected from published data, statistics on tourist trends from publications of United Nations, UNESCO, IUOTO, WTO, etc. Other statistics is obtained from national tourist organizations, trade, associations, carriers, hotel companies.[17]

(b) ***Primary Data:*** Primary data consists of information collected specially for the purpose of the investigation at hand. Primary data are supported by the following advantage and information collected is precise and current methodology of data collection is controlled, information is secret and reliable; problem of conflicting data is not there. Some of the other techniques that can be utilized in tourism sector to conduct research are as:

Research

This involves information gathered on primary sources carried out in the tourist generating market itself. The most reliable and common field research methods are: *(a)* Sample surveys *(b)* motivation research. *(a)* Sample surveys are a study of a part or fraction of a defined population. This technique consists of personal interviews of tourist, travel agents, carrier and hotel managers etc. with the help of a questionnaire through mailing, telephone contacts, at homes arrival/departure places or at temporary staying places. Surveys cover market behaviour, trends in holidaymaking, etc., cross analysed by socio- economic and other characteristics. *(b)* Motivation research attempts to investigate the motive of the population behind travel by research methods used in psychology. The questionnaire used in this research method is carefully designed at discovering the deep, subconscious and unconscious motives of human being so as not to reach the level where rational factors prevail, other techniques used are word association tests, sentence completion tests are pictorial tests and observation. Market research helps in identifying.[18]

The Best Uses of Primary Data-Collection Technique

	Technique	*Most Appropriate Uses*
1.	Survey	Determining consumer or channel member attitudes and motivation toward marketing mix factors; measuring purchase intentions; relating consumer characteristics to attitudes.
2.	Observation	Examining actual responses to marketing factors under realistic conditions; interest in behaviour and not in attitudes.
3.	Experiment	Controlling the research environment is essential and establishing a cause and effect relationship is important.
4.	Simulation	Deriving and analysing many inter-relationships among variables.

Source: Joel R. Evans & Barry Berman, "Marketing" Sixth Edition, Prentice Hall, Englewood Cliffs, New Jersey, 1994, p. 117.

Market Segmentation

Market segmentation is a recognized and universally accepted way of analysing demand. Market segmentation refers to the process by which people with similar needs and wants are grouped together for the purpose of better focusing on and serving the market.

Segmentation is based on four assumptions:

- The market for a product of service. These potential tourists can be grouped into segments the members of which each have similar and identifiable characteristics.
- A single product offering, such as a cruise, will appeal to some segments of the market more than others.
- Firms and organizations can improve their overall marketing effort by developing specific offering to reach specific segments of the market.

The process of segmenting a market can lead to much strategic management decision. Market segmentation can be more than a statistical technique used to analyse demand. It can be utilized as a management tool that leads to specific marketing decisions. The development of such a strategy begins with the identifications of

Figure No. 7.5: Tourism Market Segmentation

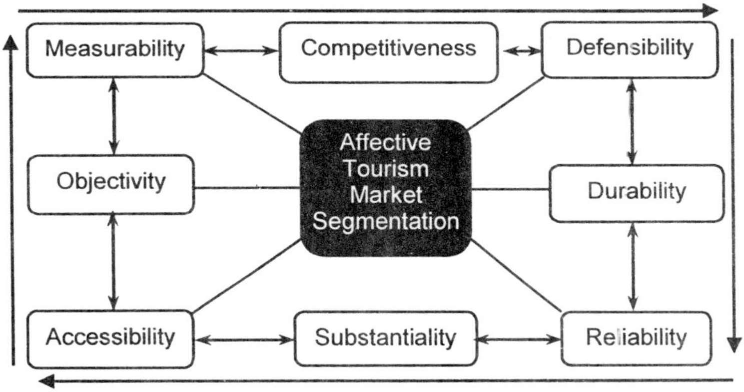

Source: A.K. Raina & S.K. Aggarwal, "Tourism Development" Sarup & Sons, New Delhi, 2004, p. 163.

profiles of segments of the market. At one extreme, a firm or destination may maximize its marketing orientation by developing a unique product offering for every potential tourist. Limitations of time and money prevent this at the other extreme, the firm or destination may save time and money by offering one basic option to everyone although that one option will undoubtedly appeal to some potential tourists, it will not to others. The compromise is to assemble potential tourists into segments and each segment having similar preference characteristics and produce offering geared to the needs of these segments.[19] Many criteria have been developed by which a market segment can be constructed. Four general categories have been developed.

Socio-economic or Demographic Segmentation

Early segmentation studies used criteria as the basis for forming market segments. These criteria remain the most commonly used today. This is probably due to the relative case of collecting data, the comparability of such information through census as well as media data, and the fact that such data is easy to understand and apply. Age and income level, in fact, has been very successful predictors of recreation participation. However the use of only socioeconomic criteria to segment markets has come under attack. It has been argued that the rapidly changing nature of society makes it impossible to rely solely on demographic data as a means of platting marketing strategy. Just because a segment of people are within a particular age or income group does not necessarily mean that they will love similar vacation preferences. Also socioeconomic information does not give the marketer sufficient information about like and dislike to properly position the product segment of the market with a product offering in the marketplace positioning refers to the decision to serve a particular that is specifically aimed at satisfying its needs and wants.

Recreation and Tourism Market Segmentation

1. *Socioeconomic and Demographic Variables*
   Age, Education, Sex, Income, Family size, Family life cycle, Social Class, Home Ownership, Second home ownership, Race or ethnic group, Occupation.
2. *Product Related Variables*
   Recreation activity, Equipment type, Volume usage, Brand loyalty, Benefit exceptions, Length of stay transportation mode, Experience Preferences, Participation Patterns.
3. *Physiographic Variables*
   Personality traits, Life style, Attitudes, Interests, Opinions, Motivations.
4. *Geographic Variables*
   Region, Market area, Urban, Sub-Urban, Rural, City Size, Population density.

Source: Daniel J. Stynes, "Market Segmentation in Recreation and Tourism", adapted from William N. Pride and D.C. Ferrel, *Marketing, Basic Concepts and Decision,* 2nd ed.

Product Related Segmentation

A major advantage of segmenting by means of product related criteria is that the information gained is directly related to the particular product in question. Indeed a major flow in some studies is that information is sought from the potential tourist that deals with general benefits sought or in the case of psychographic segmentation, general attitudes about type of product/services rather than with specific product and services. Some attempts have been made in recreation and tourism to use heavy half segmentation. Heavy half segmentation refers to the idea of segmenting a market on the basis of quantity purchased or consumed. As with other types of products heavy half segmentation has been found lacking. Benefit or attribute segmentation is fast becoming a very popular segmentation method to user in recreation and tourism. This method involves segmenting a market according to the relative importance assigned to benefits that consumer expects to realize after purchasing the product. The method entails determining the relative importance of specific product benefits to prospective consumers. Clusters are then formed of people who attach a similar degree of importance to save product benefits. Although result can have important ramifications for the development of new products and the determinations of advertising message, it is necessary to develop demographic profiles of those identified in the cluster in order to reach the market segments.

Psychographic Segmentation

Much has been made of this relatively new tool. This technique of segmentation, although expensive to use and difficult to carry out has been useful for describing segments. It can be probably best used in highly specialized and extensively developed markets to supplement the information gained from simpler analyses. Demographic data may be likened to the bones of skeleton and psychographic data may be likened to the flesh. The bones form the basis of the structure, but it is only by covering the form with flesh that the features become recognizable. Information about an individual's attitudes, interest and opinions give a much closer picture of the segment being described.

Geographic Segmentation

Geographic considerations are very important to tourism. Much of the attractiveness of a tourist destination is based on contrast, contrasting culture, climates distance or scenery. This implies there being a certain distance between origin and destination. Also we have already seen the critical role that accessibility of tourist to a destination plays in tourism. To date, destinations have used geographically based studies solely to identify primary, secondary, and in some cases tertiary markets. State and national tourist offices tend to use geographic segmentation for the purpose of determining the extent of their promotional efforts. Once market segments have been identified and profiles drawn up, it is necessary to select which segment the firm or destination will seek to attract and serve. This decision can be made only in light of an analysis of which market segments will bring most benefit to the firm or destination. Such an analysis involves four concerns.

Figure No. 7.6: Geographic Segmentation

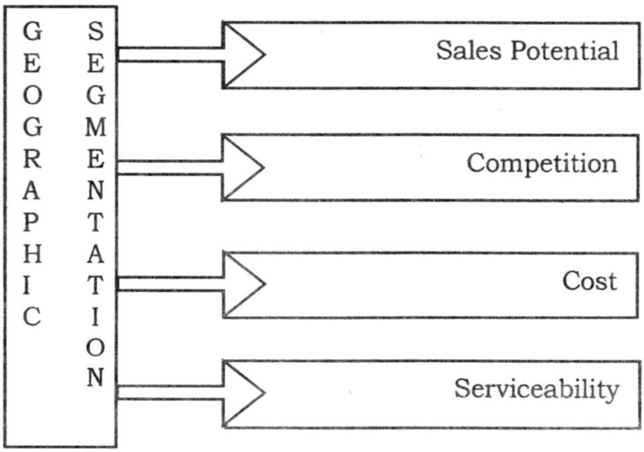

Sales Potential

What is the current and future potential for revenue from this segment? Revenue is a combination of the number of current and potential tourists and their current and potential per person spending.

Conception

To what extent does competition exist for the segment in question? How strong is our advantage compared to the competitors?

Cost

How much an investment is required to develop product to attract this segment?

Serviceability

Do we have the financial and managerial capability to design, promote, and distribute the appropriate products and satisfactorily serve the market segments attracted by the product produced?

Target Marketing

Target markets are drawn from segments. They might be called subsequent, but the word targets has a more active connotation that is important. The same precepts apply as with segmentation but they simply apply to more homogeneous markets that allow for more detailed analysis and evaluation of potential customers. This enables the creation of greater differential advantages. One travel researcher found, for example, that the vacation market segment could be broken down into ten target markets. Each one represents an isolation of interest based on benefits, usage, demographics and psychographics. Each one has requires a different package, a different positioning, and different communication. These target markets and some of their specific characteristics are as follows:

- The carriage trade: desire a change of scene but not of style, secure in wealth and position, play golf and tennis year round and when travelling, tend to vacation as a family.
- The comfortable: The largest group, insecure, seek social and psychological comfort, as in recommended restaurants, guided tours and organized activities.
- The ventures: want to see new things, have a thirst for fresh ideas, information and education; seek the new and the different; don't travel in groups; collect experiences.
- The adventurers: the venture advanced one step seek risk, danger and the unknown.
- The inners: jet setter, go somewhere because of who is there rather than what is there, they "make" destinations such as Acapulco, Majorca, Costa del sol.
- The buffs: Strongly subject-oriented, travel because of particular interest or hobby.
- The activists: not content to set by the pool and bask in the sun, want constant activities.
- The outdoor users: Campers, bikers, bird watchers, bicyclers, and other outdoor recreations.
- The restless: Travel for something to do, tend to be senior citizens, retired, widowed, collect travel experiences, travel all the time including off seasons.
- The bargain hunters: Can afford to travel but compulsively seek the best deal.[20]

Figure No. 7.7: Steps in Planning a Target Market Strategy

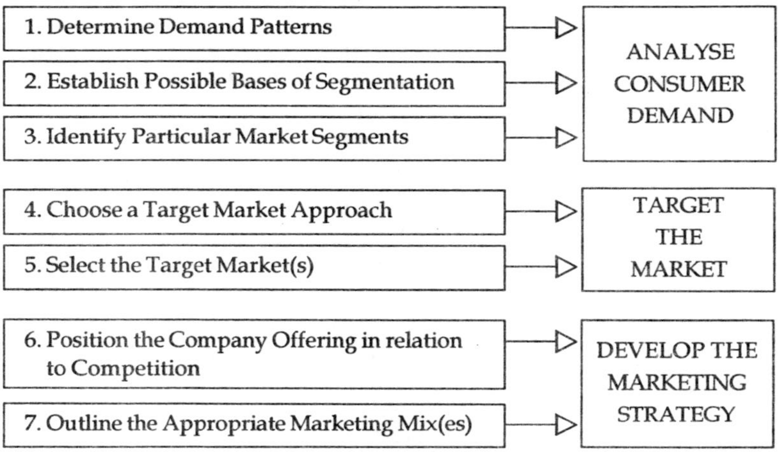

Target marketing requires analysing the sales potential of that segment or segments; that is, assessing the number of both current and potential new tourists and their pre-person pre-draw spending. Target market must also consider the competition, the cost of developing a destination for the target market, and the destination's financial and managerial capability of handling or serving that target market.[21] Developing a target market strategy consists of three general phases, comprising seven specific steps: analysing consumer demand–determining demand patterns.

1. Establishing bases of segmentation.
2. Identifying potential market segments.
3. Targeting the market choosing a target market approach.
4. Selecting the target market.
5. Developing the market strategy–positioning the company's offering relative to competitors.
6. Outlining the appropriate marketing mix.
7. Of Particular importance is product differentiation, whereby a product offering is perceived by the consumer to differ from its competition on any physical or non-physical product characteristic, including price.

Marketing Mix

In general marketing, the term 'mix' has gained prominence in the last few decades. It means mixture of element which interacts and complements each other to achieve the targeted results. The term 'marketing mix' was introduced by Prof. Neil Borders in the year 1953. Professor Borders got the cue from a study of management of marketing costs by Professor James Gulliton who described the marketing executive as a 'mixer of ingredients'. The objective of marketing is the behaviour of the enterprise in relation to its markets and customer, within the limitation given by the market situation, by the available resources and the general direction provided by the organization overall aims, there is a broad range of different activities suitable for achieving the company's goal. The form or the organization can use a variety of marketing. 'Instruments' is regard to its products or services, their pricing; their distribution or sale and their promotion. The combination of specific activities chosen by a firm is usually called the 'marketing mix'.[22]

Buell Defines Marketing Mix

"The concept of the marketing mix suggests that the company resources devoted to product, price, distribution and promotion (and the subsection thereof) should be mixed in varying proportion depending upon the industry category of the firm, its position in the market, and the competitive situation."[23] Once the target markets of a property or destination have been determined, an appropriate marketing mix can be developed. Boarden's six original elements– products, planning, pricing, distribution, promotion, servicing and marketing research were later reduced to four elements by McCarthy product, price, place (distribution) and promotion.[24] It is essential to have knowledge of various factors that are affecting these P's of market mix; the factors that affect the travel market are termed as marketing implication of tourism.

1. *Population:* It takes people to create tourism market. Today's population trends determine tomorrow's tourism. Declining birth rates do not necessarily mean less travel. As the average age increases, a greater portion of the population will be in the productive year and the economic effect will be increased in discretionary income. Industries that are sensitive to changes in discretionary income such as tourism, recreation and leisure should benefit.
2. *Age:* It is of greater interest to tourism manager than is the

actual population, because children and institutionalized elders are not travel consumer. Babies in the family have adverse effect on tourism. Nevertheless teenagers comprise an important market because they have a great deal of individual spending power and a great deal of influence on family spending pattern. They even tend to travel on their own. Baby boomers tend to be better educated and place a high priority on personal growth and experiences and have been known to consider travel as necessity. Age of 45-55 also frames an important component of travel market. Senior citizens are similar to rest of the others, when considering the purpose of travel. Outdoor recreation is not a high priority. They have an increased tendency for lodging with friends and relatives; they also are more likely to use package tour, consult travel agents, have dual residence and take cruises. Communications is difficult, their needs and desires are specific; they seek travel experiences that do not require a great deal of physical exertion, and their life style does not confine them to a specific season or length of time. Young singles travel more than the average adult does and more than other of their age. Those who are married prefer to travel by air.

3. *Income:* There is a direct relationship between family income and incidence to travel. The greater the income the more likely a household will travel. The value placed on time increases with household income which is one of the reasons air travel attracts the higher income consumer, but with husbands and wives both working it is difficult to find time for travel and vacation therefore the trend of shorter and more frequent vacation is increasing.
4. *Education:* Education broadens peoples interest and thus stimulate to travel. They prefer pleasure trips. Increased education levels lighten the propensity to travel and with expanding higher education levels air travel should also expand. As education is related with income so the rising level of education should help to increase the demand for travel.
5. *Occupation:* The managers, administrator and professionals are the largest segments forming the target markets due to their large discretionary income and education but the blue

collar segments must not be avoided totally. Budgeted travel facilities and products should be arranged for them also.

6. *Race and Gender:* It has been felt that black travel market is growing rapidly due to the increasing income; working women have increased family income, providing more discretionary income for travel; they are better customer of pleasure travel; they are better customer of working women or working wives with no children or with grown children are better customers than are working men with family responsibilities.
7. *Attitudes*: The strength of the unions, new attitudes and the paid vacation has eroded emphasis on work and reluctance to spend time and money on leisure activities. Future generation will consider leisure a birthright promoting more opportunities for travel.
8. *Time:* In today's society lack of time is a major travel constraint. Time also effects mode of transportation chosen, place visited and the activities engaged in leisure. Time is increasing due to reduction in average work week, flux time longer vacations, greater opportunities for part time work, the exodus from farming, changes in education and wider retirement opportunity to travel. Concept of paid holidays is booming up, air travel, short trips is increasing up. But due to the increasing working women force and growing propensity of managerial and technical job some problems are arising in tourism field.
9. *Fashion Custom, Habit and Tradition*: Travel experiences are now turning more important than material possessions. In the transportation areas cruise travel, air travel is now gaining popularity; resorts, cultural tourism, adventure tourism is now in fashion; travel for the purpose of visiting with friends and relatives is preferred; lower income group prefer VFR and automobiles; upper income group and business trips stay in commercial lodging and air trips, weather families trips for entertainment and sightseeing. Vacationers choose the place they never have been before. Increasing technology and faster pace of modern life make people interested in recapturing the past and history frames important tourist attractions.
10. *Changing Life-styles:* Now-a-days short trips during

weekends are preferred due to less time, more disposable income and routine may not disturb reducing work pressure etc. Adventure travel, experience travel, health travel is getting popularity. Self-fulfilment, self-gratification, self-knowledge, introspection, self-expression and self-realization are other factors promoting tourism.[25] Working couples eat out more and travel more, childless couples have greater discretionary income and travel more than do couples with children, unmarried couples travel together, single women and elder women travel alone or together for business and pleasure. There is more involvement of women in purchasing decision. People become more financially and physically mobile. There is less distinction between the social class increasing tourism and recreational life style.

Product

It has already been noted that a vacation consists of a number of different parts of products –from transportation and lodging to sight seeing and souvenirs. It is clear that a variety of providers will offer one or more of these products or services. Each provider is thus interdependent with the marketing mix. Others to offer an attractive and satisfying overall vacation experience. The philosophy of a marketing orientation suggests that products be developed to satisfy the needs and wants of those in the market.

W.J.E. Crissy has suggested several important criteria that should be met in the decision to provide a product or service.

First, there should be a relatively heavy demand for the product or service from least one important market segment, with the possibility of additional business from other segment of the market. It may be that the product can expect to break even on the basis of business from the major market segment and produce profit from business from the rest of the market. There may, of course, be a period of time before sales for a new attraction or service reach the break even point.

Second, new products and services should fit in with the general image of the property or destination area and complement existing offerings. This does not mean that a destination area must appeal to only one segment of the market and that all products must meet the needs of that market segment. A great deal obviously depends upon the size of the destination area; one part of a destination area may appeal to the jet-set, which another part may be appealing to senior citizen; within each of these parts, however, it is important that separate products and services be oriented around the one theme and market segment.

Third, any new offering should be proposed in keeping with the available supply of manpower, money and natural resources. Although new products and services should exploit on advantage that a property or destination area has, it is important that new offering be within the ability of the destination area or the management to satisfactorily provide them. A destination area may have magnificent mountain terrain suitable for skiing but may lack management knowledge in Ski area operations. Experienced management may have to be hired on a permanent or temporary basis before a ski area can be proposed.

Fourth, it is necessary that any product or service added contribute to the profit and/ or growth of the entire property or destination.

Price

Several factors influence the pricing policy set as part of the marketing mix. The price charged in any situation is unique to that situation and is affected by the combination of the factors to be discussed. In purely economic terms, price is a result of supply and demand. When supply exceeds demand, price will tend to decrease. The reverse is true also. Of greater importance is the extent to which demand changes as price changes. This refers to the elasticity involved. A 5 per cent reduction in price may result in a corresponding 10 per cent increase in the number of buyers and a subsequent increase in total sales revenue. Demand in this case is elastic. General products aimed at the luxury end of the customer scale are less susceptible to changes in price and consequently tend to be price inelastic. For destinations are properties that are open only part of the year, supply is limited and prices will have to be correspondingly higher than destination open year round. Because demand is not often uniform throughout the year, it is common to charge higher prices during the peak tourist season and lower prices when demand slackens. A product that expects a long life can be priced lower. The price charged is influenced by the competition. If our offerings are essentially the same as those of our competitors, our price must be similar to theirs. The extent to which we are unique reflects the extent to which we can charge more than the competition. Related to the influence of competition is the management policy regarding market share. If a decision is made to increase market share, prices will probably be lower than if a decision to skin a small number of tourists from several market segments is made. Pricing is obviously related to the needs of the market segment that is served.[26] If a destination or property is seen as serving the needs and wants of the market and if those needs and wants are perceived as being important to the members of the market segment, those members will be willing to pay a higher price for the destination or property. The price charged must also be perceived by the market as less than or at least equal to the value received. In certain situation the influence of the market seems to go against economic principles, with certain luxury items, demand may increase as price increases.

Promotion

Tourism promotion is one of the elements of the marketing mix and an important tool for marketing. The term promotion is interpreted and defined in many ways. Basically, the purpose of promotion is to inform, to persuade, to encourage or, more specifically, to influence the potential customer or trade intermediaries (travel agents, tour operators, reservation services, hotel) through communication to think and to act in a certain manner.[27] Many promotional tools exist to convey the message to the audience. The major part of the promotional mix is:

Advertising

Any paid form of non-personal presentation and promotion of ideas, goods, or services by an identified sponsor.

Personal Selling

Oral face-to-face presentation in a conversation with one more prospective purchase for the purpose of making sales.

Sales Promotion

Those marketing activities, other than personal selling, advertising, and publicity, that stimulate consumer purchasing and dealer effectiveness, such as displays, shows/exhibitions, demonstrations, and non-current selling effort not in the ordinary routine.

Publicity

Non-personal stimulation of demand for a product, service, or business unit by planting commercially significant news about it in a published medium or obtaining favourable presentation of it upon radio, television, or stage that is not paid for by the sponsor.[28]

Place (Distribution)

To make the tourist product easily accessible to consumers a marketer has to decide what distribution channel will be used to sell the product. The distribution channels selection is determined by the factor like location of point of sales, cost of distribution, image of the organization, effectiveness of the marketing efforts, users' motivation, regarding the product, extent of market, expected cooperation from the channel use, the extent of assistance demanded and expected by the channels used.[29] The goods and services can be read to customer by tour packagers, retail travel agents, specialty chandlers (including incentive travel firms, meeting and convention planners, hoteliers, executives, corporate travel offices etc.[30]

Figure No. 7.8: Marketing Mix

Product	Price
1. Characteristics of the product size 2. Facilities offered to staff members 3. Reputation positioning	1. Normal 2. Promoting 3. Discounted 4. Corporate 5. Wholesaler rates 6. Seasonal
Place	**Promotion**
1. Channels of distribution 2. Reservation systems 3. Intermediaries 4. Airlines 5. Clubs/associations	1. Advertising 2. Sales promotion 3. Public relations 4. Direct mail

Each intermediary can control to some degree quantity of business acquired by travel associates, they have the power of influence when, where and how people travel. The managers must study the channel choices, changes in distribution system, competitors' strategy to select the best channel. The distribution channels must not be longer, with minimum cost effectiveness and capability of achieving higher level of customer satisfaction. The width of tourism product must also be considered; new innovation must be given preference while selecting distribution channels.[31]

Introduction of Market Positioning

What is Positioning?

Positioning is a platform for the brand. It facilitates the brand to get through to the target consumer. In positioning, the firm decides how and around what parameters, the product offer has to be placed before the potential consumer. The result of your campaign depends less on how we write your advertising than on how your product is positioned. Thus, positioning is the act of fixing the locus of the product offer in the mind of the target consumer.[32] Position is a form of market communication that plays a vital role in enhancing the attractiveness of a tourism destination. The world travel and tourism council claimed that tourism is the world's largest industry. The past few years have shown a steady increased in the volume of international travel and along with this growth in travel, the number of tourism destination choices has also increase as many policy-makers have recognised the value of tourism to the economies of their regions. To some extent, this increased travel can also be attributed to an increase in advertising as tourism marketers try to enlarge their share of the global tourism pie by promoting their destinations to specific largest market. One of the most effective tools in tourism marketing as the objective of positioning is to create a distinctive place in the mind of potential customers. A position that evokes images of destination in the customer's mind, images that differentiate the destination from the competition and also as a place that can satisfy their needs and wants. Positioning is a communications strategy that is the natural follow-through of market segmentation and target marketing. Since marketing segmentation is based on the notion that different tourism destination appeal to different types of tourists, target market segments must be selected before tourism marketers can begin to attract these potential customers. An effective positioning strategy provides a competitive edge to a destination that is trying to convey its attractiveness to the target market. Positioning is more than just image creation. This important form of market communication helps to distinguish tourism destinations from similar destinations so that customers can choose the one that is the most attractive. Thus, true positioning differentiates a destination from its competitors on attributes that are meaningful to customers and it gives a competitive edge. Selection of positioning strategy that creates a distinctive or positive strategy and that creates a distinctive place in customers' minds is essential in preventing the following pitfalls:

- The destination is forced into a position of competing directly with a stranger competitor.

The destination's position is so unclear that its target market does not recognize the message that is being sent to them. This often happens when a destination tries to be all things to all people.

Market Positioning

All marketing strategy is built on STP i.e. Segmentation, Targeting and Positioning.[33] Market positioning is the natural follow of market segmentation and target marketing. Market positioning means creating an image in the consumer mind. By understanding the target market and efficient positioning strategies can be developed. The strategy to differentiate the brand or product is to place it in an appropriate cell of the human mind so that whenever the customer recalls the product, the firm's brand is the first to be recalled. This strategy is called positioning. Positioning is the act of communicating company's offer so that it occupies a distinct and valued place in the customer's mind. The goal is to locate the brand in the mind of consumer to maximize the potential benefit to the firm. A good brand positioning helps guide marketing strategy by clarifying the brands essence, what goals it helps the consumer achieve, and how it does so in a unique way.[34] The battle for your mind says, 'Positioning is what you do to the minds of the prospect. Positioning is more concerned with the customers' perception of the product offer, then the offer as such.[35] 'The aim of product positioning is to create a perception for our brand in the prospect's mind so that it stands a part from competing brands... We must cover that space in the consumer's mind as if we won a long term lease, we must find a strong position in that mind and sit on it...' Sen Gupta 'Positioning also refers to the place; a brand occupies in the mind in relation to a given product class. This place was originally a product related concept... Concerning market structure...The concept now refers to the place that the brand holds in the consumer's mind related to perceptions and preference.'[36]

There are actually two kinds of positioning in marketing: Objective positioning and Subjective positioning, sometime also called product positioning and brand positioning respectively. Each has its appropriate place and usage and is concerned with its position *vis-à-vis* the competition.[37]

Importance of Positioning

Positioning involves both launching new brands into the market place (new brand positioning), and repositioning old brands. It is concerned with the differentiation of products and services and ensuring that they do not degenerate into a commodity. Also it helps to maximize its potential into a commodity. Today, consumer is becoming increasingly confused by the huge offering of services within each market sector. These offerings are communicated by a vast number of advertising messages promoting different features of the services. The key to a successful positioning strategy is to promote the feature which the company is best at and which exactly matches the needs of the consumer because of intangibility and other feature associated with services. Successful positioning makes it easier for the customer to see a company's service as being different from other and exactly what is wanted.

Positioning is a strategic marketing tool which allows managers to determine what their position is now, what they wish it to be and what actions are needed to attain it. It permits market opportunities to be identified, by considering positions which are not met by competitors' products. It therefore helps influence both product development and the redesign of existing products. It also allows consideration of competitors' possible moves and responses so that appropriate action can be taken. The concept is often considered at the product level although it is also relevant giving the target market segment the reason for buying your services and thus underpins the whole marketing strategy. It also offers guidelines for development of a marketing mix with each element of the mix being consistent with the positioning.[38]

Main Concerns in Product Positioning

The needs for positioning arise out of the fact that a product cannot be everything to every one and have to be something to some segment. Positioning is the specific task of taking the product to a chosen orbit in the mind of the target consumers. If the positioning decision is faulty, the product suffers heavy losses. It may take a long time and enormous effort to retrieve a wrongly positioned product, while repositioning a successfully positioned product at a later stage in the light of the changes in its life cycle may be easy.

Objective Positioning

Objective positioning is concerned, almost entirely, with the objective attributes of the physical product. It means creating an image about the destination that reflects its physical characteristics and functional features. It is usually concerned with what actually it, what exists, objective positioning can be very important and is often used in the tourism industry. If a destination has some unique feature, that feature may be used to objectively position of a destination.

Less successful objective positioning occurs when the feature is not unique. This is why many destination promotions with pictures of beaches fail to create a distinct image or successfully differentiate the product. Other unsuccessful approaches may include a picture of two people looking at a mountain that looks like any other mountain or lying on a beach that looks like any other beach. One of the first rules of effective positioning is uniqueness.[39]

Subjective Positioning

Subjective positioning is concerned with subjective attributes of the destination. Subjective positioning is the image, not of the physical aspects of the destination, but other attributes perceived by the tourist. These perceptions and the resulting image may not necessarily reflect the true state of the destinations physical characteristics. They may simply exist in the tourist's mind and not all tourists agree with a particular perception or image.

In positioning, the consumer's mind is viewed as a geometric perceptual space, with different product categories and brands occupying certain position therein. These positions held by products/brand change as the available space is taken by new product/brand. How to secure a position in this perceptual space within the consumer's mind and how to retain it as the basic question in positioning? We can seek a position in the consumer's mind through several routes/propositions. We may seek a position placing our brand against another ongoing brand, or we may place it against certain expectations of the consumer nurtures. In other words, we will be placing our brand against some frame of reference as seen by the consumer. In our endeavour at meeting the desired position, we might have already endowed our product/brand with certain differentiation value. As a part of the positioning task, the firm analyses the competitor's position, sites up its own offer and identifies the best possible proposition for its product. In particular, the firm has to reckon the leader's position. It is difficult to dislodge the leading brand's position from the consumer's mind.

Basic Issues Tackled by Product Positioning

As mentioned earlier, product positioning seeks answers to the following issues:

- Where do we want our brand to be lodged in the consumer mind?
- At what should our brand be seen and considered by the consumer?
- How to ensure that the proposed brand is viewed as a superior/distinct offer against the frame of reference the consumer is having with regard to competing brands or even competing product categories?

Ways to Position the Brand (Brand Positioning)

The ways to position the brands are:

Figure No. 7.9: Brand Positioning

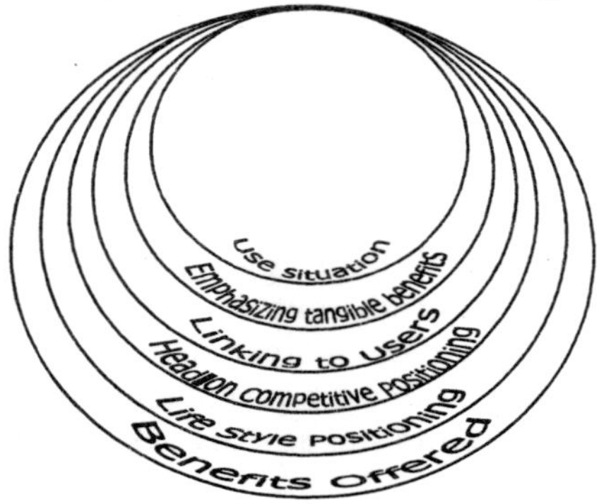

Use Situation

The marketer can identify use situation for his brand or product and analyse consumer perception of existing competitor brands in different use situations. Based on this analysis the firm can position its brand.

Emphasizing Tangible Benefits

The brand may even be positioned on the basis of tangible benefits that it offers to customers. These are in the form of specific features and sometime through price and distribution.

Head on Competitive Positioning

This is the strategy of placing a firm's brand next to leader in the market and trying to up-roof it on a specific tangible variable.

Lifestyle Positioning

A firm may even position brand as a lifestyle concept contemporary or futuristic. Many of today's new kitchen appliances, ready-made garment, textiles and watches are positioned accordingly. One of the dimensions of lifestyle is aspirations. Given the upward mobility of the Indian market is not uncommon for the marketer to use aspirations for positioning his brand. In order to do so, the brand has to communicate an exclusive image with the consumer as he is willing to pay for. Also, it should reflect the aspirations of the target market. Aspirations and other lifestyle-based positioning is today more sustainable than tangible benefit positioning.

Benefits Offered

Another way to position a brand is to highlight the benefits that customers get using the product. Emotional relationship is one of the strong reasons to buy a brand.[40]

Developing a Positioning Strategy

We have seen how companies, products and brands can be differentiated. Even in the case of a commodity product, the company must see its task as that of converting an undifferentiated product into a differentiated offering. Levitt and others have pointed out dozens of ways to differentiate an offering. But not all brand differences are meaningful or worthwhile not every difference is a differentiator. Each difference has the potential to create company costs as well as customer's benefits. Therefore the company must carefully select the ways in which it will distinguish itself from competitors. A difference is worth establishing to the extent that it satisfies the following criteria:

- *Important:* The difference delivers a highly valued benefit to a sufficient number of buyers.
- *Distinctive*: The difference either is not offered by others or is offered in amore distinctive way by the company.
- *Superior:* The difference is superior to other ways of obtaining the same benefit.

Figure No. 7.10: Developing a Market Positioning Strategy

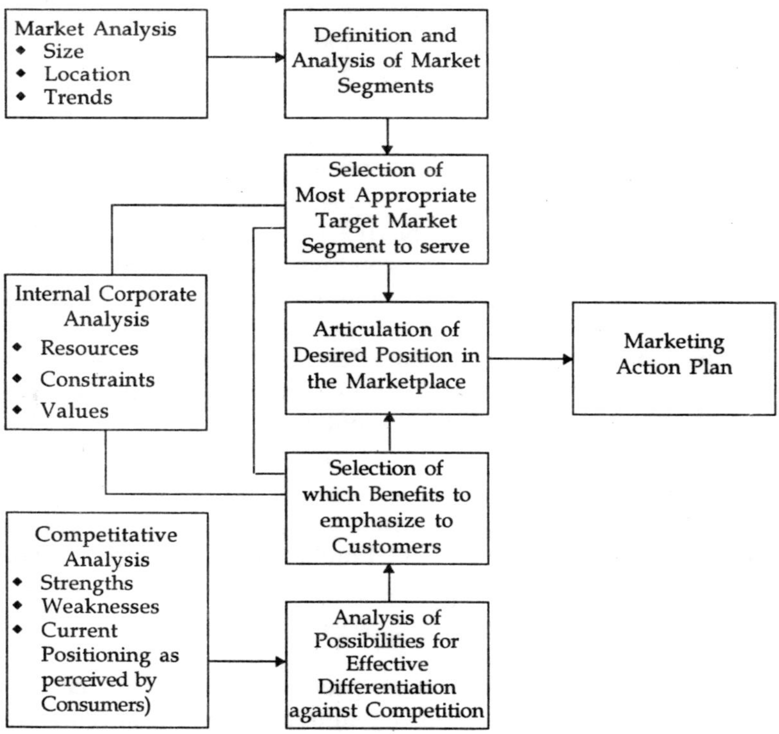

Source: (Christopher Lovelock, *Services Marketing* © 1984, p. 136, Reprinted by permission of Prentice-Hall, Inc., Englewood Cliffs, New Jersey.)

- *Communicable:* The difference is communicable and visible to buyers.
- *Preemptive:* The difference cannot be easily copied by competitors.
- *Affordable:* The buyer can afford to pay for the difference.
- *Profitable:* The company will find it profitable to introduce the difference.

Each firm will want to promote those few differences that will appeal most strongly to its target market. In other words, the firm will want to develop a focused positioning strategy.

Positioning is the act of designing the company's offering and image so that they occupy a meaningful and distinct competitive position in the target customer's minds. The most commonly promoted number one positioning are "best quality", "best service", "lowest price", "best value", "safest", "fastest", "most customized", "most convenient", and "most advanced technology". If a company hammers away at one of these positioning and convincingly delivers on it, it will probably be best known and recalled for this strength. Not every one agrees that single-benefit positioning is always best. Double benefit positioning may be necessary if two or more firms are claiming to be best on the same attribute. The intention is to find a special niche within the target segment.

As companies increase the number of claims for their brand, they risk disbelief and a loss of clear positioning. In general, a company must avoid four major positioning errors:

- *Underpositioning:* Some companies discover that buyers have only a vague idea of the brand. Buyers do not really sense anything special about it. The brand is seen as just another entry as a crowded marketplace.
- *Overpositioning:* Buyers may have too narrow an image of the brand.
- *Confused Positioning:* Buyers might have a confused image of the brand resulting from the company's making too many claims or changing the brand positioning too frequently.
- *Doubtful Positioning:* Buyers may find it hard to believe the brand claims in view of the product's features, price or manufacturer.

The advantage of solving the positioning problem is that it enables the company to solve the marketing mix problem. The marketing mix-product, price, place, and promotion is essentially the working out of the tactical details of the positioning strategy. Thus, a firm that seizes upon the "high quality position" knows that it must produce high-quality products, charge a high price, distribute through high-class dealers and advertise in high quality magazines. This is the primary way to project a consistent and believable high-quality image.[41]

Aaker and Shansby suggest that there are six major positioning approaches.

- Positioning by attribute, feature, or customer benefit
- Positioning by price/quality
- Positioning with respect to use or application
- Positioning according to the users or class of users
- Positioning with respect to a product class
- Positioning *vis-à-vis* the competition.[42]

There is another issue in regard to developing effective positioning that must be kept in mind. This is the issue of the differentiation among salient, determinant and important product attributes or benefits. One might position on a salient benefit with poor results because those benefits are not necessarily determinant or important in the consumer choice process.[43]

Competitive Positioning

In developing positioning strategies, a critical element is the positioning *vis-à-vis* the competition. It is necessary first to examine extant images and positions in the product class. One should then try to anticipate the effects of the proposed positioning and the reactions of competitors. Examining strengths and weaknesses of competitive positioning can identify niches to enter, niches to stay away from, and areas of dissatisfaction where a new positioning could generate new customers or lure others from the competition. If the segment is expanding, this process could also identify a growth opportunity. In analysing the position of the competition, marketers also want to be able to protect the position they hope to establish. This means interpreting possible competitive reactions and taking measures to reduce their impact.

Internal Positioning Analysis

Perceptual mapping, mentioned above, helps to determine positioning strategies *vis-à-vis* the competition. There are also very useful methods for analyzing one's own position on a number of different attributes or benefits that relate deliverability with any one of the constructive salience, importance and determinance. Internal analysis not only helps to determine internal positioning, but also indicates where the operations may be failing both internally and relative to the competition.

Multiple Brand Positioning

The tourism multiple brand positioning is used for growth purposes. Multiple brands provide protection from the competition against a single brand. Multiple brand positioning also helps other most chains to move from lower-tier market and threatening the middle-to-upper. Multiple brand positioning helps us to understand:

1. How we are and what for you stand.
2. To understand how products will be different from others.
3. How this multiple brand positioning will benefit the target markets.
4. How to project the right image.
5. How to create awareness.
6. Other such related questions.

Multiple brand positioning is also a common practice in other industries. In hospitality trade standardisation for common practices may be applied for obtaining desired results.

The Process of Positioning

The following are the main constituents of Process of Positioning:

A. Determine Levels of Positioning

The first step in positioning is to determining which levels are to receive explicit positioning attention.

B. Identification of Attributes

Once the level of positioning has been determined it is necessary to identify the specific attributes that are important to the chosen market segment. In particular, the way in which purchasing decisions are made should be considered. Individuals use different criteria for making a purchase decision of a service. The purpose for using the service may change the set of criteria, e.g. business insurance or personal insurance. The timing of the use of the service will also affect the choice of service. A consideration of the decision making unit is also relevant. For example, the decision may also be affected by whether a group or an individual will use the service, e.g. the amenities of a hotel may be more important for a family than for an individual.

C. Location of Attributes on Positioning Map

The positioning process involves the identification of the most important attributes and location of various companies' services, for these attributes, on a positioning map, where a range of attributes are identified. Statistical procedures exist for combining these attributes into aggregate dimensions. Such dimensions are referred to by various names such as principal components, multi-dimensional scales, factors, etc., depending upon how the data were elicited and which statistical procedures were used. Usually two dimensions are used on positioning maps and these often account for a large proportion of the explanation of the customer's preference.

D. Evaluating Positioning Options

Ries and Trout have suggested three broad/positioning options:

- Strengthening current position against competitors.
- Identifying an unoccupied market position.
- Repositioning the competition.

E. Review Alternative Perspectives of Positioning

The preceding discussion has focused on positioning of services from the perspective of how the customers perceive the company. A company's position is influenced by a group of competing companies and their customers. The network of perceptions among the company, its competitors and its customers.[44]

REFERENCES

1. Evans, R. Joel and Berman, Barry—"Marketing", Prentice Hall, New Jersey, 1994, p. 6.

2. "Testing the Effectiveness of Promotional Campaigns in International Travel Marketing", World Tourism Organization Seminar, Ottawa, 1975, p. 3.
3. Evans, R. Joel and Berman, Barry—"Marketing", Prentice Hall, New Jersey, 1994, p. 11.
4. Evans, R. Joel and Berman, Barry—"Marketing", Prentice Hall, New Jersey, 1994, p. 11.
5. Kotler, P.—"Marketing Management", PHI, New Delhi, 1990, p. 3.
6. Bukart, A.J. and Medik, S.—"Tourism, Past, Present and Future", Heinemann, London, 1988, p. 195.
7. Raina, A.K. and Jain, Neelu", Dynamics of Tourism: Concepts, Philosophy and Strategies", Kanishka Publishers, Distributors, New Delhi, 2004, p. 133.
8. Raina, A.K. and Jain, Neelu", Dynamics of Tourism: Concepts, Philosophy and Strategies", Kanishka Publishers, Distributors, New Delhi, 2004, p. 132.
9. Evans, R. Joel and Berman, Barry—"Marketing", Prentice Hall, New Jersey, 1994, p. 20.
10. Jha, S.M.—"Tourism Marketing", Himalaya Publishing House, Bombay, 1995, p. 37.
11. Mill, Robert Christie and Morrison, Alastair M.—"The Tourism System an Introductory Text" Prentice Hall Inc, Englewood Cliffs, New Jersey, 1985, pp. 357-358.
12. Coltman, M. Michael—"Introduction to Travel and Tourism and International Approach", Van Nostrum Reinhold, New York, 1989, pp. 299-300.
13. Committee on Definition, Chicago: American Marketing Association, 1960, p. 16.
14. Paul, Turner—"Using Information to Enhance Competitive Advance the Marketing Options", *European Journal of Marketing*, Vol. 25, 6 November 1991, p. 55.
15. Condiff, E.W. and Still, R.R.—"Basic Marketing Concepts, Environment and Decision", Prentice Hall Inc., New Jersey, 1964, pp. 313-314.
16. Evans, R. Joel and Berman, Barry—"Marketing", Prentice Hall, New Jersey, 1994, p. 101.
17. Makan, Dileep—"Strategies and Planning in Tourism Industry", Adhyayan Publishers and Distributors, Delhi, 2004, p. 98.
18. Raina, A.K. and Agrawal, S.K.—"The Essence of Tourism Development", Sarup and Sons, New Delhi, 2004, pp. 157-58.
19. Mill, Robert Christie and Morrison, Alastair M.—"The Tourism System an Introductory Text", Prentice Hall Inc., Englewood Cliffs, New Jersey, 1985, p. 365.
20. Lewis, Robert C. and Chambers, Richard E.—"Marketing Leadership

in Hospitality Foundation and Practices", Van Nostrum Reinhold, New York, 1989, p. 228.

21. Coltman, M. Michael—"Introduction to Travel and Tourism and International Approach", Van Nostrum Reinhold, New York, 1989, p. 301.
22. Bhatia, A.K.—"Tourism Development: Principles and Practices", Sterling Pub. (P) Ltd., New Delhi, 1982, p. 150.
23. Victor, P. Buell—"Marketing Management: A Strategic Planning Approach", New York; McGraw-Hill, 1984, p. 22.
24. Jerome, E.—"A Managerial Approach", Homewood, III: Richard D. Jewin, 1975, pp. 75-80.
25. Raina, A.K. and Jain, Neelu—"Dynamics of Tourism: Concepts, Philosophy and Strategies", Kanishka Publishers, Distributors, New Delhi, 2004, pp. 149-151.
26. Mill, Robert Christie and Morrison, Alastair M.—"The Tourism System an Introductory Text", Prentice Hall Inc., Englewood Cliffs, New Jersey, 1985, pp. 357-358.
27. Bhatia, A.K.—"Tourism Development", Sterling Pub. Pvt. Ltd., New Delhi, 1932, p. 150.
28. Marketing Definitions: A Glossary of Marketing Terms, Chicago, American Marketing Association, Committee in Definition, 1960.
29. Louis, Sterm W. and Adel, J.E.L. Ansary—"Marketing Channels", 5th Ed., Supper Saddle River, Prentice Hall, New York, 1996, p. 110.
30. Bittner, M.J. and Booms, B.H.—"Trends in Travel and Tourism Marketing. The Changing Structure of Distribution Channels", *Journal of Research*, No. 4, 1982, p. 39.
31. Raina, A.K. and Jain, Neelu—"Dynamics of Tourism: Concepts, Philosophy and Strategies", Kanishka Publishers, Distributors, New Delhi, 2004, p.157.
32. Ramaswamy, V.S. and Kumari, S. Nana—"Marketing Management Planning Implementation and Control", III ed. McMillan, 2002, p. 301.
33. Kotler, P.—"Marketing Management", PHI, New Delhi, 1990, p. 34.
34. Kotler, P.—"Marketing Management", PHI, New Delhi, 1991, p. 310.
35. Al, Ries and Jack, Trout—"Positioning: The Battle for Your Mind", Warner Books, New York, 1981.
36. Ramaswamy, V.S. and Kumari, S. Nana—"Marketing Management Planning Implementation and Control", III Ed. McMillan, 2002, p. 301.
37. Lewis, Robert C. and Chambers, Richard E.—"Marketing Leadership in Hospitality Foundation and Practices", Van Nostrum Reinhold, New York, 1989, p. 260.
38. Payne, Adrain—"The Essence of Service Marketing", Prentice Hall of India (P) Ltd., New Delhi, 1993, p. 120.

39. Singh, R.K. — "Modern Trends in Hospitality Industry", 2006, p. 110.
40. Saxena, Rajan — "Marketing Management", Third Ed., Tata McGraw Hill Publishing Company Ltd., New Delhi, 2006, pp. 285-286.
41. Kotler, P. — "Market Management Analysis, Planning Implementation and Control", Ninth Edition, Prentice Hall of India Pvt. Ltd., New Delhi, 1997, pp. 294-95, 298.
42. Aaker, David A. and Shanby, J. Gary — "Positioning Your Product", Business Horizons, May-June, 1982, p. 60.
43. Lewis, Robert C. and Chambers, Richard E. — "Marketing Leadership in Hospitality Foundation and Practices", Van Nostrum Reinhold, New York, 1989, p. 282.
44. Payne, Adrian — "The Essence of Service Marketing", Prentice Hall of India Pvt. Ltd., New Delhi, 1993, pp. 108-10, 112, 115.

8

Tourism and Hotel Industry

Tourism helps in accelerating growth by employment generation and foreign exchange earnings and opening new areas comparing a number of factors. What have always been considered the separate industries, are now integral part of much larger industries of tourism. The most important one is the HOTEL INDUSTRY.[1] In this view it will be noteworthy to consider the report of Lok Sabha Committee (1975-76) that since the hotels constitute the most important and in fact a basic element of tourism infrastructure. The committee feels that the various measures taken and efforts made for tourism promotion will not produce the desired results if the hotel accommodation in the country lags behind.[2] Tourism industry is the second largest industry in the world where it has been rightly said – *'No Hotels No Tourism'* thus hotel industry is considered as an essential part of tourism.[3] The expansion of tourism brought inevitable development to the hotel industry. The impact of tourism on hotels is clearly seen by their enormous sophisticated modern techniques. The modern Hotel Industry has become highly sophisticated and equipped with refined and systematized technology.[4]

Impact of Tourism on Hotel Industry

Hotels are the core and essential part of tourism industry. This industry has enough scope to expand further. The hotel industry has been growing its importance from economic and socioeconomic point of view. The impact of tourism on hotel industry of India focused primarily on economic and socio-cultural aspect. The impact made by tourism therefore depends upon the volume and profile characteristic of the tourists (their length of stay, their preference, purpose of visit travelling styles etc.) together with the characteristic of the Hotel Industry styles (facilities, amenities provided, its structure, cuisine etc.) is equally important as it determines the degree of its strength to tourism and tourism development.

1. *Economic Impact*

International tourism is an invisible export that it creates a flow of foreign currency into the hotel industry thereby contributing directly to the economy of the state as well like other export industries. This inflow of revenue creates industry turnover, household income, employment generation and government revenue. The generation process does not stop at this point however. Some portion of the revenue received by the hotel industry, human resource and government creating further rounds of economic activity. Domestic tourism has somewhat similar economic impact upon the host segment. International tourism brings foreign currency into the whole industry, while domestic tourism redistributes domestic currency. Money earned in other segments is spent within the host community so as to create additional resources, job opportunities for semi skilled and unskilled human resource at tourist destinations. Economic impact of tourism has diversified the economy by creating separate industries like hotel industry. Moreover, tourism seems to be more effective than other industries improving infrastructure. Indeed it is in this industry that tourism can make its most significant impact by providing monetary incentive for the continuance of the industry and by creating market for state produce.

2. *Socio-cultural Impacts*

In addition to the economic impact tourism also imposes socio-cultural impacts on the industry. The culture (the cuisine, the folk, the art, the history) of host communities is often an important factor in attracting tourists to a particular destination. Many tourists are interested in experiencing a culture, which is different from their own;[5] indeed the existence of difference between the host culture, and tourist culture is the principle, which stimulates the tourism industry. The culture of the host destination can take many different forms but most examples fall into one of the two categories:

1. Customs relating to host destination.

2. Aspects of the everyday life their history and religion. The first category includes arts and crafts, folk, dance, customs and festivals, colourful ceremonies and carnivals. The second category includes not only the local but also the national traditions and customs.

The hotel industry caters natural, homely environment and warmth. Hotel industry caters art and history, archaeology, handicraft, literature, music, dance, and philosophy of the state. Some of the impacts of tourism on hotel industry are beneficial but some can be considered to be harmful say such effect may be on culture of the host destination known as *trivialization*.[7]

This terminology can be explained as the degradation and commercialization of the host culture where the economic and socioculture impacts are favourable; they can also be explosive. Likewise the impact is seen in the feasts, festivals which tourists are encouraged to attend rather they are being high jacked and encashed by the hotel industry. With good planning, however, tourism can provide an impetus for the preservation of ancient cultures, but too often the local way of life degenerates into a commercially organized effigy of its former self.[8] The traditional dances and the skilled crafts give way to cheap imitations to satisfy the needs of the visitors and to obtain money with least possible effort.

Another impact on moral standards of the host population creates deprivation and frustration when they cannot achieve the higher level as foreign tourist. In extreme cases crime, prostitution, gambling and drug traffic are being catered by hotel industry. As Human Resource plays a vital role in the hospitality industry education and training of the resource is must.[9] So it encourages education and training of Human Resource as the industry have to cater the best products of tourism industry to the tourist. For this the hotel industry has certain duties and responsibilities for resource of the industry.

Tourism and Hotel Industry

Ellsworth M. Statler—the Henry Ford of the modern hotels says, "The guest is always right."[10] Some might contradict this but this statement reflects the ultimate challenges being faced by hotel professionals to provide services that meet ever changing need and demands of the guests. The hotel industry is a part of larger enterprises known as the travel and tourism industry. The travel and tourism industry is a vast group of businesses with one goal in common: providing necessary or desired products and services to travellers.[11]

Many hotel properties provide food and beverage service, recreational service and more such facilities. As per international standards there are, as estimated, 10 million guest rooms available to tourists around the world.[12] According to World Tourism Organisation (W.T.O.) Madrid, tourism has now become the world's largest industry, ahead of automobiles and petroleum products.[13] Further, with regards to employment, as per the world tourism and travel council report, travel and tourism industry is the largest civilian industry in the world employing one out of every ten person world wide.[14] As per the WTO report 1790 million tourist arrivals were recorded all over the world during 2004-05, registering a 4.6 per cent increase over 2000. International receipts rose to 3870 billion, registering a 7.6 per cent growth. India, however, commanded just 0.41 per cent of the global tourist arrivals and just about 0.51 per cent of the total receipts.[15]

But it is also notable that this substantial contribution of 0.41 per cent to Indian economy was equivalent to foreign exchange worth Rs. 15,000 crores.[16] Beside, the tourism sector provides direct employment to 80 lakh people and indirect employment to 2 crore people.[17]

The Indian tourism Industry has been defined to include the following segments:[18]

1. Hotel restaurants resorts and other tourist complexes providing accommodation, food and catering services to tourists.
2. Travel agencies and tour operators.
3. Units providing facilities to tourist on culture adventure, wildlife experiences.
4. Surface water and air transport facilities to the tourists.
5. Leisure, entertainment, amusement sports and health units of tourists.
6. Convention and Seminar Units.

The ninth Five Year Plan accorded industrialization to tourism. Dr. Negi writes "of the many and diverse components of the tourist industry, hotels constitute the most important segment. Hotels are the vital and essential parts of tourism industry. Without an adequate development of hotel resources all the national scenery, all the climate virtues and all sporting and recreational facilities will not suffice to sustain a good volume of tourists trade."[19]

Further, Dr. Negi writes, the expansion of tourism will inevitably bring about the development of the Hotel Industry. Hotel Industry is so closely linked with the tourism industry that it is responsible for about 50 per cent of the foreign exchange earnings from tourism."[20]

The employment avenues in the services-oriented hotel industry are quite large. As regards the direct employment it is estimated that the room to staff ratio for a hotel varies between 1:1.5 to 1:3, whereas the committee on unemployment 1993 estimated that on an average one hotel room should expect to provide employment for 2.5 persons.[21] On an average the visit of each foreign tourist provides employment to 1 person, and 6.5 domestic tourists generate 1 job.[22] Further, with regards to indirect employment there are a number of other employment avenues connected to the hotel industry viz. supply of food items, various machinery items, from kitchen to air conditioning, laundry equipments, computers, furniture, fixtures, cutlery, crockery etc. The Bhagwati Committee said it would (indirect) offer nine times employment to the number of persons employed in hotels.[23] Moreover, hotel industry seems more effective than other industries in generating direct employment. The Hotel Industry has direct impact on regional and rural development. The industry has encouraged cottage industries in many ways—handlooms for furnishings, carpets, handicraft etc. In keeping with the philosophy of self-reliance through indigenous source, the hotel industry has relied predominantly on getting the supplies and equipments fabricated in the country.[24] The hotel industry also provides an opportunity to the guests to know the regional or a country's way of life and culture. In overall terms it has multiple economic benefits, which is an urgent requirement for a developing country like India.

Origin of Hotels: A Brief History

Hotel Industry in India

India, the ancient land of civilization, culture, dance, drama, music, and hospitality has been visited through the centuries by the travellers from many countries. For facilitating the travel, the Kings and Rulers built the Dharamshalas, constructed road, planted trees, dug wells and tanks. With the advent of Muslim rulers, Sarais were introduced. In the reign of Sher Shah Suri and then Mughals it reached a level of perfection. Improvements in the means of transport and communication resulted in the establishment of inns and taverns.

Later with the advent of British the Sarais took the form of western style hotels.[25] It seems that with regard to modern Hotels, it was the British who introduced hotels in India mainly for their own use or for foreign visitors. Dr. Negi writes that the credit for opening the first western style hotel under the name of British hotel in Bombay in 1840, goes to Pallangee Pestongee. It is called the pioneer of the western style hotels in India.[26] The twentieth century was a turning point in the history of hotel industry in India. In this century there was a real growth and development of the hotel industry.

Growth and Development of Hotel Industry

The history of development of hotel industry in India dates back when the necessity and urge to travel either on foot or by horse led to the setting up of places where accommodation and food can be obtained. There are many, historical evidences about the existence of the Dharmshalas and Sarais (Inns). Some of the Sarais were built during the Tughlak dynasties. Sher Shah Suri and Mughals reached to the perfection. Akbar, Jahangir and Shajhan were great philanthropists. The Sarais built by them were unique. They afforded the best possible facilities to the travellers. Jahanara Begum built the most beautiful Sarai. The Sarai was situated in the garden of Sahibabad or Begumabad in Delhi. Although the Sarai is no more, the garden is still there and is known as Queen's Park or Azad Park. Jahanara Begum Sarai was a magnificent building.[27] In later eighteenth and early nineteenth century due to the development in the means of transportation and communication inns and taverns[28] were established in the principal cities of the country. The Sarais took the form of western style hotels in some cities during this period. David Prince who visited India in this eighteenth century stayed in one of such Sarais.[29]

The progress made by these hotels in India cannot be underestimated. In spite of the higher initial investment, costlier operating technique and comparatively lower profit margins and a number of other factors, these hotels have a continuous and steady progress. These hotels were first started about 135 years ago mainly for dignitaries and princes. Several hotels came into existence in Kolkatta, Chennai, Bangalore, Mysore, Hyderabad, Vishakhapatnam etc. The twentieth century was a turning point in the history of the hotel industry in India especially the year 1903 is remembered as a landmark. It is in this century we find the real growth and development of the accommodation industry.[30] The independently owned hotels were of traditional pattern and the typical first in the industry, but the growth and development of hotel industry has been increasingly associated with hotel groups. Hotels in different locations when placed under central management within a restricted geographical area are said to be grouped hotels. Leased hotels as agents, franchise hotels are being operated by the hotel groups. The hotel groups normally operate hotels owned by them or leased by them from their owners to whom they pay rental. Sometimes they manage hotels as agents for the owners under management contracts, which provide for the payment of expenses/ management fees and/or the sharing of profits. The groups may also operate under franchise agreements, which allow one party (the franchisee) to sell a product designed, supplied and controlled by the other party (the franchiser), in return for a fee or a share of profits. In this arrangement a hotel group may be in the role of a franchiser or in the role of a multiple franchises.[31]

The hotel groups are advantageous from various point of view say financial, marketing, managerial, technical etc. Groups extend the size resulting into various economies say financial, marketing, buying, managerial, technical economies. The financial economy is the ability of the group to have internal and external capital resources. Because of good security provided by the hotel group to its lenders, lending institutions provide a good finance. The fluctuations in working capital, revenue, and expenditure are being balanced by these financial resources, which can only be obtained by such groups. The size of the group is such that an image is created in the market, which enables the group to obtain the marketing economies say common name, facilities and standards, public relations, advertising and sales promotion. A hotel group can achieve economies of buying as goods cost keep pace with the increase in the volume and services are bought in bulk at negotiable price and range. A group can attain the availability of training schemes and benefit from interchange of staff between the hotels in a group. The advantages of group operation such as finance, personnel, purchasing and marketing can be obtained by employing specialists in the group. In a hotel group managerial economies can be enjoyed as management cost keep pace with the increase in the volume of business or businesses. Due to the size of the group various technical economies can easily be achieved which otherwise would not have been possible.

As far as the Indian Hotel Industry is concerned there are basically six groups or chains of hotels namely,

- The Ashoka Group—Indian Tourism Development Corporation
- The Welcome Group—Indian Tobacco Company
- Taj Group of Hotels—The Indian Hotel Co. Ltd.
- Oberoi Group of Hotels—The East India Co. Ltd.
- Centaur Group—Hotel Corporation of India[32]
- Clark Group.

I. ITDC–Ashoka Group

In accordance with the recommendations of Jha Committee (1963), the Government of India set up three separate corporations in 1965 namely, Hotel Corporation of India Ltd. (HCL), India Tourism Corporation and Indian Tourism Transport Undertaking Ltd. After more than a year of their working the three corporations were amalgamated into one composite corporation-India Tourism Development Corporation. This new Corporation (ITDC) commanded functioning with effect from October 1, 1966 with an authorized capital of Rs. 5 crore. Realizing the importance of tourism in the country the Government of India created a separate ministry of Tourism and Civil Aviation on 13 March, 1967 under the charge of a Cabinet Minister.[33] Today ITDC provides an incentive to travel and tourism backed by 35 hotels segmented into three different categories - Ashok Elite Hotels, Ashok Classic Hotels and Ashok Comfort Hotels and also Forest Lodges, Travellers Lodges and Beach Resorts.[34] The six 'elite' hotels of Ashok groups five star deluxe properties that cater to up market clientele. The 'classic' group comprises sixteen units that meet the expectation of the business traveller and mid market guests. The comfort category provides home comfort at eleven locations across the country.[35]

II. ITC Hotels – Welcome Group

The Indian Tobacco Company (Ltd.) entered the hotel industry in 1957 with the opening of Chola in Chennai. It has been inspired in every case by the Indian historical tradition. The philosophy of ITC is – "We enjoy people with a symbol ITC Welcome Hotels and the emblem of two folded hands in Namaskar done in flowers to be changed every day at the entrance of every ITC hotel, is the Indian way of welcoming the guests.[36] The Mughal in Agra (1976) is inspired by the red sand stone design of Fatehpur Sikri. The Maurya in Delhi (1977) is inspired by the most famous of the Maurya Emperor Ashoka. Each of the hotel is designed to have an individual character of its own, totally Indian in concept and yet ultra modern in terms of amenities and comfort. Welcome Group does not appear willing to build a chain of mass produced hotels.[37] Welcome Group is now rapidly being recognized as the most versatile and quality service hotel. Recently the president Mr. Bill Clinton of USA visited India and stayed at 'Maurya' in Delhi. The company, ITC Hotels presently operates eleven hotels under the Welcome Group banner apart from two other hotels. It owns and in all has 17 hotels in its fold.[38] The Welcome group and Travel Corporation of India Hotels and Resorts (Private) Ltd. signed an agreement to augment the Welcome Group chain by working as partners to accelerate the rate of growth of foreign tourist traffic coming to India.[39]

III. The Taj Group of Hotels

Shri Jamshedjee Tata who established Taj Mahal Hotel in Mumbai in 1904 incorporated the Indian Hotel Company, Mumbai on April 1st 1902 with an authorized capital of 30 lakh. Today Taj Group has 49 properties in 33 destinations with more than 6000 rooms in India. It is India's largest hotel chain offering Luxury Hotels, Business Hotels, Leisure Hotels, which comprise Palaces, Resorts, Garden Retreats, and Cultural Center hotels. To further consolidate its position in the industry it has won international acclaim for its quality hotels and its excellence in business facilities, service cuisine and interiors. Today, there are many hotels in the chain including Taj Mahal, Inter-Continental, President Hotel, the Fort Augada Beach Resort, the Lake Palace (Udaipur), the Rambagh Palace (Jaipur), the

Taj Coromandel, the Fisherman's Cove, the Pandyan Hotel, the Taj Mahal (Delhi) and the Taj Palace (New Delhi) in all the Taj Group has total of 55 properties in India and abroad.[40]

IV. Oberoi Group of Hotels

Mr. Oberoi the propounder of Oberoi Group of hotels was a clerk in Cecil Hotel, Shimla who soon became a partner in the Clerk Hotel Shimla. He took over Grand Hotel, Calcutta in 1933. The Oberoi Hotels Pvt. Ltd. was established with a capital of Rs. 5 lakhs in 1946.[41] Since then several hotels were built and added to his chain of hotels like Mount Everest (Darjeeling), Mount View (Chandigarh), Maharaja Hari Singh's Palace in Srinagar etc. Oberois further extended their activities internationally since 1964. They have been successfully going on with numerous ventures abroad. Kathmandu (Nepal), Singapore, Sudan, Fiji, Egypt, Indonesia, Mauritius and acquired Menna House in Cairo. Oberoi Aswan at Elephantine Island in the middle of Nile, Hotel Ya Bhawani at Zanzibar, Hotel Dammam in Saudi Arabia. In 1973 Oberoi Sheraton was opened in Bombay. The Oberoi Group has its own school of Hotel Management in Delhi, recognized by the International Hotel Association, Paris. It has an exchange programme with Lycee Technique Hoteller in France.[43] The BHEL is also moving into hotels in collaboration with Oberois and heading to established hotels at Chennai, Coimbatore, Bangalore, Pune and other commercial cities of India.[44] Oberoi has played a place setting role in developing the hotel industry since 1947. They acquired international name with elegance, personalized service and luxurious living. Mr. Oberoi the winner of the 'Agastya' award for promotion of tourism in India, the 'Victory Pillar' for promotion of hotel and catering industry, may justifiably be called the founder, promoter and builder of hotel industry on this sub-continent.[45]

V. Air India – Hotel Corporation of India

The airlines generate a substantial quantum of traffic, which feeds the hotels with business and tourist travellers. The air-passengers' natural choice is certain to be influenced by the carrier reputation and associated facilities offered by it. Therefore Air India considered it proper to enter into and give a new direction to the Indian Hotel Industry.[46] Air India in July 1971 set up a wholly owned subsidiary called Hotel Corporation of India (HCI) with a capital of US$6.5

million. Its flight kitchen is famous for the craft of crockery. The Baby of the chain HCI Group opened Centaur Hotel at Santa Cruz (presently Shivajee) Airport, Mumbai and Hotel Centaur at Delhi's Indira Gandhi International Airport. In addition, there are two beach resorts operating in collaboration with the TCI, The Centaur Beach Resort at Port Blair, and Centaur Beach Resort at Bangaram.[47]

VI. Clarks Groups

Clarks Hotel, Varanasi, was established in the eighties of the nineteenth century. In 1948 the present owner, the U.P. Hotels and Restaurant Ltd. acquired it. Within 13 years of its establishment it made a tremendous progress by establishing four luxurious hotels at Jaipur, Calcutta, Khajuraho and Kathmandu. There are plans for opening three more luxury hotels at Delhi, Patna and at a few Buddhist places.[48] Among the other hotels the prominent ones are Holiday Inn, Bombay having its franchise from Holiday Inns, Inc., USA. The New Delhi Hilton is an enterprise of Bharat Hotel Ltd., New Delhi. Asian Hotel Ltd. and Meridian, Delhi own Hotel Leela Venture at Bombay and Goa, and Hyatt Regency, Delhi, a part of Air France Hotels is there. The quality Inn and Days Inn are also expanding their business in India.[49]

Categorisation of Hotels in India

Categorisation separates accommodation into different classes. Categorising a hotel into a particular group is not easy, because of its diversity. Many hotels do not fit into any single and well-defined category. Government of India, Department of Tourism, is doing the widely accepted categorization. The hotel is classified into different star categories ranging from 1 star to 5 star deluxe. Recently a new category, heritage hotel has also been added to it. The present system of classification is based on facilities available in the concerned hotels. The Department of Tourism had constituted a committee, Hotel and Restaurant Approval and Classification Committee (HRACC), which inspects the Hotel (the applicant hotel) to assess its suitability, or otherwise for awarding the star category it has applied for. There are five such Committees – the Central Committees and four regional committees. The classification or reclassification of 4 Star, 5 Star and 5 Star deluxe hotels is handled by the Central Committees. The classification and reclassification of 1, 2, 3 Star and the regional committees do heritage hotel and approval of restaurants.[50] Further, there are many hotels, which do not apply for classification providing more or less the same facilities what these classified hotels provide. These types of hotels can be named as 'unclassified' hotels. Another category can be alternative lodging properties. It includes Rest Houses, Guest Houses, Tourist Bungalows, and Camping sites, Dharamshalas etc. At present we are having only 64,000 rooms[51] all over India whereas Las Vegas (USA) alone has more than 100000 hotel rooms.[52] Bangkok, the capital of Thailand provides more hotel rooms than our entire country.[53]

Classification of Hotels

The Department of Tourism classification is functioning hotels under the star system into five categories from 1-star to 5-star. For this purpose a permanent committee the Hotel and Restaurant Approval and Classification Committee has been set up which inspects the applicant hotels to assess their suitability of otherwise for award of the Star category applied for. Based on the recommendation of the HRACC deserving hotels are awarded the appropriate star category and are placed on the approved list of the department. Placing a hotel into a particular group is not easy. Therefore many types of classification are in existence. Here it needs to be noted that the previous researchers had taken into account only those hotels, which exist in Directories, especially in Hotel and Restaurant Guide, India, edited and published by the Federation of Hotel and Restaurant Association of India, New Delhi. For the purpose of the proper analysis of the subject a new hotel classification has been introduced with regard to Hotel Industry in India. This classification will cover every hotel unit. It is as under:

1. The classified hotels
   - *(a)* The chain hotels
   - *(b)* Independent hotels
   - *(c)* The Government owned hotels
   - *(d)* The heritage hotels.

2. The unclassified hotels
   - *(a)* Registered hotels
   - *(b)* Unregistered hotels
   - *(c)* Alternative lodging properties.

Departmentalization in Hotels

Departmentalization represents the pattern of grouping activities. Similar activities intimately related with a distinct function are grouped together to form departments. Departments however differ with respect to the basic pattern used to group activities and there is no single best way of departmentalizing that is applicable to all organizations or to all situations. The aim is to take advantage of division of labour and specialization up to a certain limit. In all categories of hotels, the base for the departmentalization is to function properly. Each major function of a hotel is grouped into a department. Sometimes, the star rating and ownership also affect the formal existence of a department into a hotel. As per the functions performed in the hotels the following departments generally exist in more or less all types of hotels:

1. Front office department
2. Food and beverage department
3. Housekeeping department
4. Accountants and audit department
5. Purchase and store department
6. Maintenance and engineering department
7. Personnel/Human resource department
8. Security department.

Front Office

Popularly known as reception is the most visible department in the hotel. It is the focal point of all activities. The front office is responsible for the sale of rooms, which is more than 50 per cent of the total revenue of the hotel. Again, on the basis of the 'function' the front office can be divided into the following sub-departments.

Reservation

It is called the 'key' of the front office department, where the demands of room-reservation are received and processed. A five star deluxe and five star hotels may or may not have a reservation manager but all have reservation assistants.

Registration

It is the focal point of the front office department where the guests are received, registered and assigned keys of rooms. Most governments and states insist on registration by the guest himself. This is a rule to protect both the hotels and the guests. It is a source of information about the foreigners in the country and also a data source for the hotels. It is done mostly by registration cards. The basic information provided in the registration card includes name of the guest, address, nationality, purpose of visit, duration of stay in the country, passport details, his place of coming and his next place of visit etc.

Information

The main function of this department is to provide information about the hotel, city, the surroundings, transportation etc. and events that are of interest to the guests. The information department also handles the mail of the guests and receive message for the guest.

Cash

The cashier maintains the guests' account, monitors the credit limit, produces guests account statement and is responsible for the proper settlement of the bills. He maintains the accounts for foreign exchange and does other miscellaneous jobs related to the cash.

Night Auditor

A night auditor audits all the revenue transactions and reconciles the revenue statements of the revenue generating outlets. They also prepare the various reports of the hotel business. Most of the hotels keep the night auditor, which is an employee of the accounts Department. To many hotels the night auditors is a part of the front office. The night auditor performs more or less the following functions:

- Verifying posted entries to guest and non-guest account.
- Balance all front office accounts.
- Resolving room status discrepancies.
- Monitoring guest credit limits.
- Producing operational and managerial reports.

The night auditor works generally in the night shift, from 11 PM to 7 AM balancing and compiling the transactions of the previous day. Each front office decides the time when it should be considered the end of its accounting day. An end of the day is simply an arbitrary stopping point for the business day.

Figure 8.1: Organizational Chart of Front Office Department in Five Star Deluxe Hotel

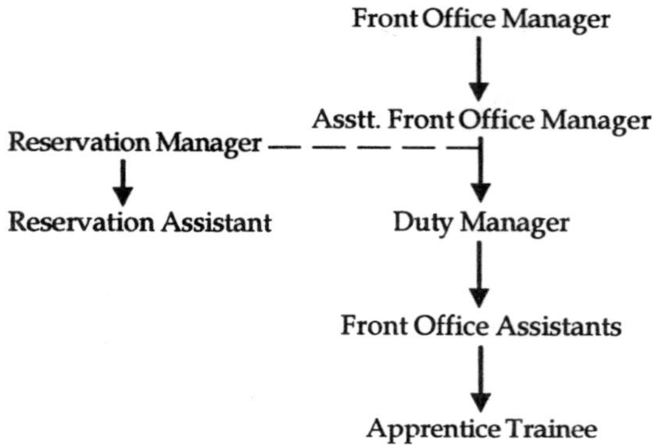

Figure 8.2: Organizational Chart of Front Office Department in 1, 2, 3 Star and Unapproved Category of Hotel

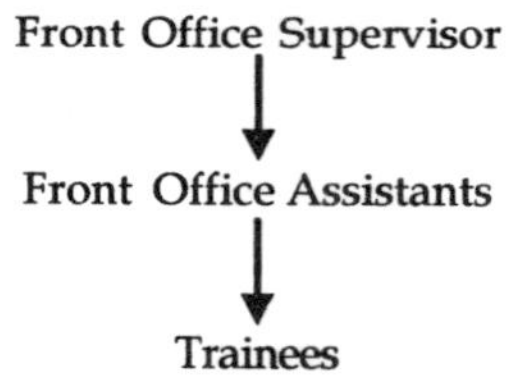

Food and Beverage Department

The hotel food and beverage department is another important section of the hotel and is considered second to the front office in terms of generating room revenue. Broadly food and beverage department can be divided into two sections–food production and food and beverage service. Food production centre basically the 'kitchen' is the place where the craftsmen and artist work to prepare the delicious combination of food. The kitchen is divided into the following sections:

(i) Continental section is responsible for the preparation of soups, roast dishes of meat, poultry, grilled dishes of meat, chicken fish and deep-frying of items. Bakery section is responsible for hot and cold sweets including pastries, cookies, cakes, breakfast items like bread rolls, muffin, banana multi bread, plain bread etc.

(ii) Indian section is responsible for a variety of Indian dishes – rice pulao, biryani, vegetables, egg, fish and mutton, chicken and tandoor items.

(iii) Pantry section is the part of main kitchen where all variety of salads (veg. and non veg.) are prepared; this section also supplies tea, coffee, fresh juice, soft drinks, mineral water etc.

(iv) Butchery section is situated a little away from the main cooking area. In this section the meat items are trimmed up to the first stage i.e. the removal of excess fat, skins and other non-edible parts from the meat items. The organization of the kitchen found in hotels is as follows:

Figure 8.3: The Organization of the Kitchen Found in Hotels

Chef de Cuisine
↓
Soups chef
↓
Chef de partied
↓
I commas
↓
II commas
↓
III commas

Food and beverage service section can be traditionally divided in Restaurant, Bar and Room Service. The restaurant basically provides table and chair for people to sit and eat food prepared by and attached kitchen. These sitting places are equipped with crockery, cutlery and linen. There are different type of restaurants – coffee shop continental, specialty restaurant, grillroom, dining room, snack bar, discotheque etc. The organization of the food and beverage service department found in hotels is as follows:

Figure 8.4: The Organization of the Food and Beverage Service

Department

↓

Restaurant Manager

↓

Head Waiter/Captain

↓

Waiter/Steward

↓

Asstt. Waiter/Asstt. Steward

↓

Bus Boy

Room Service involves the food and beverage service to the guest rooms. Today room service has become the hallmark of good hotel and most of the hotels try to provide 24 hours room service. The peak period of room service is the morning hours when the "resident guest" orders bed tea and then breakfast in their rooms. The guests call the room service though internal telephones and place their order. The organizational structure of the room service is as follows:

Figure 8.5: The Organizational Structure of the Room Service

Restaurant Manager

↓

Order taker cum cashier

↓

Waiter

Bar is the place where guest orders directly to bar man or other service personnel. Food and beverage manager heads the food and beverage department. The organizational chart of a five star deluxe hotel including the heritage is as follows:

Figure 8.6: F&B Organizational Chart for Five Star Deluxe, Five Star and Heritage Hotels

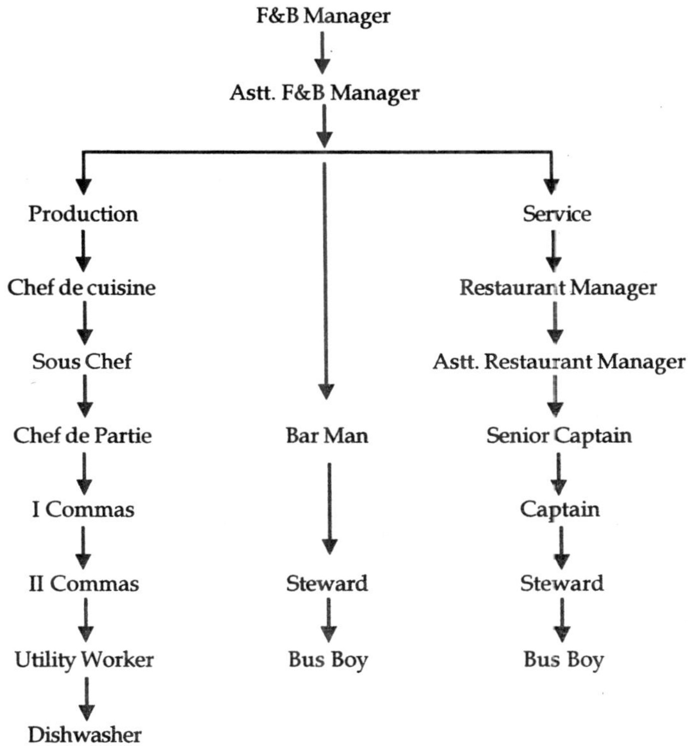

Figure 8.7: F&B Organizational Chart for 1, 2, 3 Star and Unapproved Category of Hotel

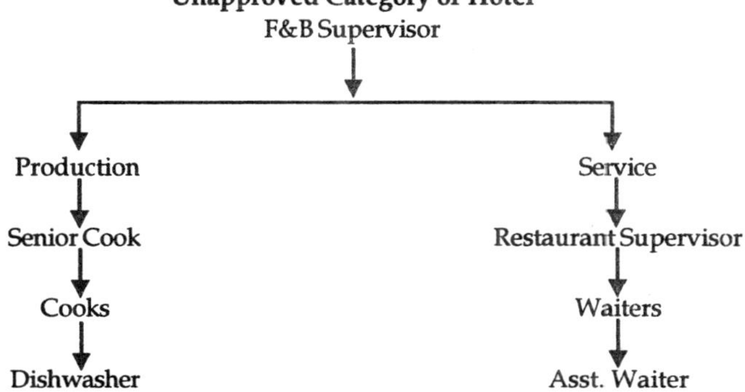

House Keeping Department

It is perhaps the most important supportive department to the front office for sale of rooms. In a few hotels, especially when the numbers of rooms are less than hundred, it has been seen that housekeeping is considered a separate department. Conceptually task of keeping of a house (Housekeeping) looks very simple but when it comes to maintaining a palace or large house of several rooms and that too balancing the taste to several hundred guests, it proves to be a Herculean task. The main task of housekeeping is to provide cleanliness, aesthetic upkeeping and maintenance that match the taste of several types of customers.

The work of housekeeping department in a hotel varies considerably according to star rating. Besides cleaning and decorating the housekeeping department is involved in laundry to the staff uniform, guest dresses and those related to rooms and restaurant linen. Among other things it also takes care of lost and found procedures, floral art, first aid etc. The head of the housekeeping department is called executive housekeeper in five star deluxe and five star hotels. The other assistants are line keeper, uniform supervisor, room boy etc. The organizational hierarchy in the housekeeping departments of five star deluxe and five star hotel sample units is as follows:

Figure 8.8: Organizational Chart of Housekeeping Department in 5 Star Deluxe and 5 Star Category of Hotels

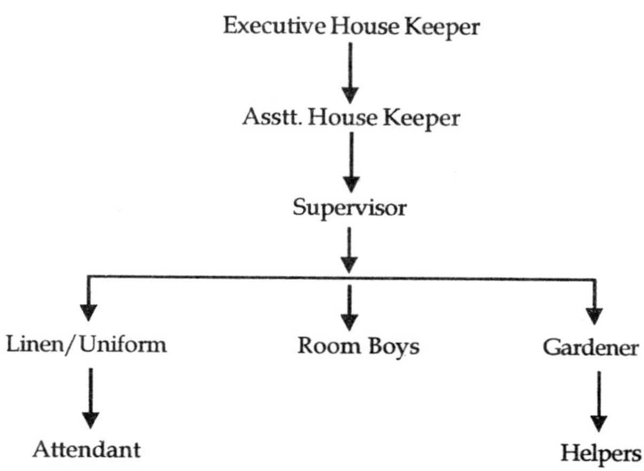

Figure 8.9: Organizational Chart of Housekeeping Department 1, 2, 3 Star and Unapproved Category of Hotels

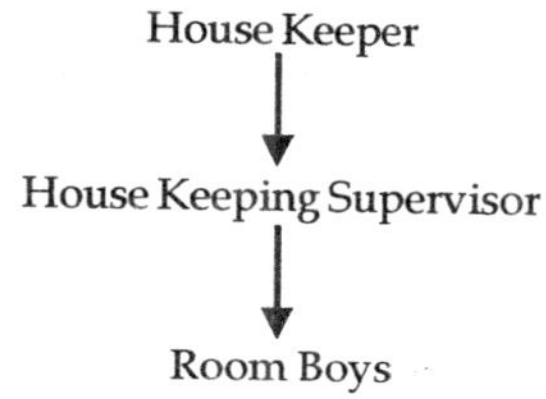

Accounts and Audit Department

The accounts department in a hotel is of vital importance owing to the special character of the business. The accounting department is concerned with the guest bills, payment of wages to the hotel employees, ledgering bills rendered for the hotel purchases and maintaining account books, recording all incomes and expenditure. At the end of the year the accounts department prepares the Balance Sheet and also measures the performance of the hotel business within the year. The accounts department also prepares different statistical reports, which are helpful for purpose of comparison of sale of rooms, sale of food and beverage outlets and income and expenditure statements. The head of this department is generally called as Chief Accountant or Chief Accounts Officer. Sometimes the Chief Accountant has to act as a dual responsibility; one he has to obey and report to the general manager and secondary he has to listen to the owner or the vice president, Finance. Organisation of Accounts Department in Five Star Deluxe, Five Star and Heritage Hotel is as follows:

Figure 8.10: Organization of Accounts Department in Fiver Star Deluxe, Five Star and Heritage Hotel

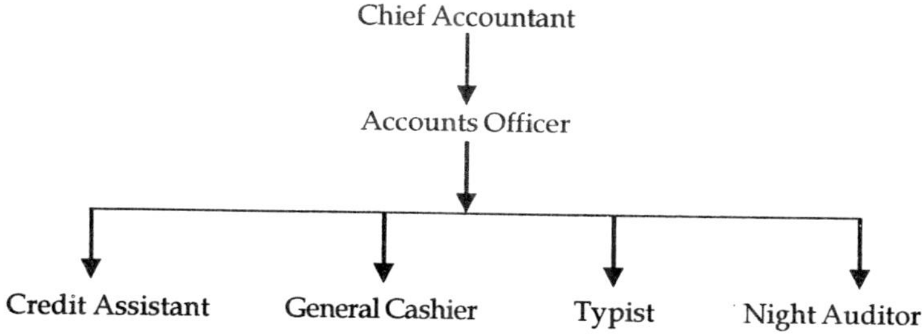

Figure 8.11: Organization of Accounts Department in 1, 2, 3 and Unapproved Hotels

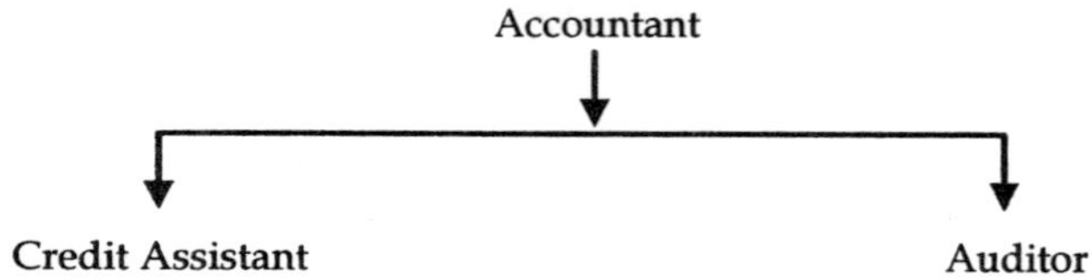

Engineering and Maintenance Department

The engineering and maintenance department in the hotel plays an important role in satisfying the guests' demand. A proper service from the maintenance department plays a significant effect on the guest motivational patterns and helps to call the guests back. There is a long list of the services provided by the Engineering and Maintenance department. Structural maintenance, heating and cooling, ventilation, air-conditioning system, refrigeration, electrical system, television and channel music, telephone and other communication system, water supply including hot water, plumbing, sewage system, swimming pool clearing, maintenance and cleaning of equipments used by the hotel, maintenance of the furniture and such many other services are looked after by this department. The maintenance department is also responsible for establishment of fire protection procedures within the hotels.

Figure 8.12: Organizational Chart of the Engineering Department in 5 Star Deluxe, 5 Star Hotels and Heritage Hotels

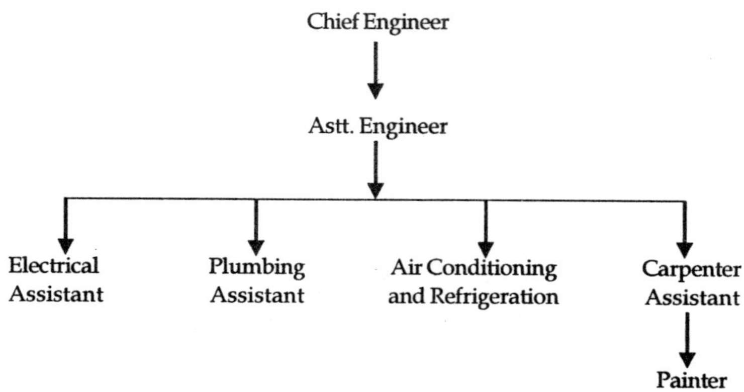

Figure 8.13: Organizational Chart of the Engineering Department in 1, 2, 3 and Unapproved Hotels

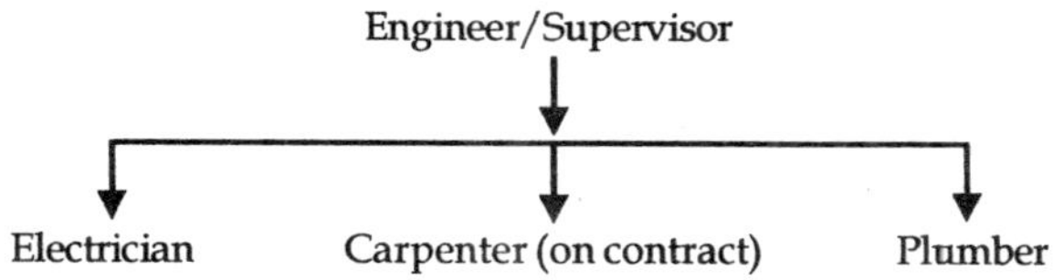

Human Resource Department

The general purpose department is to acquire, develop and maintain a competent workforce, which can accomplish the goal and objectives of the organization, what maximum efficiency and minimum expenditure. The human resource department is an integral and important part of the hotel industry but it seems that it has not acquired its due importance. The Management and the employees of a hotel, both are in need of the particular specialized department of recruitment, selection, salary, administration, discipline, grievance procedures, staff induction promotion, transfer, training and development, exit facilities, locker facilities, identity cards etc. In many one, two and three star hotels there is no such department in existence. The work of the human resources department is distributed among various persons. For example the owner and the manager himself perform the recruitment. Some other senior person does attendance, accounts department disburses salary, and provident fund and ESI are looked after by a part time professional. Thus the hotel associations and other related government officials must look in this direction.

Security Department

The hotel industry is so diverse that it is impossible to set national security standards or to totally rely on the national security system. Therefore to provide a safe and secure environment to protect guest's employees there is a great need for privately owned security arrangement and system. Now-a-days it is being felt that there is a dual or triple responsibility on the security department as the guests have started looking for safe places/destinations.

A Study of Lodging Franchising

The growth of the U.S. lodging industry is to a substantial extent due to the successful practices of business format franchises. According to *Lodging* magazine (December, 2000), between 1997 and 2000, many lodging franchise brands have doubled their size, and six brands have even grown more than five times as large among the 65 lodging franchise brands reported. Both franchiser and franchisee contribute to the success of franchising in the lodging industry: on one hand, a lodging company, the franchiser, creates a new brand name, a new type of lodging facility and operation system; while an entrepreneur invests capital, management team, and effort to pay for utilizing the brand name and operation system by signing up as a franchisee. The development of lodging franchising is largely attributed to the cooperation and contractual relationship between the franchiser and the franchisee. Building on the basis of the franchise agreement, the franchiser and franchisee create a long-term interdependent, but still independent business relationship.

Many researchers have conducted research in lodging franchises. From academic research, Withiam (2000)[1] argued the customer in a franchise system is franchisee. Brown and Dev (1997)[2] indicated that the proper relationship between franchiser and franchisee is a key to franchise performance. Roberts (1997)[3] linked franchising with strategic decision making. Roginsky (1995)[4] focused her analysis on hotel impact issues. Kliavkoff (1995)[5] discussed that hotel franchisers may encounter possible liability for their improper actions on the franchisees. Dev and Brown (1991)[6] compared franchising and chain-managed and independent hotels. Hotel industry analysts also examined the interests in the issues of franchising. Cruz (2001)[7] discussed quality, mutual trust, and franchise relations in lodging franchising. O'Connor (2000) reported that both franchisers and franchisees stress the need to work together as partners. However, all of these researches have narrowly focused on only one or two aspects of the franchise issue. This research will explore the whole franchise issue by asking the questions relative to the entire relationship.

To begin with it is our position that while there are usually two signatures to a franchise contract there are really four parties at interest in each franchise agreement. The obvious are the franchiser and the franchisee. But other parties interested in the franchise relationship between the franchiser and the franchisees are other franchisees of the franchiser and the general public. With regard to other franchisees, what they do or do not do reflect positively or negatively on other franchisees in the franchise system and what they all do determines whether or not the group keeps its covenant with the public which has been premised the bounty from the franchiser and franchisee relationship. We will examine the elements of the relationship which will lead to the satisfaction of the four parties involved in the franchise relationship.

The only good contract is a fair contract. A fair franchising agreement is one of most important factors for long-term relationship. Dailey (1998)[8] discussed about franchisee rules. He stressed that "the Uniform Franchise Offering Circulars (UFOS) is the principal disclosure document to guide prospective franchisee with their investments". He argued that the franchisers should provide accurate and unambiguous language in the document. He also addressed the issue of territorial protection. Historically the UFOS documents were required by the law in order to protect a franchisee from him. During the franchise craze in 60's and early 70's, the franchisee's desire to be "his own boss" and make huge annual salaries drove prospective franchisees into a feeding frenzy that caused them to throw all caution to the winds and sign any contract based solely on the unsupported representation of a franchiser.

The FTC disclosure laws did not require a franchiser to get permission from the FTC in order to sell franchises; however, what it did require was that the franchiser to divulge information about itself: its operation, the number of franchisees it has, its financial statements, litigation history, and various other information. The whole idea of the law is neither to encourage or discourage the individual to become a franchisee, rather it is to supply an individual with all of the information to make educated decision on all of the facts and have time to seek the guidance of business professional and speak to existing franchisees to find out about their experiences with the franchiser. Territory protection is extremely important and very often there is absolutely no information at all contained in either the disclosure documents or the franchise contract itself. It is up to the perspective franchisee to make direct inquiry of the franchiser to find out their policy relative to how close to an existing franchise, if they will need to either open a company store or establish a new franchise. One of the leading franchisers in the United States did not have any written policy concerning the opening of competitive franchisee of company stores in close proximity to an existing franchisee. However, they did have an unwritten policy that they would not open a competitive unit close enough to an existing unit if it would reduce its gross sales to less than 80% of what it was before the competitive unit opened. It behaves a prospective franchisee to determine the franchiser's policy on this issue in order to avoid any future unexpected financial devastating surprise.

Franchisees should watch closely for possible hidden costs. Sometimes the costs are indirect and may take the shape of paying higher prices for goods and services when a franchiser fails to pass volume purchase discount for goods and services that the franchiser requires its franchisees to use. There is nothing illegal about a franchiser being rebated a commission on the goods or service being supplied to franchisees in the franchiser's organization provided however that the franchiser does reveal that this practice is going on between the supplies and the franchiser. If the franchiser is having such a relationship with one or more supplies and does not disclose it to the franchisees, then the franchiser will be liable to the franchisees in damages. Recently, one of the major hotel franchisers was discovered to have been receiving such rebates without disclosing these commissions to the franchisees, and was sued by the franchisees and a court awarded $50,000,000 in damages to the franchisees and against the franchisers. The disclosure document mandates that such rebates be disclosed. Storholm and Scheuing (1994) believed that the basis of the franchiser and franchisee relationship is a trust-worthy franchise agreement. A close look at the UFOS becomes very important for any potential investors who plan to sign up as a lodging franchisee. They need to give an in-depth review and analysis of each clause in the initial franchise offering including the product, service/support, costs, controls, terminations, renewal and transfer standards, franchise advisory boards, franchise sales processes, dispute resolution and performance obligations. They should evaluate the initial offerings based on the contents of the offerings, clarity of each clause, easy understanding of the languages, accuracy of terms, if any, hidden or vague meanings. They should read the disclosure documents carefully.

However, just reading the disclosure documents, no matter how thoroughly, does not reveal all of the information necessary to arrive at a decision as to whether or not to sign on to any particular franchise commitment. A prospective franchisee should look into all of the litigation reported in the disclosure documents. Investigate the grievances of the complaints filed against the franchiser by the plaintiffs. Read all of the pleadings filed in the lawsuit, they are public records and unless sealed by the court, copies are available either for viewing at the clerk of court's office or photo static copies may be procured at a nominal costs. Examine each of the case to determine the validity of the complaints and whether or not the plaintiff prevailed and check and follow upon the litigation history of the company and randomly check existing franchisees.

A successful franchise operation largely depends on continuous support and cooperation, a long-term relationship between a franchiser and franchisee after they both have signed the franchise agreement. Emerson (1998) argued that "the franchise relationship creates rights beyond the contract itself". He stressed the success of franchising is dependent upon "combination of business know-how, market knowledge, capital and manpower. For a potential franchisee, many questions need to be asked. For a lodging franchiser, it should prepare to respond accurately the requests from a future franchisee. Here are some of the questions need to be addressed:

Get to know the Franchiser

- How long has the franchiser been in business?
- Who are officers and key members in the management team of the franchiser?
- How many hotels and motels does the company own?
- How many units does the company franchise?
- How well is the brand name recognized by the travelling public?
- How effective is the company's reservation system?
- What type of market/s does the company try to target at?

Services/Support

- What training does the company provide for its franchisees?
- What is the training cost?
- How prepared is the company to provide the training services?
- How and where does the company conduct such training?
- What measures does the company take to assure the quality of the products and services?

- What services does the company provide its franchisees?
- What specific measures does the company take to help each individual franchisee market its products and services (advertising nationally/locally)?
- To what extent, does franchisee enjoy economic scale of purchasing power and reservation network provided by the franchiser company?
- What commission arrangement does franchise has with suppliers of products and services that franchisees are required to use by the franchiser?
- What are the regulations of redecoration and equipment improvement?
- What are the product limitations and availability?
- What are the inventory requirements?
- Who owns the signage?

Communication

- How does the company communicate quality assurance issues with its franchisees?
- How frequently, how well, and to what extent, does the company communicate with its franchisees for the operation?
- How good a listener is the company?
- How responsive is the company to the franchisee's concerns?
- To what extent, does the company accept a franchisee's constructive suggestions and operational ideas?
- If there is a communication break-down, what effort does the company make to restore its line of communication with its franchisees?

Costs

- To what extent, does a franchisee receive the value it has paid for?
- What are the actual costs associated with the franchise contract: the initial set-up cost, operating capital, royalty fees, marketing fee and reservation cost?
- How reasonable are the various fee charges?
- Is there any flexibility for the various fees?
- What incentives the company may give to the franchisees to obtain more favourable fee charges?

Controls

- How is the company controlling in the matter of site selection?
- What measures does the company take to avoid impact/ encroachment issues taking place?
- How well does company handle disputes with franchisee for territorial right issues?

Termination, Renewal and Transfer Standards

- What happens when the franchise expires?
- How reasonable are the standards of termination, renewal and transfer of a franchise operation?
- If there is a disagreement in the standards, how does the company resolve the problem?
- What happens to franchisee's assets in case of termination of a franchise by the franchiser because of contract violation?

Franchise Advisory Board

- What position does the company take on the board?
- How are the members of the board selected?
- What are the responsibilities of the board members?

Franchise Sales Process

- How does the franchise sales activity process?
- Is there any money from the franchisees' advertising fund used by the company to promote new franchise sales?

Dispute Resolution

- What effort does a company make to resolve disputes between the company and its franchisees?
- What procedures are provided for the resolution of disputes?
- What law is applicable to the resolution of disputes?
- Does the franchise agreement designate a certain state laws to be used in resolution of dispute?
- Is mandatory arbitration or mediation required for the resolution of disputes?
- What procedures are provided by the company for the resolution of conflicts between franchisees?
- How does the company resolve these disputes?

- What protection does the company provide the franchisee for competitions from either the company's units or other new franchisees?
- Are there mandatory arbitration clauses?
- Are there mandatory jurisdictional litigations?
- What if a franchiser changes its name?
- How well does the franchiser act in settling disputes between franchisees?

Performance Obligations

- What performance obligations does the company need to fulfill?
- What are the required performances obligations that a franchisee needs to accomplish?

Ethical Consideration in Franchising

- What are the ethical concerns of the company?
- What are the ethical concerns of the franchisees?

Research and Development

- What effort does the company make in understanding customer needs and wants?
- What effort does the company make in product development?
- How does the company encourage the franchisees to research on customers' needs?
- How well does the company accept the customer research input provided by franchisees?
- How prone is the company to field test new products?

Effectiveness of Franchise Association

- How effective does a franchise association help its members?

Research on Future Trends in the Industry

- How sensitive is the company toward future change in the industry?
- What effort does the company take to forecast the future trends?
- Does the company have environmental scanning system to analyse the changes in the industry?

- What effort does the company make to communicate the future trends with its franchisees?
- To what extent, does the company utilize the input from franchisees in the future trend analysis?

Conclusion

By searching answer for the questions, the potential franchisees will prepare themselves for fair franchise contracts, pave the roads toward successful franchise operations and build good relationships with franchisers. For franchisers, they should prepare to respond to the questions and understand the franchisees' concerns and establish fair franchise policies and standards. The questions can be a basis of the communication between franchisees and franchisers. These questions will help the researchers to explore the problems and issues in the field of hotel franchising.

Stakeholders in the Lodging Industry

Freeman (1984)[9] created a comprehensive stakeholder approach to understand strategic management. He stated "a stakeholder in an organization is any group or individual who can affect or is affected by the achievement of the organization's objective" (1984: 46). He discussed how each industry or company or even a department manager may have a specific group of stakeholders that impact on or are impacted by the business operations. Moreover, the stakeholders in each entity might change over time in its organization life cycle. He identified the common groups of stakeholders as owners, financial community, employees, customers, advocates, competitors, trade organization, union, suppliers, government, media and local community, etc. Since then, hundreds of articles have been published in various research journals to contribute to stakeholder theory.

The research has stemmed from the traditional management theory of shareholder as management's sole responsibility to a broad range of stakeholders' interests for which management must be responsible.[10] As Freeman (1999: 233) stated "if you want to maximize shareholder value, you should pay attention to key stakeholders". Many researchers agreed that it is vital for a business organization to understand its stakeholders and maintain trustful relationships in order to survive and succeed in this ever-changing and very competitive world.

The lodging industry depends upon its stakeholders for survival and growth. Lodging companies have gradually realized the importance of understanding their stakeholders and build relationships with them. With the complexity and uncertainty of the business environment, more stakeholders have become involved in lodging operations. If you compare the two research white papers of the global lodging industry published by the International Hotel & Restaurant Association[11] (Olsen, *et.al.*, 1995 and 2000), you will find in the 2000 white paper that the lodging industry leaders added two new driving forces—sustainable development and social responsibilities of the global lodging industry besides the driving forces discussed in the 1995 white paper, such as capital market, safety and security, technology, capacity control and new management. This means that the environmental and local community stakeholders have begun to play more important roles and demand that their interests be accounted for in the industry's future development.[12] Thus, lodging companies need to pay close attention to these stakeholders' demands that they might have ignored in the old days. Although there is some research in the area of managing business relationships between lodging firms and their customers, or franchisees, or suppliers, most of the research is about managing a single pair of the relationships. No attempt has been made to neither explore fully the stakeholder approach in strategic management nor holistically analyse the key stakeholders in the lodging industry. Therefore, there is an urgent need to study stakeholder theory in order to better understand stakeholder management in the lodging industry. Like Frooman (1999)[13] raised the questions of a general business, we need to ask: who are the stakeholders in a lodging company? What do they want? and how are they going to try to get it; keeping in view the following objectives:

- Identify key stakeholders of a lodging firm
- Create a framework of the stakeholders of a lodging firm
- Understand the stakeholders' interests and demands
- Discuss how a lodging company may manage the relationships among its stakeholders.

Literature Review

Donaldson and Preston (1995)[14] summarized previous research of stakeholder theory into three typologies: descriptive, instrumental and normative approaches. The descriptive approach describes how an organization manages the interests of its stakeholders. The instrumental approach prescribes what impact stakeholders may have on corporate effectiveness. The normative approach discusses the reason why a company ought to treat its stakeholders based on ethical (moral) grounds.

In order to describe and better understand the stakeholders, researchers categorized them into different groups. Clarkson (1995)[15] classified an organization's stakeholders into primary groups (shareholders and investors, employees, customers and suppliers) and public (the government and communities); and secondary stakeholders, such as media and a wide range of special interest groups that do not have direct transactions with the corporation but can influence or be influenced by the corporation. He argued that all the interests of primary stakeholders should be treated fairly without favouring one group at the expense of others. Carroll (1993)[16] defined that stakeholders with a formal, official or contractual relationships are primary ones, otherwise they will be secondary stakeholders. Deavenport (2001: 12)[17] clearly discussed that an industry needs to balance among the stakeholders such as customers, employees, suppliers, investors and the many publics. He argued that the industry's success "has less and less to do with market share, manufacturing plants, interest rates... but more and more to do with people, the stakeholders" and build relationships with the stakeholders.

While Clarkson (1995)[18] and Jones and Wick (1999) argued the organization need to treat all the stakeholders fairly, Jawahar and McLaughlin (2001)[19] used organization life cycle theory to propose that an organization needs to use different strategies to treat its various stakeholders based on the importance of stakeholders to the organization at the specific stage of its life cycle. Gioia (1999)[20] stated that an organization should favour certain stakeholders. Cohen (1999)[21] believed that a company needs to prioritize the interests of its stakeholders. Mitchell *et.al.,* (1997)[22] contributed to the stakeholder theory by providing a systematic identification of stakeholders. They created three criterions to judge stakeholders: the power of a stakeholder to influence the firm, the legitimacy of the stakeholder's relationship with the firm, and the urgency of the stakeholder's claim on the firm.

From the normative perspective, Freeman's (1984)[23] stakeholder theory extends the management responsibility from solely for the stockholders to the society as a whole. Management needs to shoulder the social and environmental responsibility and care not only about the company's financial performance but its social performance as well. If it does not address the social and environmental issues, it may be faced with boycotts, lawsuits and protests, which will eventually cut the shareholder value and hurt the company's bottom line.

With the fast changing business environment, the old economic perspective of social costs needs to be realized as strategic investment in stakeholders' demands, as Ruf, *et.al.,* (2001), argued that such strategic investment will help firms develop additional, inimitable skills and gain competitive advantage. This investment will lead to higher financial success. Ruf *et.al.,* (2001), Waddock and Smith (2000)[24] , Harrison and Freeman (1999) and Berman *et.al.,* (1999)[25] all suggested that researchers could use the Kinder, Lydenberg and Domini (KLD) database to evaluate corporate social performance. Waddock and Smith (2000) suggested companies should use a responsibility audit to check how a corporation takes care of employee relationships, quality systems, community relations and environmental practices. They argued that there could be a positive correlation between corporate financial performance and social responsibility practice. Malvey, Fottler and Solvensky (2002) suggested a firm should use a stakeholder report card to evaluate stakeholder management performance. Davenport (2000)[26] used the Delphi Method to identify three indicators of a good corporate citizenship which can be used for assessing corporate social performance including ethical business behaviour, stakeholder commitment and environmental commitment.

From an instrumental perspective, the study by Ruf *et.al.,* (2001) suggested that if a corporation improved its social performance, it could lead to improvement in its financial performance. Berman *et.al.,* (1999) found two stakeholder relationship variables (employee and product quality and safety) have a positive and significant relationship with the firm's financial performance and other stakeholder relationship variables (diversity, environmental responsibility, and community relations) had moderate effect on a firm's performance. Szwajkowski (2000)[27] analysed the Fortune

Reputation Survey (FRS) and found employee and product quality and safety were the most reliable indicators of corporate reputation. The author (2000: 384) further stated that shareholders make their investment bet on "how effectively corporate managements can predict, anticipate, satisfy and balance stakeholder issues". However, if a company neglects the interests and demands of its stakeholders, the stakeholders will use their power and resources they control to directly and indirectly influence corporate business strategies (Frooman, 1999).[28]

In regard to the interests and demands of the stakeholders, researchers discussed the issue in various directions. Wood (1994)[29] categorized the stakeholders' interests into concrete versus symbolic, economic versus social, and local versus domestic versus international. Frederick *et.al.,* (1992) generated a list of stakeholder interests. Some researchers focused on one specific interest, such as Stead and Stead (2000) focused on green stakeholders' interest – protection of Planet Earth. Deavenport (2001) clearly spelled out the interests of five major stakeholders: customers are interested in "the right product in the right amount delivered at the right time at the right price" (2001: 12); employees expect job opportunity, good payment and benefits, further training and education; suppliers want to build a long-term business relationship with your operation; investors demand for high return on investment and industry growth; the public holds an industry accountable for its social and environmental responsibility. Freeman (1984: 92) discussed that stakeholders have economic, technological, social and political effects on the firm. Frooman (1999) argued that it is important to reorganize the divergent interests of stakeholders, however, what management ought to do is to manage potential interest conflicts among the stakeholders.

In terms of how to manage the stakeholder relationships, LaBerge and Svendsen (2000) argued that an organization must create trusting and cooperative relationships, and effectively communicate with its stakeholders. Effective communication is very important in building the relationships among stakeholders and in response to the needs and interests of stakeholders. Szwajkowski (2000) offered several principles, such as actively monitoring all legitimate stakeholders' concerns, openly communicating with stakeholders, adopting processes and modes of contact with each stakeholder, recognizing the interdependence among stakeholders and treating them fairly, etc.

When taking closely look at the application of stakeholder management in the hospitality and tourism industry, the authors found only a few papers in the tourism research and one study mentioned the stakeholder issue in lodging research. Sautter and Leisen (1999)[30] and Bramwell and Sharman (1999) used stakeholder theory as a tool to promote collaboration among stakeholders in the tourism planning process and policy making. They believed that tourism planners must actively pursue the interaction with their stakeholders such as: local businesses, residents, activist groups, tourists, national business chains, competitors, government, and employees. Markwick (2000)[31] analysed benefits and costs a stakeholder might have in a golf course development. He believed the stakeholders, such as developers/shareholders, hoteliers, potential employees, customers and government, would receive benefits from the development. However, the development would have predominant costs for farmers and environmentalists. Buhalis and Flectcher (1995)[32] created a wheel of tourism stakeholders, which links the stakeholders' interests, benefits and responsibilities among the host population, tourists, public sector and government, tourism operators, and tourism enterprises together. Buhalis (2000) argued that it is very important to balance the interests of all the stakeholders and the sustainability of local resources when marketing a destination. Enz (2001) found that aligning stakeholders' interests was one of the concerns of lodging managers. However, the stakeholders in her study seemed narrowly defined as political entities and owners. She treated customers and employees, those important stakeholders as separate issues.

Mapping Stakeholders in a Lodging Company

Stakeholder mapping is an important tool for a lodging company to understand who are the stakeholders, what are their interests and demands, and what position each stakeholder may have in a specific strategic issue of the company.

As Freeman (1984) discussed, different industries or different companies may have different groups of stakeholders, different lodging companies may have different groups of stakeholders who influence or are influenced by lodging operations. Figure one maps all the stakeholders involved in the lodging industry. They include financial stakeholders: stockholders, private investors, franchisees, banks, creditors, institutions and pension funds, etc.; distribution channels: Global Distribution Systems (GDS), internet support, management contract companies and travel agencies, customers, employees, suppliers, political entities, trade associations, competitors, environmental advocates, local communities, industry analysts and media. The industry analysts and media may not have a stake or demand in the lodging operation, however, what they do may impact a lodging company.

Financial Stakeholders

From the financial perspective, the financial structure of a lodging company can be very complicated as many stakeholders may invest in the company. A public traded company obtains its financing through its stockholders, pension groups, institutional investors and private investors. A private lodging company may have one or many owners. Whether it is a public or private lodging company, it gets loans for hotel projects from banks and creditors. There is a tendency for many lodging companies not to own lodging properties so as to avoid real estate investment risk and take tax advantages. Some public-traded companies may only own lodging brand names and business know-how but their affiliated properties are owned by franchisees or other owners. These lodging companies may act as agents to operate lodging properties through management contracts and/ or franchise agreements, but the real owners could be real estate developers, institutions (pension fund, bank, etc.) or even trade unions. The advantages for lodging companies are to use others' money to develop their brand names, sell-management know-how and fast grow their market shares with little investment risk in the lodging industry. However, lodging companies must also remember when you sign an agreement with whoever the owner is you have a legal and ethical responsibility to the owner.

Shareholders of a lodging company are interested in maximizing return on investment, earnings per share and the growth of the company. With the free flow of the global capital, they can simply switch their investment into other companies or even other industries if their demands are not met. This exerts enormous pressure for hotel managers to add value and generate a future stream of cash flow to meet the investors' demands. These stakeholders increasingly demand their involvement in decision making of the lodging firm to avoid the investment risk they are facing. Banks and creditors demand that hotel companies make their interests and principal payments on the loans in a timely manner. This could result in enormous pressures for a lodging company loaded with heavy debts in an economic downturn. It is very important to build a very good relationship with banks and creditors in order to finance a company's new projects, borrow for immediate cash need, facilitate merger and acquisition activities, or refinance its loans and delay payments. However, if a company cannot fulfill its pay-back obligations, it cannot accomplish its ambitious plans and even may be forced into bankruptcy.

One of the unique features of the lodging industry is that many lodging firms do not own lodging properties; their franchisees are the property owners and operators. Through signing franchise agreements, the franchisees become a group of very important stakeholders of a lodging company. By paying various kinds of fees, they demand that their interests be taken care of by the lodging company, such as advanced reservation system, marketing and promotional services, assistance in development planning, assistance in opening, and operational aids and dynamic support services, such as training, on-line support, information management, purchasing system and yield management, etc. Without franchisees' investment, the lodging company is just a name without properties. It is very important for a lodging firm to fulfill its obligations and commitments to its franchisees and maintain a good relationship with its franchisees in order to continue its growth. There have been some disputes and conflict of interests between a lodging company and its franchisees in recent years. For a lodging company as a franchiser, it must realize that franchisees are investors. The owners' interests and demands must be taken care of. If their interests are not met, these lodging property owners may switch their brand flag to competitors.

Employees

Employees look for better compensation and benefits, opportunities for progression, training, job satisfaction and good diversity practices from a lodging firm. With the labour shortage and scarcity of talented employees, a lodging company must treat its employees as among its most valuable assets, enhance internal service quality, empower them, provide them competitive payment and benefits, satisfy their needs and demands. In turn, the company will increase productivity and efficiency, reduce costs, maintain its competitive advantage, add value to its shareholders, obtain higher profit margin and market share as suggested by Heskett, *et.al.*, (1997) in their book—*Service Profit Chain*. If the employees are mistreated, they can simply join your competitor which treats them better.

Customers

A lodging company with multiple brands attracts customers from different segments of the market. They can be business or leisure travellers. Unlike the old days when the customer was looking for a room and its physical amenities, today's travellers equipped with information and knowledge about lodging operations are increasingly purchasing "experience" and "services" and they have hundred of brands and properties to choose from. Customers focus on their interests on better price/value relationship and safety and security of hotel products and services. Failure to meet customers' expectations and needs means that a lodging operation may lose their business forever. Moreover, many customers may represent certain advocacy groups and demand specific attention; if their needs or demands are not accommodated, they may simply switch their business to a competitor, or launch a campaign or boycott against the company. The recent boycott of Adams Mark Hotels by NAACP is a good example of what an advocacy group can do to lodging operations.

Intermediaries as Stakeholders

The complexity of the lodging business arises because that there are two kinds of intermediaries involved in the operation: one lodging management contract companies interposed between the owners and a brand-name lodging firm; the other intermediaries are many distributional channels between the lodging firm and its customers. From an operation's perspective, although many owners could franchise a brand name and accept a management contract from the same lodging company, they could probably franchise the brand name but have a thirty-party management contract company run the operation. Thus there are a large number of management contract companies serving as intermediaries between brand-name lodging companies and the actual owners of the lodging properties.

Management Contract Company

A lodging management contract company is a unique entity in the lodging industry. It helps an owner to operate property/properties whichever brand of a lodging firm the owner desires. As a management contract company plays an intermediary role between a lodging company and owners, it may help or break a lodging company. If the relationship between a lodging company and a management contract company is good, the management contract company may suggest that the owner continues to flag the brand name of the lodging company, otherwise, it may advise the owner to switch to a competitor's brand.

From marketing perspective, because of the fragmentation of the lodging industry and the needs for a lodging property to be located for the convenience of the customer, a lodging company relies upon many distribution channels as intermediaries to promote and market its products and services.

Distribution Channels

Unlike many other industries, a lodging company establishes a large network of marketing alliance to distribute its products and services. Besides its own reservation system and web-site, a lodging company needs to build distribution channels through travel agencies, Global Distribution System (GDS), internet providers, professional marketing agents, convention and visitor centres at destinations. Such collaborations are very important for the success of a lodging operation. For an example, travel agencies provide over 20 per cent of hotel room bookings for lodging companies (Rich, 2002). It also needs support from airlines, restaurants and cruise-lines to reach to its customers.. However, some internet search engines may try to take over the entire reservation system of a lodging company and offer cut-throat low room rates to the customers. These stakeholders could become competitors of lodging companies. Lodging companies need to be careful and control these stakeholders.

Suppliers: Architecture and Construction Companies and Raw Materials

A lodging company depends upon architects and construction companies to provide high quality designed and well functioning properties to attract its customers. A lodging company cannot afford badly designed or poor functioning nor delayed hotel constructions. A good relationship between these companies and a lodging firm should start from the very beginning. A good support from its materials suppliers is vital to a lodging company's operations. Building a win-win relationship with its suppliers will help the lodging company obtain needed quality materials, safety products and speedy delivery, reduce costs and increase profit margin.

Competitors

A rival lodging company competes with other lodging firms for the market share, customers, talented employees, investors and franchisees. The intensive mergers and acquisitions in the lodging industry in the 90s created several larger multinational lodging companies dominating the lodging market. However, there may be many common stakeholder management issues that make it useful for competing lodging companies to work together. They need one voice to deal with laws and regulations that may not be in favour of lodging operations. They need cooperation when handling issues, such as environmental protection and social responsibilities. Because of the scarcity of financial resources and competition from outside players, lodging companies have been building marketing and purchasing alliances to collaborate together rather than fight each other.

Political Stakeholders

The political stakeholders of a lodging firm are various levels of governments, law makers and judiciaries. Multinational lodging firms need to obey both domestic and foreign governments' laws and regulations, such as taxes, labour, immigration, environmental protection laws and regulations. Failure to follow the laws and regulations can only jeopardize the operations of hotel companies.

Trade Associations

A trade association is a collective voice for lodging companies to lobby political issues and make them favourite rather against lodging companies. In the meantime, trade association can also establish rules and regulations to guide the proper conducts of lodging operations. A lodging firm should actively participate in the associations and gain all the benefits provided by the association and support its operations.

Advocate Group, Environmental Group, Social Organizations and Local Community

The interests and demands cannot be overlooked. It is now the responsibility of a lodging corporation to protect the environment, reduce waste and help resolve social problems. Proactively working on environmental issues can lower the costs of complying with environmental regulations. Ecofriendly products and services appeal to customers, thus enhance loyal customers and create a competitive advantage for the lodging firm. The society requires a lodging firm to be a good corporate citizen. Helping the local community through charity contributions and volunteer work will win a positive image for a lodging company, which is the best way to promote its business. Although these groups may be treated as secondary stakeholders, they could heavily influence the strategic direction of a lodging firm.

Union

Generally, trade unions play a minor stake in the lodging industry. However, on behalf of employees, they negotiate with a lodging company for a better package of compensation and benefits for the employees.

Industry Analyst and Media

Although they may not have any stake in the lodging company, they definitely can influence the company as well as its investors, customers and other stakeholders through their analysis and reports. All these stakeholders make stakeholder management very complicated for a lodging company as each stakeholder may have different interests and demands. Table one summarizes the stakeholders, their interests and their possible impact on a lodging firm.

Freeman (1984) stated that stakeholders have economic, technological, social and political effects on the firm. Most of the stakeholders of a lodging company discussed herein have an economic effect on the success and failure of a lodging firm. They are associated with a lodging company through different contractual relationships, such as buyer and seller relationship with customers and suppliers through products and services, investor and operator relationship with stockholders, institutional and individual developer through stocks and ownership interests, lender and borrower relationship with banks and creditors through loans and credits, contractual relationship with franchisees and management contract companies through franchise and management agreements, contractual relationship with IT companies, travel agencies, distribution channels through technological and marketing support, and worker and employer relationship with employees. Even political entities have economic interests by collecting taxes and political contributions. From the managerial perspective, because of heavy financial involvement in a lodging company, stakeholders, such as stockholders, institutional investors, banks and creditors, and franchisees are increasingly interested in having a seat on the board of directors or having their voice heard in the lodging company by which they may influence the strategic directions and operations of the lodging company. Technologically, IT companies, GDS, travel agencies, marketing alliances, even competitors and customers have an impact on the technological development of a lodging company. Politically, political entities, such as various levels of governments, trade associations as well as unions do have influence on the lodging firm. Socially and environmentally, environmental advocates, local communities, employees, customers, governments as well as investors demand that a lodging firm should shoulder its social and environmental responsibilities and commitments. As preserving the cultural and physical environment is increasingly becoming the norm, a lodging company must demonstrate sensitivity to environmental concerns, quality life of the community, crowd control, sustainable development and other ethical practices. Media and industry analysts may not have any stake in the lodging company but their analysis and reports could support or break a lodging operation.

Building Trustful Relationships

Based on the above analysis of the stakeholders and their interests and demands it is clear that a lodging company must build a trustful relationship with its stakeholders in order to survive and grow. To be trustful, a lodging company must clearly define its vision and core value, goals, expectations and commitments, make its operation transparent to all its stakeholders. A lodging company needs to truthfully and ethically present to its stakeholders information about its financial performance. The recent Enron, Anderson and Worldcom scandals surely alert the heavily economic related stakeholders to closely look at the commitments that a lodging firm claims to have and the truthfulness of its management practices and commitments. In order to build trustful relationships, a lodging company must understands the following points:

- Holistically analyse and understand its stakeholders
- Openly communicate with all the stakeholders
- Proactively and fairly addresses stakeholders' interests
- Strategically invest in stakeholders' demands
- Effectively pursue collaborations and partnerships and resolve conflicts among stakeholders
- Successfully shoulder both economic and social responsibilities.

It will be interesting to investigate how a lodging company manages and balances the relationships among various stakeholders. As stakeholders adopt different positions in the strategic decisions of a lodging company, it will be a worthwhile effort to examine how lodging actually deals with the stakeholders with conflicting interests and demands. Researchers may also use KLD database to analyse if a lodging firms' financial performance benefits from balancing economic and social responsibilities demanded by stakeholders.

Table–1
Lodging Industry Stakeholders and their Interest and Impact

Lodging Industry Stakeholders	*Interests or Demands*	*Impact or Effect*
Employees	Compensation, benefit, career development	Economic-Social
Stockholders	Capital growth, ownership & EPS, ROI	Economic-Managerial
Franchisees	Capital growth & asset ownership	Economic-Managerial

Contd...

Lodging Industry Stakeholders	*Interests or Demands*	*Impact or Effect*
Financial Institutions	Wealth creation, ROI, interest payment	Economic-Managerial
Customers	Level of services satisfaction & loyalty Price/value relationship	Economic, technological, social, environmental
Suppliers	Profit sharing & creation of value	Economic
Environmental Advocates (Green Corporations)	Ecosystem	Environmental social
Political entities	Power, legitimacy, tax	Political, economic, environmental
Competitors	Competing for customer, employee, franchisee, Technical advantages Market share	Economic technological
Management Contractors	Profit sharing	Economic
Technological Support	Cooperation, support, profit sharing	Technological Economic
Marketing Alliances	Invested capital & profits	Economic Technological
Local Community	Support from the firm Economic prosperity Environmental protection Less social problems	Social Economic Environmental
Unions	Power, legitimacy & urgency	Economic Social Political
Trade Association	Support	Political
Industry Analysts Media	Report good or bad of the firm	Economic Social, technological, political, environmental Managerial

REFERENCES

1. Negi, J., "*Hotels for Tourism Development*", Metropolitan Book Co. Pvt. Ltd., New Delhi, 1984, p. 8.
2. *Ibid.*, p. 4.
3. *Ibid.*, p. 8.
4. *Ibid.*, p. 14.
5. Kaul, Virender, "*Tourism and the Economy*", Har Anand Publications, New Delhi, 1994, p. 95.
6. *Rajasthan Patrika*, 15 January 2001, p. 14.
7. Virender Kaul, "*Tourism and the Economy*", Har Anand Publications, 1994, p. 96.
8. Mohammed Zulfikar, "*Introduction to Tourism and Hotel Industry with Special Focus on Font Office Management*", Vikas Publishing House Pvt. Ltd., 1998, p. 60.
9. Written Document of Taj Group of Hotels.
10. Floyd Miller, Statler America's Extraordinary Hotelman, Statler Foundation, New York, 1968, p. 36.
11. Kasavana, M.L. and Brooks, R.M., "*Front Office Procedures*", 4th Ed. Educational Institute of AHMA, Michigan, 1996, p. 3.
12. Joseph D. Fridgen, "*Dimensions of Tourism*", Educational Institute of AHMA, Michigan, 1996, p. 193.
13. Indian Management, A Blueprint, Welcoming more Tourists, May 1997 p. 54.
14. Travel and Tourism: "*The World's Largest Industry*", World Travel and Tourism Council Report, 1992.
15. Indian Management, A Blueprint, Welcoming more Tourists, May 1997, p. 54.
16. *Yojna*, Paryatan Vikas Ke Avsar, August, 1998, pp. 52-53.
17. *Yojna*, Paryatan Vikas Ki Sambhavana, June, 1998, pp. 2-3.
18. Indian Management, A Blueprint: Welcoming more Tourists, May 1997, p. 55.
19. Negi, Dr. J.M.S., "*Hotels for Tourism Development*", Metropolitan Book Co., New Delhi, 1997, p. 17.
20. *Ibid.*, p. 3
21. *Ibid.*, p. 8.
22. Indian Management, A Blueprint: Welcoming more Tourists, May 1997, p. 58.
23. Report of the Bhagwati Committee on unemployment, 1973.
24. Negi, Dr. J.M.S., "*Hotels for Tourism Development*", Metropolitan Book Co. New Delhi, 1997. p. 9.
25. *Ibid.*
26. *Ibid.*

27. Negi, Dr. J.M.S. "*Hotels for Tourism Development*", Metropolitan Book Pvt Ltd., New Delhi, 1984, p. 18.
28. *Ibid.*, p. 19.
29. *Ibid.*
30. *Ibid.*, p. 21.
31. Zulfikar Mohammed, "*Introduction to Tourism and Hotel Industry with Special Focus on Front Office Management*", Vikas Publishing House Pvt. Ltd., 1998, pp. 77.
32. *Ibid.*, p. 87.
33. Sharma, K.K., "*Tourism In India (Centre-State Administration)*", Classic Publishing House, Jaipur, 1991, p. 141.
34. Hotels & Restaurants Guide India'98-Advertisement.
35. Kamra, K.K., Mill, R.C., Kaushil. Si, "*Hospitality Operations and Management*", Wheeler Publishing A division on of A.H. Wheeler & Co. Ltd., New Delhi, Allahabad, 2000, p. 27.
36. *Ibid.*, p. 25.
37. Negi, J.M.S. "*Hotels for Tourism Development*", Metropolitan Books Co, New Delhi, 1997, pp. 79-92.
38. Kamra, K.K. Mill R.C., Kaushil. Si, "*Hospitality Operations and Management*", Wheeler Publishing A division of A.H. Wheeler & Co. Ltd., New Delhi, Allahabad, 2000, p. 25.
39. Negi, J.M.S., "*Hotels for Tourism Development*", Metropolitan Books Co, New Delhi, 1997, pp. 79-92.
40. Kamra, K.K., Mill R.C., Kaushil. Si, "*Hospitality Operations and Management*", Wheeler Publishing A division of A.H. Wheeler & Co. Ltd, New Delhi, Allahabad, 2000, p. 23.
41. *Ibid.*
42. *Ibid.*
43. Negi, J.M.S., "*Hotels for Tourism Development*", Metropolitan Books Co, New Delhi, 1997, pp. 79-92.
44. *Ibid.*
45. Kamra, K.K., Mill R.C., Kaushil, Si, "*Hospitality operations and Management*", Wheeler Publishing A division of A.H. Wheeler & Co. Ltd., New Delhi, Allahabad, 2000, p. 23.
46. *Ibid.*, p. 27.
47. Negi, J.M.S., "*Hotels for Tourism Development*", Metropolitan Books Co, New Delhi, 1997, pp. 86-99.
48. *Ibid.*
49. *Ibid.*
50. Hotel and Food Service Review, Hotel Classification, August, 1997, p. 25.
51. *Yojna,* Paryatan Vikas Ke Avsar, August, 1998, p. 54.
52. Kasavana, M.L. & Brooks R.M., "*Front Office Procedures*", 4th ed., Educational Institute of AHMA, Michigan, 1996.

53. *Ibid.*
54. Withiam, G. (2000). "Who's the customer?: the franchisee". *Cornell Hotel & Restaurant Administration Quarterly*, 41 (3) (June), p. 12.
55. Dev, C. & Brown, J.R. (1991). "Franchise and other operating arrangements in the lodging industry: a strategic comparison." *Hospitality Research Journal*. 14 (3), pp. 23-41.
56. Roberts, C. (1997). "Franchise and strategic decision making". *Journal of Hospitality and Tourism Research*, 21 (1), pp. 160-178.
57. Roginsky, R. (1995). "Focus on impact: a critical analysis of hotel-impact issues". *Cornell Hotel and Restaurant Administration Quarterly*, 36 (4), (August), pp. 18-26.
58. Kliavkoff, G.T. (1994). "Law: Controlling the vicarious liability of hotel and motel franchisers: hotel franchisers can become caught up in the improper actions of their franchisees." *Cornell Hotel and Restaurant Administration Quarterly*, 35 (1) (February). pp. 59-73.
59. Dev, C. & Brown, J.R. (1991). "Franchise and other operating arrangements in the lodging industry: a strategic comparison." *Hospitality Research Journal*, 14 (3), pp. 23-41.
60. Cruz, T.D. (2001). "Kinder, gentle franchising." *Hotels*, (March), pp. 51-56.
61. Dailey, (1998). "Franchise rules you should know." *Journal of Accountancy*, 186 (3), (September), pp. 57-61.
62. Freeman, R.E. (1984). Strategic Management: A stakeholder approach. Boston: Harper Collins.
63. Freeman, R.E. (1999). Divergent stakeholder theory, *Academy of Management Review*. 24 (2), pp. 233-236.
64. Olsen, M.D., Zhao, J.L., Sharma, A. and Choi, J.G. (2000) Leading Hospitality into the Age of Excellence—Expansion, Competition and Vision in the Multinational Hotel Industry, published by International Hotel and Restaurant Association.
65. Olsen, M.D. (1996). Into the new millennium. A White Paper on the Global Hospitality Industry by the International Hotel Association, pp. 27-49.
66. Frooman, J. (1999). Stakeholder influence strategies. *Academy of Management Review*, 24 (2), pp. 191-205.
67. Donaldson, T., & Prestib, L. (1995). The stakeholder theory of the modern corporation: concepts, evidence, impactions. *Academy of Management Review*, 20 (1), pp. 65-91.
68. Clarkson, M.B.E. (1995). A stakeholder framework for analyzing and evaluating corporate social performance. *Academy of Management Review*, 20, pp. 92-117.
69. Carroll, A. (1993). Business and Society: ethics and stakeholder management. Cincinnati: South-Western Publishing.

70. Deavenport, D. (2001). Balancing the five: the petrochemical industry and its stakeholders. *Executive Speeches*, 15 (6), pp. 11-14.
71. Clarkson, M.B.E. (1995). A stakeholder framework for analyzing and evaluating corporate social performance. *Academy of Management Review*, 20, pp. 92-117.
72. Jawahar, I.M. & McLaughlin (2001). Toward a descriptive stakeholder theory: An organizational life cycle approach. *Academy of Management Review*, 26 (3), pp. 397-414.
73. Gioia, D.A. (1999). Practicability, paradigms and problems in stakeholder theorizing. *Academy of Management Review*, 24, pp. 228-232.
74. Cohen, D. (1999). Taking a risk: Max Clarkson's impact on stakeholder theory. *Business and Society*, 38 (1), pp. 39-43.
75. Mitchell, R.K., Agle, B.R. & Wood, D.J. (1997). Toward a theory of stakeholder identification and salience: defining the principle of who and what really counts. *Academy of Management Review*, 22 (4), pp. 853-887.
76. Frederick, W.C., Post, J.E. & Davis, K. (1992). Business and society: corporate strategy, public policy, Ethics (7th ed). New York: McGraw-Hill.
77. Waddock, S., & Smith, N. (2000). Corporate responsibility audits: doing well by doing good. *Sloan Management Review*, 41 (2), pp. 75-83.
78. Berman, S.L., Wicks, A.C., Kotha, S. and Jones, T.M. (1999). Does stakeholder orientation matter? The relationship between stakeholder management models and firm financial performance. *Academy of Management Review*, 42 (5), pp. 488-506.
79. Davenport, K. (2000). Corporate citizenship: a stakeholder approach for defining corporate social performance and identifying measures for assessing it. *Business and Society*, 39 (2), pp. 210-219.
80. Szwajkowski, E. (2000). Simplifying the principles of stakeholder management: the three most important principles. *Business and Society*, 39 (4), pp. 379-396.
81. Frooman, J. (1999). Stakeholder influence strategies. *Academy of Management Review*, 24 (2), pp. 191-205.
82. Wood, D.J. (1994). *Business and Society* (2nd ed.) New York: Harper Collins.
83. Sautter, E.T. & Leisen, B. (1999). Managing stakeholders: A tourism planning model. *Annals of Tourism Research*, 26 (2), pp. 312-328.
84. Markwich, M.C. (2000). Golf tourism development, stakeholders differing discourses and alternative agendas: the case of Malta. *Tourism Management*, 21 pp. 515-524.
85. Buhalis, D. & Fletcher, J. (1995), Environmental impacts on tourism destinations: An economic analysis. In H. Cocosis, & P. Nijkamp, Sustainable Tourism Development (pp. 3-24). England: Avebury.

Bibliography

BOOKS

Aaker, David A. and Shanby, J. Gary—"Positioning Your Product", *Business Horizons,* May-June, 1982.

Akhtar, Javed—"Tourism Management in India", Ashish Publications, New Delhi, 1990.

Al, Ries and Jack, Trout—"Positioning: The Battle for Your Mind", Warner Books, New York, 1981.

Anand, M.M.—"Tourism and Hotel Industry in India: A study of Management", Prentice Hall of India Pvt. Ltd., New Delhi, 1976.

Baker, Michael J.—"Marketing", Fourthly Edition English Language Book Society, McMillan, 1985.

Bala, Usha—"Tourism in India Policy and Perspectives", Arushi Publications, New Delhi, 1990.

Batra, K.L.—"Problems and Prospects of Tourism", Printwell Publishers, Jaipur, Rajasthan, 1990.

Batra, G.S. and Chawla, A.S.—"Tourism Management–A Global Perspective", Deep & Deep Pub. (P) Ltd., New Delhi, 2000.

Batra, G.S. and Dangwal, R.C.—"Tourism Promotion and Development: New Advances", Deep and Deep Pub. Pvt. Ltd., New Delhi, 2001.

Bendra, V.P. — "Tourism in India", Parimal Prakashan, Aurangabad, 1979.

Bhalla, L.R. — "Geography of Rajasthan", Kuldeep Publishing House, Jaipur, 2005.

Bhardwaj, D.S., Kamra, K.K., Chaudhary, Manjula, Bhushan, Ravi K., Boora, S.S., Chand M., Taxak, R.H. — "International Tourism: Issues and Challenges", Kanishka Publishers, Distributors, New Delhi, 2006.

Bhatia, A.K. — "Tourism Development: Principles and Practices", Sterling Publishers Pvt. Ltd., New Delhi, 1982.

Bhatia, A.K. — "International Tourism: Fundamental and Practices", Sterling Pub. Pvt. Ltd., New Delhi, 1991.

Bhatnagar, S. — "Front Office Management", Frank Bros. & Co. (Publishers), New Delhi, 2002.

Bittner, M.J. and Booms, B.H. — "Trends in Travel and Tourism Marketing: The Changing Structure of Distribution Channels", *Journal of Research*, No. 4, 1982.

Bryden, John M. — "Tourism and Development", Cambridge University Press, London, 1973.

Burkart, A.J. — "The Management of Tourism", Heinemann Publishing House, London, 1976.

Burkart, A.J. and Medlik, S. — "Tourism: Past, Present and Future", Heinemann Publishing House, London, 2nd edition, 1990.

C.Y. Gee, Dester, J.L. Choy — "The Travel Industry", The AVI Publishing Company, Westport, Connecticut, 1984.

Campbell, J., Dunnette, M., Arvey, R. and Holervick, L. — "The Development and Evaluation of Behaviourally Based Rating Scales", *Journal of Applied Psychology*, Vol. 57, No. 1, February 1973.

Chandan, J.S. — "Management Concepts and Strategies", Vikas Publishing House Pvt. Ltd., New Delhi, 1997.

Chib, Somnath — "Essays on Tourism" Cross Section Publications Pvt. Ltd., New Delhi, 1989.

Chris, Argyris — "Personality and Organization", Harper and Row, New York, 1957.

Colly, G. — "International Tourism Today", *Lloyds Bank Review*, 1967.

Condiff, E.W. and Still, R.R. – "Basic Marketing Concepts, Environment and Decision", Prentice Hall Inc., New Jersey, 1964.

Cornell, Williams, B. — "Organisation and Management in Industries and Business", Ronald Press, New York, 1947.

Davis, H.D. — "Potentials for Tourism of Developing Countries", *Finance and Development*, London, 1968.

Dharmarajan, S. and Seth, Rabindra — "Tourism in India–Trends and Issues", Haranand Publication, New Delhi, 1994.

Dixit, Manoj and Charu, Sheela – "Tourism Products", New Royal Book Co., Lucknow, 2001.

Evans, R. Joel and Berman, Barry – "Marketing", Prentice Hall, New Jersey, 1994.

Foster & Douglas – "Travel & Tourism Management", McMillan, London, 1985.

George, B.P. and Swain, Sampad Kumar – "Advancements in Tourism Theory and Practice", Abhijeet Pub., Delhi, 2005.

George, Young — "Tourism Blessing or Plight", Harmonds Worth Penguin Book Ltd., England, 1973.

Ghosh, Biswanath – "Tourism and Travel Management", Vikas Publishing House, Delhi, 1998.

Gupta, Vijay Kumar — "Tourism in India", Gyan, New Delhi, 1987.

Harold, Koontz and Cyril J.O. Connell — "Principles of Management", 3rd Edition, McGraw Hill Book Co., New York, 1995.

Harrison, D. and Price M. – "Fragile Environments, Fragile Communities? An introduction in price M (ed.) *People and Tourism in Fragile Environments*, Chichester, 1996.

Hicks, M.K. and *et. al.*, – "Tourism", Heinemann, London, 1968.

Howard, N. — "A New Way to View Consumers", *Dun's Review*, No. 2, August, 1981.

James Stoner, Edward Freeman and David Gilbert — "Management", Prentice Hall, 1995.

Jerome, E. — "A Managerial Approach", *Homewood, III*: Richard D. Jewin, 1975.

Jha, S.M. — "Tourism Marketing", Himalaya Publishing House, Bombay, 1995.

Kaul, R.N. — "Dynamics of Tourism" (Vol. 1: *The Phenomenon*, Vol. 2 *Accommodation*, Vol. 3 *Transportation and Marketing*), Sterling Publishers Pvt. Ltd., New Delhi, 1985.

Kershaw, A.G. and Lundberg, D. — "The Tourist Business", Cahners Book International Inc. Boston, 1974.

Kotler, P. — "Market Management Analysis, Planning, Implementation and Control", Ninth Edition, Prentice Hall of India Pvt. Ltd., New Delhi, 1997.

Lewis, Robert C. and Chambers, Richard E. — "Marketing Leadership in Hospitality Foundation and Practices", Van Nostrum Reinhold, New York, 1989.

Lickorish J.L. — "The Travel Trade" Practical Press, London, 1958.

Louis, Sterm W. and Adel, J.E.L. Ansary — "Marketing Channels", 5th Ed., *Supper Saddle River*, Prentice Hall, New York, 1996.

Makhan, Dileep — "Tourism as an Economic Enterprise", Adhyayan Publishers and Distributors, New Delhi, 2006.

Malhotra, R.K. — "Nature and Tourism", Cyber Tech Pub., New Delhi, 2006.

Maslow, A.H. — "Motivation and Personality," Harper and Row, New York, 1954.

McIntosh, R.W. — "Tourism Principles, Practices and Philosophies" John Wiley, New York, 1986.

McMurray, R.N. — "Avoiding Mistakes in Selecting Executives", *Michigan Business Review*, Vol. 22, No. 4, July 1970.

Medlik, S. — "Profile of Hotel and Catering Industry", Heinemann, London, 1972.

Michael, Coltman — "Travel and Tourism", Van Nostrand Reinhold, New York, 1989.

Mill, Robert Christie — "Tourism: The International Business", Prentice Hall, New Jersey, 1985.

Morrison, A.M., Negi, J.M.S. — "Tourism and Travel Concepts and Principles", Gitanjali Publishing House, New Delhi, 1982.

Mridula, Dutt Narayan — "Ecology and Tourism", Universal Publishers Distributors, Delhi, 1991.

Norval, A.J. — "The Tourist Industry, A National and International Survey", Pitman, London. 1980.

Ogilivie, F.W. — "The Tourist Movement: An Economic Study, Staples Press Ltd., London, 1980.

Page, Stephen J. — "Tourism Management System", Butterworth-Heinemann, 2003.

Pande, Ram — "History and Growth of Tourism", *Shodhak*, Jaipur, 2006.

Paul, Turner — "Using Information to Enhance Competitive Advance the Marketing Options", *European Journal of Marketing*, Vol. 25, 6 November, 1991.

Pawar, R.S. and Rai, Vinay Kumar — "Tourism and its Development a Geographical Analysis", Sonali Publications, New Delhi, 2006.

Payne, Adrain — "The Essence of Service Marketing", Prentice Hall of India (P) Ltd., New Delhi, 1993.

Peter, Douglas — "Tourism Development", Longman, London, 1981.

Peter, Michael — "International Tourism, Hutchinson, London, 1981.

Piffner and Sherwood — "Administrative Organisation", Prentice Hall, New Delhi, 1964.

Pimlote, Jar – "The English Man's Holidays", Faber & Faber, 1947.

Pizam, Abraham – "The Social Impact of Tourism", *Recreation Research*, Vol. II, Publication House, Lucknow, 1986.

Puri, G.K. — "Travel and Tourism for All", New Delhi, 1986.

R. Naronha – "Social and Culture Dimensions of Tourism: A Review of the Literature in English", Tourism Projects Department, World Bank, May 18, 1977.

Raheja, Banwari Lal – "Tourism and Hospitality Services", Arises Publishers and Distributors, New Delhi, 2004.

Raina, A.K. — "Tourism Industry in Kashmir", Shipra Publication, New Delhi, 2002.

Raina, A.K. and Agarwal, S.K. – "The Essence of Tourism Development", Sarup & Sons, New Delhi, 2004.

Raina, A.K. and Lodha, R.C. — "The Fundamentals of Tourism Systems", Kanishka Publishers, New Delhi, 2004.

Raina, A.K., Jain, Neelu — "Dynamics of Tourism-Concepts, Philosophy and Strategies", Shipra Publications, New Delhi, 2, 2004.

Rajuvedi, V.P. – "Tourism in India", Yojna, Vol. 46, Ministry of Information and Broadcasting, New Delhi, 2003.

Ram, Acharya — "Tourism in India", R.B.S.A. Publishers, Jaipur, 1977.

Ramaswamy, V.S. and Kumari, S. Nana – "Marketing Management Planning Implementation and Control", III ed. McMillan, 2002.

Richard, Henderson — "Performance Appraisal", Reston Publishing, 1984.

Robinson, H. — "A Geography of Tourism" MacDonald and Evans, London, 1979.

Saxena, Rajan – "Marketing Management", Third Ed., Tata McGraw Hill Publishing Company Ltd., New Delhi, 2006.

Seth, Pran Nath — "Successful Tourism Planning and Marketing", Cross Section Publishers, New Delhi, 1978.

Shah, K. and Gupta, G. — "Tourism the Poor and Other Stakeholders: Experience in Asia: Overseas Development Institute (ODI) - Fair Trade in Tourism paper, the Sustainable Livelihood Working Paper Series, ODI, London, 2000.

Sharma, Hemant — "HRM in Hospitality Industry", ABD Publishers, Jaipur, 2006, 6.

Sharma, J.K. — "Tourism Planning and Development: A New Perspective", Kanishka Pub. Distributors, New Delhi, 2000.

Sharma, K.C. — "Tourism Policy Planning and Strategy" Pointer Publisher, Jaipur, Rajasthan, 1996.

Sharma, K.K. — "Tourism in India", Classic Publishing House, Jaipur, 1991.

Sharma, Vivek — "Tourism in India", Arihant Publication, Jaipur, Rajasthan, 1991.

Singh, R.K. — "Modern Trends in Hospitality Industry", 2006.

Singh, Ratandeep — "Tourism Today, Structure, Marketing and Profile", Vol. II, Kanishka Publishers, Distributors, Delhi, 1994.

Singh, Tej Veer — "Tourism and Tourist Industry in India", New Heights Publishers, New Delhi, 1995.

Singhal, Ravi Shankar Kumar — "Ecotourism and Sustainable Development", Abhijeet Publications, Delhi, 2003.

Smith, Stephen, L.J. — "Tourism Analysis: A Handbook", Longman, London, 1989.

Victor, P. Buell — "Marketing Management: A Strategic Planning Approach", New York, McGraw-Hill, 1984.

W. McIntosh — "Tourism Principles, Practices and Philosophies, John Wiley, New York, 1986.

W.W. Hunter — "The Indian Empire: Its People, History and Products", Smith Eden and Co., London, 1987.

Wahab, S.E. — "Tourism Marketing and Management Handbook", Prentice Hall, London, 1975.

Williams, J.O. — "The Philosophy of Management", Wiley & Sons, New York, 1930.

Journals, Reports, Brochures, Periodicals, Magazines, Articles in Newpapers and Websites

- International Union of Official Travel Organisation: Conference on International Travel and Tourism, Geneva, 1963.
- Tourist Statistics, Government of India, Department of Tourism, New Delhi, 1998.
- OECD Tourism Committee, International Tourism and Tourism Policy in OECD Countries Report Organisation for Economic Co-operation and Development, Paris, July, 1973.
- Express Travel World, Business Pub. Div., Indian Express Newspapers (Bombay) Ltd. Ist Floor, Express Tower, Nariman Point, Mumbai, November, 2006.
- Inputs from the article published in *Times of India*, New Delhi, August 13, 2006, by Subodh Ghidiyal.
- Annual Report—Department of Tourism, Government of India, New Delhi, 2005–07.
- Tirthas of Pre-historic Rajasthan, Article by R.K. Tyagi, *Shodhak*, Vol. 4, B, Sr. 11/1975.
- Discover Rajasthan, Tourism Arts & Culture, Government of Rajasthan, 1997.
- Department of Tourism, Art & Culture, Jaipur, Brochure.
- Key part of the Market, Business Travel, Financial Times Survey, *Financial Times*, 23rd May, 1973.
- "Testing the Effectiveness of Promotional Campaigns in International Travel Marketing", World Tourism Organization Seminar, Ottawa, 1975.
- Committee on Definition, Chicago: American Marketing Association, 1960.

- Goodwin, H.—Pro-poor Tourism: Opportunities for Sustainable Local Development. D+ C Development and Co-operation, No. 5, September/October 2000.
- The inputs from the article published in *Times of India*, June 3, 2006 by Amitabh Kant, Joint Secretary, Ministry of Tourism Government of India.
- Inputs from the article published in *Times of India*, November 5, 2006 by Arun Kumar Das.
- Quoted by H.P. Smolks in forty thousand against the article, 1937.
- Managing Business Enterprises, Module-V.
- Tourism Development and Economic Growth, OECD, 1966.
- WTO Travel and Tourism Barometer, Madrid, May 1993.
- World Tourism Organisation, 1996.
- Tourism Society in Britain, 1999.
- Census of India, 2001, Rajasthan.
- Travellers India, National Geography, 2001.
- Employment News, September, 2004.
- The *Times of India*, New Delhi, November 8, 2006, Wednesday.
- Time out Jaipur, September-October, 2005.
- Destination Rajasthan Atithi, October, 2000.
- Jovice, Zivadin – "Articles on Tourism and Geography in the International Travel and Recreation," Journal No. 3.
- http://www.tourindia.com
- http://www.indiaculture.org
- http://www.udaipurplus.com
- http://www.rajasthan-tourism.com
- http://www.tourismofindia.com

- http://www.rajasthantourism.gov.in
- http://www.clipperholydays.com
- http://planningcommission.nic.in

Index